For
Lorie!
Blessed Be!

THE
HOLY BOOK
OF WOMEN'S
MYSTERIES

Z. Budapest
Sept 2 w '89

THE
HOLY BOOK
ᴼ WOMEN'S
ᶠ

MYSTERIES

(Complete in One Volume)

**Feminist
Witchcraft,
Goddess
Rituals,
Spellcasting,
and other
womanly
arts...**

Zsuzsanna Budapest

Wingbow Press,
Berkeley, California

Originally published by Susan B. Anthony Coven No. 1.

Cover art: *Wolf Woman* by Suzanne de Veuve; from the collection of Elizabeth Wolfe-Held.

Book Design by Paula Morrison
Typesetting by ExecuStaff
Printing by Intercollegiate Press

ISBN 0-914728-67-9

Wingbow Press books are published and distributed by Bookpeople, 2929 Fifth Street, Berkeley, CA 94710.

First Wingbow edition: 1989

Table of Contents

I like to dedicate this twentieth anniversary edition of The Holy Book of Women's Mysteries to all those women who organized, published and pioneered on behalf of the Goddess for the past two decades.

May we be remembered with love and honor by those who follow us and take our calling and dedication to the Goddess into the 21st century. May the Goddess never be forgotten again!

How This Book Was Born

Once upon a time, somewhere in Virginia, there were two ex-nuns, Laura and Beach, who embarked on the adventure of following the path of the Goddess with a precious and rare copy of a book in their hands. This book was called *The Feminist Book of Light and Shadows*.

They also had with them a basket filled with candles and food to share, and Peppy, their trusted mutt. And so they set out in the middle of a windy Halloween night. Beach was reading avidly by flashlight about the ritual for Halloween, when a gust of wind dislodged the book from her hand and carried it triumphantly toward the nearby woods where they were headed.

Laura dropped the basket immediately, and began to chase the airborne copy, but to no avail. For a moment, Beach thought God the man was getting even with them for heresy. Laura thought the Goddess was sending the book ahead of them as a sign for their newly-found faith. But Peppy was delighted with the chase, which she punctuated with wild barks and gruffs at the ever-flying winged book that flew with such ease, each female following it, caught up in her own way in the night's excitement.

Finally, in the woods, a birch tree snatched the book out of the wind's hold and dropped it on the wet autumn grass. Peppy immediately snatched it up and brandished it between her teeth. This was the last copy in the world of *The Feminist Book of Light and Shadows*.

I'm telling you this story because these two women were instrumental in our continuing to publish *The Feminist Book of Light and Shadows*, which later became *The Holy Book of Women's Mysteries*. They wrote us a letter of such vivid detail that we realized that the hunger for this information was greater than we had thought. We needed to raise funds, turn the pamphlet into a more permanent form and keep it in print.

The Susan B. Anthony Coven No. 1 was just an experiment at the time, started on the Winter Solstice of 1971 with a handful of friends, later growing into a fluctuating group of between twenty and one hundred twenty women. We met every Sabbath (the solstices, equinoxes and high points in between) and every full moon, which occurred thirteen times a year. This was a vigorous pagan practice of observing twenty-one major holidays per year. What we put on paper was pretty much what we were doing in the mountains in Malibu. But by the time we wrote it down, we had already changed one practice, so we kept telling readers not to slavishly follow the patterns we suggested but to internalize the patterns and then improvise what suited them best.

We met on Sundays at Mama's Cafe in Malibu. There were about eight of us in the core group, and I'd like to thank each of them—those who came and practiced with us and those who helped create *The Holy Book of Women's Mysteries*. Janet Roslund, of course, was the most instrumental in holding us together with her seriousness as an organizer and her bursts of mediumship. She channeled the Goddess as the Dean of the College. Of course, the college was the universe. She would close her eyes and her voice would come out sounding prim and higher than usual. "Now girls," she would say, "you must learn all of the curriculum here at the college: the herbs on my back, the trees in my hair, my nature which is yours. And we want no tardiness in attention. Graduation is close."

Janet also found a remark written by Florence Nightingale, whom we all admired. She posed a very potent question: "Do you think it is possible for there to be a religion whose essence is common sense?" This question prompted us to respond to her across time and say, "Yes, the earth religions are such that their essence, their dogma, so to speak, is common sense that glorifies practical things and the improvement of our lives right now, not later, after death, which is absurd."

In Malibu, we sat around a weatherbeaten old table outside Mama's Cafe eating our eggs and potatoes, drinking coffee, talking and fantasizing and laughing, and knowing that we were new and doing something revolutionary that was going to influence the world around us. However, we didn't know to what great effect. The sun beat down on our backs and we scribbled our notes. And so *The Holy Book of Women's Mysteries* was born after many such meetings, contributions, suggestions, stimulation, nourishment, and a lot of bacon and eggs at Mama's Cafe.

I want to thank Nina Ramona, who always prayed in the circles for the oppressed countries around the world. She constantly made us remember what a special place we lived in and our responsibility to the rest of the world.

One afternoon I was having a talk with Joan, who never failed to inspire me. She was grilling me.

"What about this witchcraft religion?" she asked. "What is it that we believe in? What is it, Z?" She always had a great effect on me, and I realized I'd never really pulled it together before: feminist witches—what do we believe in that's different from the rest of the pagan community? Why are we new? And I just sat down and channeled the Manifesto of the Susan B. Anthony Coven No. 1, right on the edge of 1972, reflecting all of our moods and times. As I'm reading it today, so much later, I'm amazed.

The only thing that I would change—and we have changed—is the part about men. We do work with men now. The men are changing rapidly, thank heaven. We recognize this historical fact. The feminist movement is still alive and many men work for it now and many more will in the future. The work with men is usually done in workshops—men's mysteries. Dianic circles are still for women only.

Around this same weatherbeaten wooden table, there was a great debate: "What do we mean by 'Dianic'? What is it? What does this tradition mean for women?" We decided that it is a women-centered, female-only worship of women's mysteries, but not confined to the worship of the goddess Diana alone. Diana is a European name for the Goddess of the Moon. Her name means "Holy Mother," and we loved the name. Many rivers, such as the Danube, are named after her, as are several other natural areas. As women, however, we relate to the global Goddess as She was worshipped by ethnic groups around the world. She is more like the Goddess of the Ten Thousand Names, but each time we talk about the Goddess, what we really mean is Life—life on this earth. We always recognize, when we say "Goddess," that She is the life-giver, the life-sustainer. She is Mother Nature.

Valerie, who was leading workshops in assertiveness and prosperity consciousness, always encouraged us to make the book more action-oriented, connecting political and personal. We tried to do this in its tone and direction.

Lhyv Oakwomon came to us from Colorado. She was a natural priestess coming from a black woman's experience, finding it compatible and nurturing to work in the Dianic tradition. She contributed what she had learned in the desert while studying with Native Americans.

Annu sat around the table, too. She was a partner in the Feminist Wicca candle shop, which the coven also ran. She was the strangest of all witches because her nose was dead. She could not really distinguish between rosemary and cinnamon. Her contribution is about dreams, where her nose doesn't matter but her inner self is quite clear and she can distinguish very well between images. She contributed by giving us steadiness and keeping the Feminist Wicca's books in order. Essentially the candle shop moved back into her house, where she still runs it as a mailorder business.

Anna Kria, a tall, queenlike lady, was our astrologer. She turned us on to stargazing astrology, also known as sidereal astrology. She made us look at the stars with new eyes, new interpretations, and see it as a precise science, not merely legends and lore passed down since Babylon.

Noel Brennan was a sister we didn't meet in person. Only through the mail did we receive her correspondence, her poems, her spells, her practices. We recognized her as a great soul. Finally, in 1985, I met her and found her to be everything I thought she was going to be—a sacred poet, a devoted priestess.

Chris Carol also contributed to the book. I initiated her in 1978 at Beltane, although by then she was conducting her own circles in Portland and had also organized the Changing Women Chorus, a Goddess choir. Her contributions to the *Song of Amergin* are very moving, especially when you hear them. There is a tape of the Changing Women Chorus singing all those verses.

One day Starhawk was driving down Lincoln Boulevard in Santa Monica, wondering why feminism and witchcraft hadn't found each other yet. Just as she thought this, she drove past the Feminist Wicca and the name caught her eye. She stopped her car and came into our candle shop for the first time. I happened to be staffing that day, so I told her about the Susan B. Anthony Coven No. 1, and invited her to our upcoming Spring Equinox Festival. Starhawk attended her first ritual with us, and the impact on her life was glorious proof of why we should never close circles to anyone new. She quickly became a great teacher and priestess. She educated herself in different traditions, and is now contributing to the literature of Goddess religion. I've included her piece about the dangers of magic because it was so needed and it shows Starhawk's approach, always looking through everything with humor.

Helen Beardwoman typed and edited the first edition of *The Holy Book, Part I*. She served as the Maiden Artemis in the coven. She was there the first time the police arrested us on the mountaintop for candleburning and trespassing. We found out that the land we were trespassing on was owned by Iranian interests. This infuriated us. We did not believe that Iran had any business owning this beautiful place of power, and we, as California women, felt that being thrown off this land was most unjust.

It was an absurd night. Over a hundred candles were burning in fireproof containers, because in our practice we usually lit two candles for each woman; there were about thirty-eight of us. Below us lived the Malibu rich with their kidney-shaped swimming pools. One of them, closest to the mountain, called the police, saying that there were strange cars parked outside. Just parking "strange cars" in Malibu was enough to mobilize eight police, armed with rifles. They came for us over the fire roads, because this place was hard to approach, and we'd climbed the mountain to get there. Just as Nina Ramona was reading her list of purposes for her new high coven (this was a Candlemas), we heard a chorus of coyotes howl at us from the mountain in great warning. It was so loud and eerie that we stopped the ritual and listened. Women were looking to me for guidance. I had never heard anything like it. I thought there might be another coven worshipping somewhere else on the mountain because I heard deeper, male voices mixed in with the higher, female voices. It was a tapestry of solid sounds with human elements. I went on with the ritual, ignoring the sound. Five minutes later the police arrived. I will never again ignore coyotes, wolves or whoever else is howling and disrupting my ritual; from now on I will take it as a warning. I advise you to do the same.

Helen Beardwoman took the rap when the police pointed their car lights at us and asked, "Who is the leader of this group?" At the time, I was on probation for reading Tarot cards to an undercover policewoman, so I could not come out and say I was. Besides, we were not into leaders and followers. We were learning from teacher, but we regarded each other as equals. Helen Beardwoman stepped out and said, "I am." At the time, Helen sported a lifelong beard. She was tortured during her childhood with electrolysis, trying to kill off her follicles and make her beardless like a girl. She looked like a girl all her life—beautiful, gentle, strong, but with a beard.

This was when we were all liberating ourselves from bras, corsets and high heels. She decided to liberate herself from electrolysis and see just what she looked like as she was designed by Mother Nature. Her beard was not too visible, since it was very blond. However, the police were immediately fascinated by it. They questioned her about how she grew it, did she take hormones, and was she a man. There was only one policewoman among them, and all thirty-eight of us lined up to be arrested by her. It took a while. My students who were attending this Candlemas ritual for their own initiation saw the pitfalls of practicing the earth religions.

At the trial, a sign at the entrance to the courtroom said "No bare feet or bathing suits, please." That's Malibu for you.

Our lawyer, who was part of the group and present at our arrest, made a very strong case that there was no fire danger and no private property signs had been posted. Nowhere were there indications that we were not allowed on the land. It was not a state park with a curfew. It was wilderness, and we respected it. We took extensive pictures of our altar and proved beyond the shadow of a doubt that there was no danger of fire.

However, all this groundwork and preparation didn't interest the judge or the district attorney. All they kept talking about was Helen's beard, whether it was real, if she was a man. It just fascinated them no end. Our case was pushed through as an afterthought, and we were fined thirty-eight dollars—a dollar apiece.

Mary Farkas contributed the chapter on nutrition to *The Holy Book*. She is a countrywoman of mine. I met her in Venice, California. She looked at what I ate—namely, Hungarian soul food—and said. "Listen Z, if you continue eating our Hungarian cuisine, I'll tell you, in about a year or two, first you'll get a little neck pain and then you're going to have shoulder pains, then back pain. Because what you're eating is a lot of fats from animals, and they're going to accumulate in your body and you're going to be stiff from them before your time."

As she was speaking to me, I realized that I already had small back and shoulder pains. In great fright, I said, "Oh, no—I already have them? What shall I do?" She and her lover came over and cooked me a wholesome meal with barley and salad, and for protein they taught me to eat more soya curds. It was very delicious, and she converted me to vegetarianism for the next ten years. (However, watch out for eating too much barley, because that can put the pounds on you very quickly; also, beware eating too much cheese to replace the meat. Essentially, I learned not to eat a lot. When you are a vegetarian, just eat smaller portions. Today, I do with a little chicken and I certainly eat all the seafood I can get my hands on, but I avoid red meat and fatty foods.)

Mary then disappeared from my life. The last time I saw her was in Boston at the First Women's Spirituality Festival, but her impact on my life still lingers, and her impact on many women's lives is furthered by her work in *The Holy Book*.

Carol Christ and I met in New York when she and Naomi Goldenberg were just graduating from Yale Theology School. Carol invited me there for a talk and we found great sisterhood around the Goddess. She and Naomi had a difficult time at an all-male, God-oriented school, holding up the Goddess flag, and we helped each other to stay strong. Her contribution to the daily practices is very valuable. She was involved in teaching rituals at San Jose State, and she now leads tours to Anatolia (Turkey) and Lesbos (Greece) to perform rituals in ancient Goddess temples around the Mediterranean area.

My most beloved contributor to *The Holy Book* was my mother, Masika Szilagyi, who passed away in 1979. I consulted a psychic to know what she's been up to. (Doctors don't treat their own children, and psychics go to other psychics to talk to their psychic relatives.) The psychic located her and said, "Well, I don't know if it means anything to you, but I see what appears to be a soul that is making sculpture out of light and is leading groups of people through the sculptures and they feel better when they come out the other end."

I recognized my mother and said, "Yes, that's her. She's having shows again." Of course, when you're dead you don't have clay to work with, so Mother uses light. I'm sure it's a great challenge, working with the other great artists on the Northern and Southern Lights. And she's helping other souls.

My mother had a large collection of folklore and items relating to Hungarian paganism. I inherited her love of pre-Christian religions; my pain at not being able to talk to her is fierce and deep, and will never be appeased.

I'm very much a Persephone type. I feel I manifest that goddess, and my yearning for my mother, Demeter, is great, she of the clay, she of the earth. I believe she is waiting for me, and when I die, she will help me cross the space between life and death. Before her death, my mother sent me her *Book of Sorrows, Book of Spells*, and I translated it into English. This was one of the last collaborations we managed to bring about. Her beautiful art, which is included in *The Holy Book*, is all on the second floor of my house in Budapest. The government promised her a permanent museum, but somehow it never materialized. So her pieces are waiting for a home. Right now my stepfather dusts them off every day and tries to keep them in shape.

Many people ask me why I use the word "witch" so often in *The Holy Book*. Why don't I call it "Womanspirit" or "Goddess's Inner Guide"? Safe, New Age-ish words that don't threaten anybody. My answer is, I like the word "witch." It is the only word in English that denotes "woman with spiritual power." I know that Hollywood propaganda, Christian propaganda, have made people think that witches are totally evil.

Even in Hungary, the word *boszorkany* means somebody who can hex. In German, the word *hexe* is negative. We find the spiritual woman relegated to the realm of the negative, but it doesn't mean you cannot reclaim the word. So every Halloween, the media call me and want to know what the witches are up to and why we call ourselves witches. I explain to them that this word means "priestess", that it has suffered a great deal of bad-mouthing and propaganda, and we are aiming to reclaim dignity for witches and educate the world about witchcraft. If you insist on educating about a word, it takes about twenty years, but you can do it. Look what happened to the word *woman*.

When we began the Susan B. Anthony Coven No. 1, we used to watch the Olympics. The announcer would come on and say, "Well, the girls are doing real good in swimming," and then the women appeared, and they were all over twelve years old, nothing like girls at all. We wrote strident letters to the commentators and demanded that women be called women, since they didn't call men boys. Eventually, the men changed, because the women changed in their attitudes, and today we have *women's* events.

What happened to "chicks" and "broads"? Remember those words? We just got rid of them, that's what happened. Language is a living tool and in the English language it's particularly important to be conscious of how we use words. When calling for help, don't say, "Oh, my God," say "Oh, my Goddess." If you do it often enough, in time it will roll naturally off your tongue. It's just habit. If you use these expressions around your friends, they soon pick them up unconsciously and they also begin to talk differently.

The last question I'm always asked is why we named our group the Susan B. Anthony Coven No. 1. "Don't you know," they ask, "that Susan B. Anthony was a Quaker and had nothing to do with witches?" (By the way, her best friend, Elizabeth Cady Stanton, was the spiritual forerunner who spent ten years reclaiming women's spirituality. She disclaimed the validity of the Bible by proving that it was written by clerks and therefore was not the word of God but a political tool to keep women in their place.) So why do we say Susan B. Anthony Coven No. 1?

We chose her name because Susan B. Anthony was a suffragist whom we all respected. She had her limitations; she was not perfect. And neither are we. Susan B. Anthony attended a fundraiser for Victoria Woodhall, who was a well-known psychic and the first woman to run for the Presidency. This fundraiser took place in New York, and a reporter spotted Susan in the corner. She was not drinking, because she didn't like to drink; she also didn't like Victoria Woodhall. She was there because she wanted to support this outrageous act of running for president, since she was working for the vote for women.

The reporter taunted Susan and said, "Well, Susan B. Anthony, what are you going to do in the afterlife?" Susan was sizzling by then, and she turned to the reporter and said, "I'll tell you: When I die I shall go neither to heaven nor to hell, but stay right here and finish the women's revolution."

As witches, we need a guardian spirit, someone who is devoted to the same cause that we are. When I came across this story about her, I said, "Susan B. Anthony, we've got a job for you. You'll be our Lady of the Coven. You shall be leading us in a political/spiritual way." And that's what's been happening ever since. We have never regretted taking on her name, and I think by now she's reconciled to the fact that her spirit is called upon by women's circles all over the world.

Foreword
by Phyllis Chesler

We are blessed by Z's presence among us. Long may she live!

Ah my Priestess: mother, daughter, sister, friend, "thou hast ravished my heart" with the courage of thy womb and with thy redolent pagan ways.

> *How fair is thy love, my sister, my spouse! How much better is thy love than wine! My beloved is gone down into her garden, to the beds of spices, to feed in the gardens, and to gather lilies.*

When Z laughs, she means it. Her howls soar high above manmade rafters and peal more sweetly than church bells. Tolling ancient female pleasures. "I am here. I am still here. You can't kill me. But your guilt worries me still..."

When Z yells, she roars. The winds of lamentation gather in her soft mouth. She "commands me with truth more terrible than an army of banners." Her blue eyes pale into pain. She moans of Matricide and of Amazons, caged. Of rape and of Motherless daughters. Of women's cowardice and of the persecution of wise and religious women.

> *Oh my dove, that art in the clefts of the rock, let me see thy countenance, let me hear thy music; for sweet is thy voice, and thy countenance is comely.*

When Z reads the cards or priestesses a ritual, she is like this book: sacred *and* accessible, fiercely political and endearingly personal.

The Holy Book of Women's Mysteries is every woman's Spiritual Survival Guide. It is filled with Mother Goddesses, Sacred Sons, Amazons, and tortured witches. It is also a "cookbook" filled with useful recipes: how to form a coven, how to use herbs and candles, how to cast a spell, how to eat well. All within a radical feminist context.

There is no other body of information presented and interpreted in this way anywhere. It is our heritage, passed down by Z to each of us, a family heirloom.

> *Thy navel is like a goblet, which wanteth not liquor: thy belly is like a heap of wheat set about with lilies.*

Z says women must bless and love themselves. Without this, they cannot love their sisters or their leaders—which we must do, or die as slaves.

She says "Self-love is where liberation begins" and "Honor the High Priestess"—although here Z is not talking about "adoring one leader and ignoring others." In her "personal experience nobody is getting kissed on her silk slippers like the male gurus are."

For women to imagine and honor a female deity is a sign of mental health. How sane can we be if we honor God as a tall white male—we who are relatively short, mortal, female, and of many colors. Imagine if women understood that Mary is not a virgin (in the Christian sense) and that she has a daughter, not a son. Listen to Z: "A self-created god who has no mother is a totally unsupportable concept." To deny motherhood is to deny women, and there are two kinds of people: mothers and their children.

> *Thy lips are like a thread of scarlet, and thy speech is comely; thy temples are like a piece of pomegranate within thy locks. The roof of thy mouth like the best wine that goeth down sweetly, causing the lips of those that are asleep to speak.*

Women are spiritually starving. Psychoanalysis, a job, a lover, a "career," a political support group, a patriarchal religion—none alone, all together are not sufficient to strengthen us or "cure" us of the indifference, hostility, betrayal, and violation that are our daily fate.

Z's rituals will strengthen and heal us. For example, instead of being shamed, terrified, and even slapped when we menstruate for the first time, how about a pagan ritual for first menstruation? for menopause? Instead of doing a nosedive into isolated new-born motherhood, how about a ritual to welcome the new mother into the circle of mothers? These rituals, and many more, are found in *The Holy Book of Women's Mysteries*.

Z describes rituals for naming newborn children, for healing ourselves after surgery, after a miscarriage or an abortion, and for finding a home, a job, a lover. Perhaps she is at her best in describing attitudes in the craft toward Death. How to die, how to feast and bury the dead, how to be reborn. Here Z is stately, sure-footed, and sacred.

I love her more serious spells: how to hex a rapist, to free political prisoners, to regain psychic balance after rape, and weatherwork.

> *The mandrakes give a smell, and at our gates are all manner of pleasant fruits, new and old, which I have laid up for thee, O my beloved.*

Feminists in conflict or at a grim standstill should pay attention to craft ethics: "Do as thou wilt and harm none;" "Don't think you're omnipotent, don't waste time in self-importance, guilt, or paranoia, and maintain a sense of humor;'' ''Don't throw a spell in anger;'' ''Build up the inner temple (the body), which is portable and all we have;'' ''Do no evil—but act in self-defense and self-affirmation;'' ''A witch bows to no man.''

> *My dove, my undefiled is but one; she is the only one of*
> *her mother, she is the choice one of her that bore her. The*
> *daughters saw her and blessed her.*

Z of the dashing phrase, the silver laugh, the unmistakable eyes of the Sibyl. Where do you come from?

From Budapest. From your mother Masika's womb. (Gypsy-steppes, a lone wolf, women's precise embroidery.) Before that: from emerald-shimmering Atlantis. Always, from your own strong will, spring into being. Against the odds, as usual.

Z: I remember us walking in 1976, bathed in Santa Monica pastels, talking about your being arrested for ''fortune telling'' in California. In California! where the weirdest of patriarchal sects and churches are tax exempt...

I knew then how witchy you really are.

> *Set me as a seal upon thy heart, as a seal upon thine arm:*
> *for love is as strong as death. Jealousy is cruel as the grave.*
> *Thou that dwellest in the gardens, the companions hearken*
> *to thy voice: cause me to hear it.*

Introduction

Many books have appeared about witchcraft in the past few hundred years. Some presented the Craft as a curious pastime; they highlighted its "cookbook" aspects, such as how to get a lover or do in your enemy, while missing the dignity and majesty of Earth religion. Some presented the Craft as a highly ceremonious pageantry which required you to invest your life savings in the proper tools, robes and glittering chalices, as if the power lay in the high quality of the objects you used. Such attitudes missed the humble common sense originating in the Craft, which made it such a desirable religion for peasants and Earth-loving folks. And some books presented the Craft as a fossilized, hierarchical power structure of those who were "adept," "third degree" or who had otherwise achieved "guruhood". The rest of us weren't fit to tie the laces on their sandals. Reminiscent of another religion or two? Precisely! Such books missed the all-pervading idea of equality in the Craft.

Finally, there are many books which perverted the Craft to such a degree that in presenting it, they even forgot or wrote out the major deity concerned with the Craft of the Wise: the Female Principle of the Universe. Those writers reflected their own sexism and fear of women, no matter how learned their books seemed to be. Taking out the heart of the theology destroyed people's images of this gentle path.

And these were the "friends" of the Craft. Now for the enemies.

Here we go back to the very invention of printing. When Gutenberg printed the first book in 1456, it was the Bible. Western culture still holds a cultivated fetish for the printed word, regarding it as gospel. If it's printed, it must be so.

This historic invention was immediately turned against women. The *Malleus Maleficarum* (*The Witches' Hammer*) of James Sprenger was published in 1485. Like television in its early years, this book had wide exposure and taken as gospel. It was the demented, sadistic fantasy life of the male collective consciousness in the repressed sexuality of two Jesuit priests. It ended up killing eleven million women, men and children. It was a very *un*holy book. It would fit in well with today's pornography. The tortures of women were often sexual, under the pretense of holiness. Today, some men get off on such tortures. You can tell if someone is burning leaves blocks away. Imagine what a city must have smelled like when they burned four hundred women at the stake in one day. Why is the killing of women allowed in a "religious" document today?

There should have been a *Holy Book of Women's Mysteries* hundreds of years ago. Ours started as *The Feminist Book of Lights and Shadows*, which I wrote in 1975. The Holy Book Collective always knew it was a "dictated book." We held our meetings on the Malibu mountaintop, and ate breakfast at Mama's Cafe, brainstorming about how to resurrect, remember and invent women's religious experiences. Every Sunday morning we advanced the work in a fabulous, speedy fashion, unencumbered by our normal limits, writing down our ideas concerning Women's Religion and what we thought could be communicated. To this date we have not stopped building and collecting material. A *Woman's Holy Book* is never done! Women relate to creativity in religion, in a changing, ever-growing, blooming stream of consciousness. Our Book is alive, not a fossilized concept from the dark past.

It is a historical book because it contains the memories of the ancient ways, such as the Women's Festivals, the Trysting Ritual and the Sabbat celebrations. Yet it is infused with such modern practices as freeing political prisoners and welcoming a new mother into the circle of mothers.

Sprenger (of *The Witches' Hammer*) will spin in his grave when women learn about the Great Rite, a sexual ritual, and no doubt he's right to call all women witches. Most women don't think they're witches because it's too dangerous to think so. There is a horror of ultimate annihilation connected to it in the deep mind. But were we not better off as a species practicing the life-affirming religion, acting out life-oriented rituals, regarding each of us as children of the Goddess? Enfolded into a celestial motherlove, would we not spin healthier dreams, societies, relationships, lives? Is the male principle of the universe not death without the tempering, inclusive force of the Goddess? Pre-patriarchal religions, practiced universally not too long ago (5000 years is generous) yielded a saner and more comfortable life for all. People focused on life rather than war. Today's obsession with death is a direct result of the exclusive male value system, often referred to as "progress", and its degradation of women. A *Women's Holy Book* is but one of the utterances of the awakening Goddess in Her many guises. The sense of the prophecy, wonder and sacredness articulates through the Mysteries, as the Lifegiver becomes more visible in defense of our endangered species, mothers and their children.

When women and men look at Goddess religion, they expect to find earmarks of the religions with which they were previously involved. They are confused when they don't find anything like it, and so it is even debatable if we have a religion or a tradition.

Witches prefer to call it their Tradition. There are many traditions. We are not divided by color (such as black and white witches); rather, we follow different traditions: Dianics, Druids, Gardnerians, Welsh, English,

Pictish, Nordic, eclectic and more. None of these witchy traditions worship the devil. The devil, poor thing, is a Christian, not a pagan, invention. Devil worship is a measly 150 years old, and was the backlash result of witch burnings.

In witchcraft, the most important cornerstone philosophy is a *trinity*, not a duality. This alone colors everything explaining life. Since we have no duality, there is no concept of "apartness" separating male-female, black-white, good-evil. The Trinity multiplies into three times three, as in the Nine Muses, and from then on explodes into the diversity of nature, accepting the *different* as a religious concept.

This means there is no division between body and soul. One is not despised and the other glorified. There is no division of the sexes; both come from the same source, the Mother. There is no division of spiritual and profane; all is related in the universe, and none stands apart from nature. All is Nature.

When you commit a crime against life, killing the "enemy's" daughters and sons (because there has never been a war in which only the men were killed), you have to finish the enemy's karmic burden. As an example: the Vietnam war coming home. Veterans of that war suffer from physical and psychological scars—they call it "ghosts riding on our backs." There is consequence to all sins against Nature. Nothing goes unnoticed. It is not a sin to kill in self-defense. But going to war "obeying orders" is to be blamed because there is a moment in all people's lives when they can actively choose against it with their free will, the Goddess-given sense of morality and decency. This moment of choice needs enlightening circumstances to reveal itself, without which the person misses her or his destiny. When there is ignorance about the choice, the conditions are evil. Deliverance from this evil comes from information: knowledge, experience, collective consciousness. The Goddess within all.

The Life Force manifests in us, so it's never hopeless. But it isn't always easy to tune into ourselves, especially when we are driven by meaningless work, bored to death by repetition and deprived of living teachers who can pass on information about how to get what we want while we're alive and how to seek truth in harmony with others. This excludes the teachings of the "Our God has the answer and all others are evil" variety, as we find coming from Judeo-Christianity, Islam, Krishna, Buddhism, Moonies and gurus. Does this worry the Goddess Religionist? Only to the extent that these patriarchal religions may gain the political power to outlaw others.

Unfortunately, this is happening right now in this country. It does not surprise me, since it's clear how militaristic the so-called leading religions are. If they followed their Good Books, the Christians would stay out of politics and people's bedrooms and stick to their own lives. I wonder where they have the time to tend their own qualities of the divine, when they spend so much time marching on Washington against the ERA, organizing against gay rights, keeping the blacks down, the Latinos out, the Asians in (new immigrants provide cheap labor) and the war machine running full speed. All this in the name of the Prince of Love?!

We have seen four centuries of systematic torture and killing, mainly of women, whom the church decided were witches. We have seen the Good Book waved at us as we were tied to the stake. We see the conservatives rising in this country, with their lobbyists convincing Congress that God wants it to uphold the Good Book's values as they rage into murder any day. We have seen it before.

Women, witches or not, have had to live with religious oppression. We experienced it on our skin; some were burned, some mutilated. Even today, cutting out the clitorises of females at the age of six or seven is a common practice in India, Africa and Muslim countries. We are kept pregnant against our will, and punished everywhere for being poor. Why would a respectable religion be obsessed with the hatred of women? The hatred of anybody? I don't know. It only makes sense if you see it as a militaristic effort to set up a social system in which women are controlled, with no choice on abortion, no jobs for equal pay. Sound familiar? When women are controlled, the empire is controlled. Women's product is citizens. Consumers. Lovers.

Chapter 1

Feminist Witchcraft

Politics of Women's Religion
Manifesto of the Susan B. Anthony Coven No. 1

We believe that feminist witches are women who search within themselves for the female principle of the universe and who relate as daughters to the Creatrix.

We believe that, just as it is time to fight for the right to control our bodies, it is also time to fight for our sweet woman souls.

We believe that in order to fight and win a revolution that will stretch for generations into the future, we must find reliable ways to replenish our energies. We believe that without a secure grounding in women's spiritual strength there will be no victory for us.

We believe that we are part of a changing universal consciousness that has long been feared and prophesied by the patriarchs.

We believe that Goddess-consciousness gave humanity a workable, long-lasting, peaceful period during which Earth was treated as Mother and women were treated as Her priestesses.

We believe that women lost supremacy through the aggressions of males who were exiled from the matriarchies and formed the patriarchal hordes responsible for the invention of rape and the subjugation of women.

We believe that female control of the death principle yields human evolution.

We are committed to living life lovingly toward ourselves and our sisters. We are committed to joy, self-love, and life affirmation.

We are committed to winning, to surviving, to struggling against patriarchal oppression.

We are committed to defending our interests and those of our sisters through the knowledge of witchcraft: to blessing, to cursing, to healing, and to binding with power rooted in woman-identified wisdom.

We are opposed to attacking the innocent.

We are equally committed to political, communal, and personal solutions.

We are committed to teaching women how to organize themselves as witches and to sharing our traditions with women.

We are opposed to teaching our magic and our craft to men until the equality of the sexes is a reality. We teach "Pan" workshops today and work together with men who have changed themselves into brothers.

Our immediate goal is to congregate with each other according to our ancient woman-made laws and to remember our past, renew our powers, and affirm our Goddess of the Ten Thousand Names.

Women's Religion, As in Heaven, So on Earth

What people believe (faith-religion) is political because it influences their actions and because it is the vehicle by which a religion perpetuates a social system. Politics and religion are interdependent.

Every new social structure strives to come up with some kind of mythology of divine origin for its values and aims. The mythology is passed on for generations, and often its validity goes unquestioned for centuries. For example, a self-created male god who has no mother is a totally insupportable concept. It is, to say the least, not supernatural, but merely unnatural. Nothing in nature parallels, let alone substantiates, such an absurdity. Everything, even a star, originates somewhere—every creature in the world has a mother force. Obviously, to deny motherhood is to deny women.

Patriarchal religion is built on this denial, which is its only original thought, the rest of the edifice having been ripped off stone by stone from the Old Faith of Paganism. The Christian Trinity is a word-by-word reversal of the Fates, the Three-Fold Mother, the Three Graces. The Dove is the sacred bird of the Great Mother. The Great Mother was eventually incorporated into the new Christian religion in the form of the Virgin Mary, who is today worshipped in an "idolatrous" fashion in the Catholic Church.

Who absorbs whose culture is a crucial issue on the cultural battlefield. Those who refused to accept this accommodation and continued to practice the ancient art were persecuted.

Women's spirituality is rooted in Paganism, where women's values are dominant. The Goddess worship, the core of Paganism, was once universal. Paganism is pleasure-oriented, joy- and feasting-prone, celebrating life with dancing and lovemaking. Working in harmony with Mother Nature, we discover and recover the All-Creatrix, the female power without whom nothing is born or glad.

Male energy pretends to have power by disclaiming the female force. Today, given the patriarchal society within which we live, witchcraft with a feminist (Dianic) politic says clearly that the real enemy is the internalized and externalized policing tool that keeps us in fear and psychic clutter.

The craft is not only a religion; it is also a lifestyle. In the time of the Matriarchies, the craft of women was common knowledge. It was rich in information on how to live on this planet, on how to love and fight and stay healthy, and especially, on how to learn to learn. The remnants of that knowledge constitute the body of what we call "witchcraft" today. The massive remainder of that knowledge is buried within ourselves, in our deep minds, in our genes. In order to reclaim it, we have to open ourselves to psychic experiences in the safety of feminist witch covens.

A new kind of trust is the most important contribution that women's spirituality has to give to the women's movement. We learned we can trust our bodies when we learned we had the right to control them. We are learning we can trust our souls through learning that our right to have them is rooted in our recognition of the Goddess, of the female principle within the universe and ourselves.

It is from this source that our independence comes.

The Turning of the Tide: How We Lost It

Reprinted from *Sister,* February 1974

Spirituality in humans occurs from the earliest times, and some scientists call our species a religious animal.

Spirituality isn't necessarily religion. It can be a spontaneous communication with spirits around us. Eventually this process is formalized and then we've got religion.

Mythology is the mother of religions and grandmother of history. Mythology is humanmade by the artists, storytellers, entertainers of the times; in short, culture-makers are the soldiers of history, more effective than guns and bombers. Revolutions are really won in the cultural battlefields.

Women have understood this very well since we became aware of how women's culture had been ripped off by the ruling class. This resulted in a stunted self-image of women, which caused insecurities, internalizing the cultural expectations of us created by male culture-makers. Most of the women in the world still suffer from this spiritual poverty.

Neither was this reasoning unknown to the early patriarchs who gave us today's sexist society. Alexander the Great (the Pig) burned down the libraries that contained the sacred scrolls of the matriarchy, the maps, the astrological discoveries, the medicine, the entire knowhow of the woman-oriented culture that went before him. He knew that this would stop the propagation of the ideas of woman's supremacy.

When pastoral tribes from the north first started coming south to what we know as Greece, they too had to deal with the culture they found: high priestesses and temples dedicated to the Triple Goddess (Isis, Diana and Hecate), sacred shrines, and women in power.

For the first three hundred years, these newcomers to Greece were assimilated by the Triple Goddess culture, Hera (meaning courage), so much so that the Greeks gave up their notion of "marriage" as indecent. Priestesses took over and evenly distributed their favors among all tribes at appropriate sowing times to ensure fertility of the barley, figs and dates. The Greeks learned that this magic worked, and discarded their patriarchal ways. Their male god, whom they called Dios, was formally adopted by Hera as her son, and renamed Zeus after her real son Zagreus. It was all right until more of the same northern tribesmen started to come down from the south side of the Danube, discovering to their horror that their cousins wore jewelry and sometimes women's clothing and were ruled by women. The effort of cultural warfare became at this point a very conscious campaign.

Sthenelus, the leader of the Achaeans, disavowed Zeus as the son and therefore subject to Rhea (Hera), the Triple Goddess, and declared that he had no mother! This was an important political move. He popped out of the sky all by himself; therefore, he was the Almighty Creator, with no dependency on Hera's or Rhea's motherhood for life.

A full-scale religious war ensued. On the Goddess's side, the high priestesses of Rhea and Athena were hung from an oak tree by their hair with anvils tied to their feet until they swore to accept Dios and not insist on the supremacy of Rhea. However, the worship of the Goddess was not discontinued for the sake of the harvest!

But this was not all. Sthenelus called for a conference to agree on and fix the new pantheon once and for all. These religious leaders gathered at Olympia to make up the deities to be worshipped by their offspring for centuries thereafter. Father Zeus became the Almighty ruler; Poseidon used to be a forest god, but now with the forests vanishing, he had to be given a new territory, and he got the sea; and the thunder he had wielded was taken away from him and given to Zeus. He was married to Amphitrite, the Mother Goddess in Her marine aspect, to make his rule stick.

The Triple Goddess, in Her gracious character as Nymph, could not quite be excluded, but they ripped off Her ancient name Marianae and forced Her into a "marriage" with the lame god Hephestus, the sooty-faced blacksmith god, and renamed Her Aphrodite (foam-born). The Triple Goddess's very important aspect as the *Maid* also had to be included in response to public demand. After some dispute, She was admitted into the new patriarchal family as Artemis of the New Moon, the huntress of the wild. This was the correct name She bore among the Palasgians.

But there was a rub. The new Artemis was reborn as the twin of Apollo (who used to be a mouse god) to elevate him into some glory by association.

The patriarchs needed all the glamour they could steal. This concession didn't satisfy the Boeotians and Athenians, on whose affections the Maiden Goddess had a very powerful hold. They demanded Athena be included in a seat of importance. After long and drawn-out meetings, it was decided that she could be included with her own name as Athena only if she also suffered rebirth, denounced her mother, Rhea, and was born from the head of Zeus as a fully-formed maiden in armor.

In the question of the Underworld, a traditional realm of the Triple Goddess, Hecate, the patriarchs really went wild. This was the muscle of the matriarchy. The goddess of Death could be invoked to plot against the new-fangled gods of Olympus, so they abolished her. This caused a big public outcry, and since the name of the game was ''who shall absorb whose culture,'' the patriarchs included Persephone as the wife of Hades, brother of Zeus. The bereaved Palasgians considered Her marriage nothing less than rape. And so the stage was set for a sexist society. The entire Western world lifted the values and male domination structure from the Greek model.

Mythmakers, poets, singers and artists talked about these new deities from then on. They told of the rapes of Zeus as he populated the pantheon with semigods, offspring of his clandestine affairs with mortal women, because Hera, forced into this new institution called ''marriage'' with him, would not give him any children except Hephestus. And we call these works classical knowledge and art, and revere them. What a pity!

I concentrate on the story of Greek culture because it had the most influence on our own society. But the Greeks were not the only ones who made the change-over from Mother Goddess worship to denial of motherhood. As a tool for upsetting female lineage and female inheritance, the Egyptians also made up their own cockeyed stories about Re, the sun god, and deposed Hathor, the mother of all life—symbolized by the white cow—and Isis of the thousand breasts, mother-lover of Osiris, a god who died and was resurrected annually.

In Sumer, where the matriarchies were most ancient and successful, new myth-makers changed Nammu, the sea goddess, into Enlil, a kind of grandson of hers, concentrating mythology around the male figure. In Babylon, where the patriarchy was at full blast, stories circulated that Marduk brought forth the entire Universe, and represented Order (Law-and-Order isn't new either), while Tiamat, the Triple Goddess, was made to represent Chaos. Marduk chopped up his mother's body and made the world out of her limbs. What a grisly mother-hating myth this is. Shades of Jack the Ripper.

Christianity is rather naive compared with the earlier patriarchal yarns. Eve (whose name comes from Havla, life), doubtless the Goddess in Her mother form, eats from the apple tree! This is most absurd, since the apple (or quince) always belonged to Her and symbolized wisdom. The tale that the snake made her do it is transparent as well. The snake belongs to Her; it is the Goddess's symbol of death and rebirth. At Her shrines, the sacred snakes used to be consulted by the priestesses for oracles. Hecate, Mary, Medusa and Eve—they are never without their sacred animal, the snake, just as Life is never without Death as a necessity.

Such is the power of mythology. It fixes the society that the ruling class wants perpetuated. That's why, dear sisters, we must get on with our own myth-making. I propose a story, ancient in its roots, but not often repeated nowadays, except at witches' festivals, where the Mother Goddess is dispensing Psychic Energy, in this energy-crisis-ridden world, to Her daughters, who turn to Her.

The Great Goddess is stirring again in the hearts of Her daughters. Thousands of wicca covens exist today as the spiritual poverty of male culture turns off more and more women. Church women are in revolt, demanding to be ordained, and individual women are discovering the magic their womanhood gives them if they only listen to the Goddess' instructions.

I believe, as a revolutionary, that the women's movement is badly in need of just such an energizing. To reclaim our souls is the next step in achieving the goals of the movement, after taking back our bodies.

We now have to gradually turn the same weapons of culture-making that defeated us against our oppressors.

The Slothwoman as Ancient Magician

Reprinted from *Thesmophoria*, Spring Equinox, 1986

My friend Carla didn't believe in anything, not god or goddess or spirits; she even doubted that she had a soul herself. One day, Carla had to face a great challenge. She fell in love.

Since this was not something she had done often in her life, something inside her wanted reassurance, wanted some protection against the affair falling apart. On that day she called me up.

"Can you do a protection spell on me, Z?" she asked.

"I don't do spells for others," I said. "It's not empowering if I do it for you."

"I'll give you money."

"Carla, that isn't the point. I don't do spells for you or anybody— unless you want to learn how, in which case I'll be happy to teach you."

"But you know, Z, I'm not a believer," she said. "My spell wouldn't work."

"Your spell will work fine even if you don't believe in it. Witchcraft is not a matter of faith, it is a matter of observation. We work with natural laws. You can think the sun won't rise or the moon won't shine, but they still do whatever they're supposed to do in the universe, regardless of what you believe. But since this love affair is close to your heart, your emotional investment far outranks mine, so it's your work that's needed," I explained.

"Whatever you say. Teach me then," Carla finally agreed.

I listened to her problem, which was simply about this man who didn't want to be tied down with a lover. In other words, he just wanted sex, but not to be tangled up with the care and emotions that come with a committed relationship.

She performed a spell called "lover come near," using two cherry red candles, with each candle bearing their names. I told her to walk up a mountain under the full moon, burn the two candles to the Goddess and ask Her to blend these two hearts into one. Placing the candles on the ground, she was to move them closer and closer together until they touched and burned down together.

The spell worked within two weeks.

The reluctant lover came to see her more and more often, blending their energies together, making commitments, and they finally relaxed with each other.

There are many ways to get interested in magic, but falling in love seems to be the biggest recruiter for the Goddess.

Still, how did she do it? A woman who had no preparation, who just followed a spell like a recipe?

My theory is that deep within ourselves, there lives a creature I call Slothwoman (or Slothman). She is our ancestral brain that is the repository for all our racial memories, that controls healing; a sturdy creature, to be sure, but speechless. She is into the elements, this brain: fire, water, and earth. She controls our instinctive behavior. Our sex life would be boring without her help, and generally she is what we deny in ourselves in this modern life.

In order to impress our Slothwoman, we have to do tricks, like making up little rhymes, easy ones she can rock to back and forth, and make a pretty little altar that would turn her on. We use candles and incense to fascinate her within—use magic, which is her language, her form.

This sweet gentle giant is the key to our lives; she is body, health, sex, instinct, creativity, and love. She wants security from us. She wants to be regarded. She wants to be called forth. Otherwise, she can sleep through our modern lives and do nothing. She is Slothwoman, ancestor.

I visualize her as a tall, hairy, ungainly creature, my Slothwoman. She lumbers as she walks. She is clumsy. She howls at the moon and hums when happy. She likes food and cooking smells, the company of others, and family kinds of gatherings. If I take care of her, she lets me have all I need to maintain myself body and soul. If you can turn on this ancient brain within, you can turn on the magic.

I think it's natural to look at spellcasting as a process much like cooking; you use a cookbook and follow the steps. It isn't the tools that make the magic come to pass, it is your own brain. Intellect, however, is not this magical brain. Imagination, the dark night, the full moon, wild environments, woods, mountains, rivers, oceans—these are the places where the Slothwoman comes alive.

Faith healing works the same way. You create a situation where the priestess gets access to your old brain and a circle of friends builds a giant fire, makes sounds with rattles and drums, and opens you up to the healer's words.

Then, while the energy is quite high, an experienced priestess knows when she can command the evil spirit (a.k.a. sickness) to leave the body. Our brain is so powerful that if you can make her reject the sickness, she can lower fevers, get up and walk even if she was at death's door.

The same is true with this brain if she chooses to die. Suppose this part of our brain feels "hexed." Slothwoman hates that. She may not even want to get up in the morning. In Tahiti, there were priests who would hex an individual and no Western doctor could cure him. The only cure was to have the hex removed by the person who put it on him.

Our old brains are gullible, cannot be "hip." No amount of consciousness raising can help. This brain doesn't have the power of speech. It only understands the old moves, rituals, rhymes, fire, water, stars. Only out of these elements can a cure be constructed. Speeches and psychologists are meaningless.

It is important to keep communicating to our own inner Slothwoman. If you are a friend to her, she is less fearful, less gullible. If you provide her with the appropriate rituals she is satisfied and will provide you with robust health, a lusty sex drive, and a love of life. Slothwoman, however, is not the one who gets up each morning to go out and get a paycheck. That's our new brain, devoted to speech and the opposed thumb.

Scientists say we only use ten percent of our brain power; the rest must be cultivated by design. In nature, what you don't use, you lose.

Spellcasting is what other religions call prayer. To cast a spell on a mountain means to pray for something. In the Craft, we pray to an immanent Goddess; She permeates all walks of life. We do not just pray to Her "above," but also "within." When patriarchal religions talk about the "grace" that comes to those who pray, they are talking about the same things we did thousands of years before them.

Cultivate your deeper mind and be well.

"Dangers" of Magic
by Starhawk

There are real dangers to the practice of magic, most of them found within ourselves, particularly before we have a full and deep understanding of how magic works. I have listed here some of the major problems which trip us up, with some suggestions for protection. However, it is a necessary part of everyone's magical education to occasionally fall victim to one's character traits. We all find ourselves ego-tripping, do-gooding, showing off, and all the rest from time to time, but how else could we learn compassion and tolerance for others who go off on the same tangents? Falling victim to one's own illusions eventually confers a sort of immunity, much like the result of a childhood disease, and with luck, recovery is rapid and complete. Here, then, are the "mumps and measles" of magic.

Omnipotence. This is quite common when first discovering that your Will can effect events. You may feel a tremendous rush of power and believe that you can do anything and everything. Experience will cure this fallacy quickly, however, but the condition of omnipotence can lead to...

Guilt. You may believe you can do everything, but sooner or later you will fail. Sometimes it is the people you care about most whom you are unable to help. Unless you realize that magic has its limitations and works within the framework of laws (just as standard medical science does), you run the risk of feeling responsible for everything that goes wrong in the universe. Relax. You are not that powerful, nor are you that important.

Paranoia. As your awareness grows and you become more conscious of negative energy and impulses in others, you may become oversensitive and begin jumping at shadows and protecting against dangers that don't exist. There is also the dodge of ascribing every negative thing that happens to you to "psychic attack." A healthy stream of cynicism is a good defense against this one. Remember that magic that is real rarely conflicts with common sense. If you feel beset by evil forces, look within yourself to see what is drawing them.

Saintliness. It is hard to resist the temptation to be more-spiritual-than-thou, to offer unasked-for advice to your acquaintances, and to look down on others who have not "seen the Light," all the while trying to appear humble. With any luck at all, you will come back to earth before you lose all your friends.

Showing Off. This, like Saintliness, is hard to resist. When the fanatic Jehovah's Witness in your chemistry class spouts off about religion, how can you NOT tell her you see a hypocritical green spot in her aura? With painful experience, however, you will discover that people will not hear or listen to your advice or commentary unless they have asked for it, and that magic only works when it's real, not for show.

Going Half-Astral. When you get so caught up in magic and psychic work that you neglect the earthly plane and your physical body, you will become drained and weakened. In extreme cases, people who lose touch too completely with earth can have what amounts to a psychotic "break." This is easily avoided, however, by making certain you stay grounded and centered when you do any magical work or meditations. Also, it is vital to have a satisfying and rewarding earth-plane life, including a good sex life and a love of good food.

The Craft should not cause any loss of pleasure or ability to function in your daily life. On the contrary, pleasure and capabilities in ordinary things should only be heightened by your increasing awareness.

Your very best protection against all of these ills and any others you may meet physically or psychically is to maintain your sense of humor. As long as you laugh at yourself, you cannot head too far down the wrong path, and you always have an immediate ticket back to truth. Whenever you find you are taking yourself too seriously, or whenever you meet someone or something who encourages you to do so, beware! Remember, laughter is the key to sanity.

Tools of the Craft—Material

Altar: It represents the deep mind. No one else is allowed to touch your private altar, not even lovers or relatives. Sabbath altars, on the other hand, are built by all participating.

Setup: A table cover with a clean white cloth and a Mother Goddess image in the middle (a single rose, pictures, even postcards are used to represent the Goddess). We don't worship the image; witches are not fetish worshipers. We use the image to awaken in our deep minds the Triple Goddess, Who rules over life, death and beauty. On two sides there are two white candles. In front of the image, there is a censer or incense burner. A shell makes a nice burner. Magical work takes place in front of this setup, be it black or white magic.

Athalme: A knife, preferably black-handled, with a blade that can be magnetized. It represents the air element, and is used to separate the sacred grounds from the rest by casting the circle.

Wand: It represents the fire element. Place it to the south on your altar. It is used in love magic, and can also be used to cast circles. The magic wand does willpower work.

Cord: The cord is made to measure, wrought to bind. It is used to cast the nine-foot-radius circle for ritual work.

Chalice: It represents the water element and the grail. It is the Goddess symbol of plenty and blessings.

Pentagram: It represents the five-fold path. It is the ancient sign of protection. It also stands for the earth element.

How to Make Your Tools

It is best to make all your tools from scratch. If that is impractical, try to invest as much energy in them as possible. When you buy them, never haggle over the price.

Athalme: Take magnets and stroke the knife toward yourself until it is magnetized. Strengthen the magnetic force at each new moon.

Wand: A branch, from a special tree you love, as long as the distance from elbow to third fingertip, taken under a full moon, which you pay for with one drop of your blood. There are thirteen sacred trees, any of which is great for wands. Most often used are: rowan, oak, elder, willow, blackthorn, hazel, mistletoe and elderberry. Dig out a little hole in one end of the branch and stuff it with a piece of cotton and a drop of your menstrual blood. Seal with candlewax drippings. Put your witch's name in runes upon the opposite side of the wand and a pentagram at the top and bottom. Consecrate it in the name of Diana with water, wine, fire, incense and oil at new moon time.

Biolline: White-handled knife to carve with.

Cauldron: Iron pot to burn your herbs in or cook meals for feasts in.

Cord: Red yarn, braided into a nine-foot long girdle worn around the waist.

Necklaces, rings and jewels are all used according to inclination. Shells, stones and seeds such as acorns were traditionally used to make necklaces, which stand for the "circle of rebirth."

Candles, Oils and Incense

These are three important tools in the practice of magic. The flickering of candlelight and the aroma of burning incense awaken and stimulate the deep mind, the source of the power we work with in doing spells. It is the ancient part of us that knows no language, communicing through instinct and intuition.

Candles

Candles represent the fire element, which is associated with the south. They are used to mark that corner of the universe, both on your altar and in your circle. A candle's color is important because we naturally ascribe different meanings to different colors:

Attraction: Yellow and orange
Concentration: Purple and white
Dispelling (blessed): Black
Happiness: Blue, orange, pink
Holidays: White
Friendship: Blue
Influence: Brown and pink
Love: Pink and red
Novena: Nine-day candle
Prosperity: Red or green
Peace: White
Protection: Reversible (Black with red center)
Revenge: Reversible (Black snake with red center)
Special devotion or supplication: Nine devotional candles
Special spiritual message and readings: Red and white
Special favors: Brown
Success: Triple action (Red, white, blue)
To pray for the sick: White
Work: Purple
Improve vibration: White and pink

Candles are also designated by color to the months of the year:

> January: Red and gold
> February: Yellow and blue
> March: Blue and green
> April: Pink and orange
> May: Blue and gold
> June: Red and blue
> July: Red and green
> August: Pink and orange
> September: Pink and gold
> October: Pink and gold
> November: Yellow and blue
> December: Red and orange

The month you were born determines your astral colors. Choose astral candles to represent yourself (or others) in your spell.

Image Candles

Image candles can be used in a spell by themselves, or they can be used along with regular candles.

Black Cat: To stop slander and gossip.
Green Female or Male Images: For money, anoint with Money Oil during

waxing moon. Burn a little each morning and night.

Red Female or Male Images: For love, anoint with Musk, Attraction or Lover's Oil. Burn a little bit each morning and night.

Black Snake Reversible: To send back evil vibrations.

Black Skull: To stop an attack on your mind.

Purple Skull: To influence the mind of others; anoint with Control Oil.

Grey Images: To cancel out bad luck; anoint with Uncrossing Oil for purification and health.

Red Snake: To burn away obstacles between lovers.

Yoni (the female genitals): Ancient symbol of freedom and rebirth; green for health and growth, red for love.

Candles should be anointed and blessed before they go on the altar. The appropriate oils to use are described below. To anoint your candle, pour the oil on your fingertips and stroke it upward from the center; then turn it around and stroke it upward again. Be sure to get the top and bottom and the wick. To bless the candles, lay them down all together and hold your hands over them, thumbs touching. Feel them all over with your bioplasma (not touching). Imagine your energy going into them. Breathe deeply a few times, and holding your hands over the candles, say:

> *In the name of Isis of the thousand breasts,*
>   *may my purpose be blessed;*
> *In the name of Diana, may my spell be strong;*
> *In the name of Hecate, Queen of Heaven, Queen of Hell,*
>   *may my purpose be accomplished.*

Close your hands tightly around the candles, saying "So mote it be!" Here, as in all blessings, the spirit is the thing; improvise!

Oils

In addition to being used to anoint candles, oils are the body's incense. Use them instead of perfume; they are more organic and they manipulate the aura by stimulating the deep mind.

Ava Rosa: To bind your enemy.

Bast: Sacred to the Sun Goddess. Use as a powerful good-luck vibe.

Bat's Blood: Breaks hexes. (It is an herb.)

Bewitching: Amplifies willpower. Use it only with clear purpose.

Black Art: Used in self-defense to zap. Sacred to Lilith.

Bergemont: Protection and money drawing.

Cleopatra: Heavy love vibration with control.

Cinnamon: Attracts lovers, good luck, health.

Come-inside: To be visited often by great people.

Double-Crossing: For revenge.

Dove's Blood: An ink used to write commands on parchment paper.
Fast Luck: For special projects, gambling.
Forget Him/Her: If an affair is best forgotten.
High Joan: For sacred candles.
Lover's: Freshens up love affairs.
Money Drawing: Anoint your purse, candles.
Musk: Excites sexuality. For love spells.
Priestess: Ritual oil; anoint candles with it; further spirituality.
Protection: Wear it daily against danger on all levels.
Patchouli: Sacred to Pan.
Rosemary: Protection; wear it to battles.
Rose: Sacred to Diana.
Success: Wear it to make your goals come true.
Uncrossing: Wear it if bad luck strikes.
Violet: Sacred to the Fairy Queen.
War Water: For attack, used in spells with war powder.

Incense

Incense represents the air element, associated with the direction of the east, and is used to mark that corner of the universe in a ritual setup. The aromas of different incenses put different vibes in the air. Burning incense is a good way to control your psychic space. Powdered incense burns very well when you pour it into a cone-shaped pile in your censer and hold a match to it. The pebble-form incenses (Isis, frankincense) and the incenses that include herbal mixtures burn better on charcoal. See the section on Spellcasting for incense recipes.

Tools of the Craft—Psychic

The number one tool that we have is imagination. Do you remember when you were a child, how you could populate an empty space with things, people and conversations; experience total transformations within by just imagining them? This childhood imagination is stifled during the school years. We are socialized, forbidden to fly with our thoughts.

I visited the place in Hungary where I grew up, and I saw the beloved backyard of our traditional yellow building. As a child, I lived on the ground floor of a four-story apartment house. Of course, the yard was much smaller than I remembered it, but it was still there and just as dark. Many people tried to plant flowers there, but because of the shadow from the apartment house, nothing grew.

But I remember playing there with a red brick representing a train. I pushed it around on the ground for hours and hours on end, making little tracks. And I stopped in make-believe places, and I called them whatever I knew. For instance, I went to Africa and visited the jungles and saw the tigers and the elephants. Other times, the train stopped in Paris and I got out and I became a grown-up lady, shopping for clothes. I went to Australia in the backyard, watching the kangaroos hop around, catching them and playing with them. I remember the backyard transforming into a stage for ballet, where I was the prima donna and I danced for hours in front of a giant, roaring, applauding audience. Other times I went on quiet walks and transformed myself into birds and flying creatures. I battled dragons. I won battles and generally had a grand time. This is the precious faculty we use in magic; we use it in everyday life, and in creating our reality—our imagination.

The second tool is breath. When you sit in front of your altar, you become conscious of your breathing. You imagine your lungs becoming like wings and you fill them with air. You see, your being is connected to life through breath. When you gather with others, holding hands and breathing in unison, you become as one. It's very easy to unify with many people by just breathing together. Even if you are not doing the Craft, but gathering to discuss an issue or have a meeting, it's a very good idea to hold hands and breathe together a little while before you begin. You will find people becoming friendlier and more focused, and the work being done faster. Then, at the end, close the meeting by breathing together.

The third tool is something I call "clear targeting." To find purpose is a gift. You have to work for it. It's not just "Oh, here it is. I'll pick it up and it's mine." If you think about attaining peace, you have to meditate on that, too. You have to meditate first before you can find the proper target. Whatever you do, you can always find a positive way to get to it, even if you are in great trouble.

The answer is not to smite your enemy to the death, because Mother Nature does not work like that. You are better off finding a positive way to attain what you need. Just meditate on your purpose. To find your purpose and for proper targeting, get yourself a skyblue candle. The color blue is a relaxing color. It's easier to find answers (your purpose) when you are relaxed. Write your name on the candle three times and meditate on your purpose three nights in a row. Burn a little incense as well.

Basic Witchy Setup

Be it for Sabbats, Esbats, or private devotional rituals, the basic elements of the ritual are the same and follow the same sequence. The basic witchy setup is:

1. Determining the boundaries of the circle.
2. Consecrating the grounds with fire and air (incense), water and salt.
3. Drawing the circle separating the grounds of worship.
4. Purifying those who enter the circle.
5. Closing the circle after all are admitted.
6. Invocations to the corners of the universe.
7. Sealing the circle.
8. Raising witches' power.
9. Inviting the Goddess.
10. Blessing on all tools, food, people.
11. Ritual work appropriate to the event.
12. Feasting: first thanks and libation to the Goddess, then personal business with the Goddess.
13. Dancing and "Pleasure Now!" celebration.
14. Dismissing the spirits.

Why Should a Woman Cast a Spell?

Why not? Everything else has been done.

Casting a spell is a willful act, some say. It is interfering with the natural order of things. I say casting a spell is observing and participating as an equal partner in the natural order. A woman is part of the natural order. Her directed willpower is part of nature. I recognize the reluctance toward casting a spell. It is against every kind of social conditioning you have ever received. So I advocate doing this; go ahead and scare yourself. It's good for you.

Casting a spell, in self-defense or in self-interest, is not selfish but positive, life-affirming. You have been given powers, the very same powers that society devalues. Your right-brain activity, your hunches, come in handy in this activity. Now is the time to use this very oppression, like Aikido, in your own favor. All your life as a woman you have been encouraged to be intuitive, sensitive, nurturing and inventive. In spellcasting, that is all that you need.

"But Z, what if it comes back to me tenfold?" Well, don't be a fool. Never use your magic to attack the innocent. Then you have nothing to fear. Always target wisely, finding a positive approach toward what you seek. Don't be frivolous or cowardly. If your course is righteous, and your tools ready, go to it. Women have enough trouble worrying about being powerless without wasting time worrying about a little power we can use right away. Did I say "little"? Not at all. A lot of power. Women can call down nature in their own behalf. For example, we once cast a spell for a custody case.

The father hired a very expensive lawyer and the trial date was only three days away. The mother gathered us in a circle and we raised energy around a sassafras tree, performed spontaneous prayers, chanted the names of the Goddess, and offered a small libation of milk to the Earth. Three days later, this woman called to say her husband and his lawyer set out for court and never arrived! She won by default. (We still don't know where they went instead.)

A young woman in Venice, California came to us after her rape. She knew the man and wanted him prosecuted. We shared a hex with her to bring this man to justice so he could not weasel out from punishment. She performed the hex, with our help, and buried the remnants in a nearby cemetery. The rapist was caught while eating in a greasy-spoon restaurant after raping someone else. The police put him away for all his crimes. He is still in jail.

In San Francisco, we performed a spell against the Briggs Initiative, which would have made it illegal for gays to teach. The initiative bit the dust.

The success stories are endless and miraculous. Spells are powerful prayers and they do work. Practice your powers and you will never again believe you're inferior.

Casting the Circle

The Casting of the Circle is crucial for any ritual work. The ritual work must correlate the correct planetary aspects with the purpose of the work.

Gather the sisters participating in the ritual and measure a circle by holding each other's hands and standing at arm's length. Mark the circle by gathering a stone to replace one's foot space. Gather more stones and build an altar in the middle of the circle, slightly to the north (power corner). Upon the stone altar, set your representation of the Mother Goddess; an image, or a single rose, is fine. Place two white candles (one to the east, one to the west) of the Goddess image.

Each woman now places one white candle on the altar, and one on the outside circle stone.

Women are needed to mark out the circle with flour and barley, and write the names of the Goddess within the circle. They are also to consecrate the grounds with fire and air by walking around with incense in the circle (frankincense and myrrh are traditional; herbal incense is fine).

The High Priestess (HP) purifies all the grounds and herself with water and salt (or seawater, if it is available). Her priestesses leave the circle to meditate. The HP draws the circle with her witch's knife on the ground in an uninterrupted way, separating the grounds of worship from the rest. It is drawn from east to south to west to north, leaving a gate to the east open for the women to enter.

Women gather to enter, oldest first, youngest last.
The HP sprinkles purifying water on each one, saying:

> *I purify you from all anxiety, all fears, in the name of Diana.*

Woman answers:

> *I enter the circle in perfect love and perfect trust.*

HP kisses and embraces the woman:

> *Welcome to the Goddess's presence.*

With incense, HP consecrates each woman with a pentagram in the air. Each woman then attends to lighting her candle on the altar and outer circle. When the last woman has entered, the HP closes the gate with her knife and says:

> *This circle is closed. The Goddess blesses Her women.*

To unify: Form the circle with linked bodies, hands on napes of necks. Breathe deeply to oxygenate. Every woman makes a sound with her body that can manifest as a low hum, or Goddess names, or just variations of the sound the group uses.

Backing the HP, the women turn to the east, drawing a pentagram in the air with their witches' knives.

HP walks to the east corner, drawing a pentagram in the air with her athalme, kissing the blade after each invocation:

> *(East:) Hail to thee, powers of the East! Hail to the great eagle, corner of all beginnings! Ea, Astarte, Aurora, Goddess of all Beginnings! Come and be witness to our rite as we perform it according to ancient rites!*

> *(South:) Hail to thee, powers of the South! Corners of great fire and passion, Goddess Esmeralda, Goddess Vesta and Heartha! Come and be witness at our rite as we perform it according to ancient laws!*

> *(West:) Hail to thee, powers of waters! Life-giving Goddess of the Sea, Aphrodite, Marianne, Themis, Tiamat! Come and guard our circle and bear witness to our rite as we perform it according to ancient rites!*

> *(North:) Hail to thee, corner of all powers! Great Demeter, Persephone, Kore, Ceres! Earth Mothers and Fates! Great sea of glass! Guard our circle and bear witness as we perform our rite according to your heritage!*

HP moves back to the east corner and seals the circle with her kiss. Now the circle is really closed, and nobody can leave it until the spirits evoked are properly thanked and dismissed.

The Ritual

All place their knives down. Arms are linked one more time—it's time to raise the witches' power. First a low hum is produced, but then creativity and imagination can be used to embroider on the overall sound of everyone. Unusual sounds can come up, animal sounds, howling at the moon like dogs or hooting like owls.

While this is happening, the HP feels when the time is right (energy has been raised) and invites the Goddess's appearance. This part is always improvised, but there are ancient lines to memorize, if you are so inclined (see the Sabbats for details):

> *Blessing upon all tools, food, people.*

All extend hands in the sign of the Horn (little finger and thumb extended, rest tucked under), never interrupting the hum, which is the energy to use throughout the ritual:

> *Gracious Goddess Diana! Eternal Sister! Bless this food to make us strong! Bless our tools, too, and hearts! We gather together to receive your teachings and draw near your presence.*

All coveners say:

> *Blessed be!*

HP pours the wine into the chalice, holding it up to the moon:

> *Lovely Goddess of the bow! Lovely Goddess of the arrows! Of all hounds and of all hunting. Thou who wakest in starry heaven when the sun is sunk in slumber. Thou with moon upon thy forehead, who the chase by night preferest unto hunting in the daylight, with thy nymphs unto the music of the horn—thyself the huntress, and most powerful: I pray thee think, although but for an instant, upon us who pray unto thee! Fair Goddess of the rainbow, of the stars and of the moon, the Queen most powerful of hunters and of the night. We beg thee thy aid, that thou mayest give to us the best of fortune ever!*

HP pours wine upon the earth as a libation and all coveners, when receiving the chalice, do the same. She sips of the wine and says,

20

"Blessed be!" or gives us a short blessing, or whatever is close to the heart.

Practical Advice for Circling

We have gathered practices based on improvisation. So, rule number one is to improvise any time you feel as though creative juices are flowing. This is very important. Spontaneous praying is more powerful than the memorized, out-of-the-book kind. What comes through the soul in the moment is more powerful than what is hammered into the brain.

When you recite poetry, don't worry about forgetting a line or two. Do not read from a piece of paper. Nothing can ruin high energy more than somebody whipping out a flashlight and starting to read. It's different when you are settled down at the last part, the feast part of your circles, and there is free-flowing conversation. You can read your poetry then. Remember the earth's religions preceded writing and they invented it.

Take some time alone and walk through rituals in natural places to find out what works for you. Try to worship outdoors as much as possible. Don't let yourself become too much of a backyard pagan or a livingroom witch. That's missing the point.

Indoor gatherings are more practical when the weather is cold and you intend to go sky-clad. Sky-clad means taking your clothes off, remembering that in the craft, the naked human body represents truth—the goddess Maat, for example, is always shown nude, with feathers only; and she's the goddess of truth. Remember that it is a great equalizer, not a sexual thing, to take your clothes off. It also teaches you love for your body, respect for your body, and acceptance of the variety around you.

Do not lend out your *Holy Book* to other people. It is notorious for disappearing from people's homes. Put your name on it right away, and if you have to lend it out, write down the name of the person to whom you lent it. I have seen people buying new copies because they lent them out and never got them back. Others say the books were stolen. Now, that's a bad idea—to steal *Holy Books* from each other. There are enough copies for everyone, so please buy your own copy and don't lift it from others.

The Feast

The chalice goes around to each woman, who toasts the Goddess with libation. Thanks for received favors and praises for Her wisdom are in order. The second round of wine is used for sisters' wishes, a dialogue between Goddess and Woman. Communal and personal help might be asked here. All coveners listen intently to each woman's words and seal them with "Blessed be!" or "So mote it be!" Before the women grow tired of standing, the HP takes the bread or cakes, as the case may be, and offers them to Diana. It is then passed from woman to woman. All think about the significance of the Moon as governor of waters and, therefore, of organic life on Earth.

The feast is done in happy tones, with much praise for the Goddess, and celebration of Her among us, Her women. All can then sit on the ground.

After the feast, dancing begins.

Ancient Meeting Dance

The circle of women holds hands and steps in rhythm from the east towards the north. At one point, the HP whips around and, as she moves from north to east, she kisses each woman. The women follow and kiss each other likewise.

Dance music can be made with sacred instruments: cymbals, drums, flutes, tambourines. Recordings of women's music are fine. Partying and general merriment continue until energies are depleted.

Then the circle is formed one more time. The HP draws her pentagrams starting from the north, then moving toward the west, south and east, as in the beginning.

> *(North:) Goddess Demeter, we thank you for your presence. Watchtowers of the North bless us before you leave! Blessed be!*

> *(West:) Great Goddess of Life, watchers of the West, thank you for attending, please bless us before you leave! Blessed be!*

> *(South:) Great Goddess of Fire and Passions, thank you for guarding us! Please bless us before you leave! Blessed be!*

> *(East:) Great Goddess of All Beginnings, grant us our prayers! Thank you for attending! Please bless us before you leave! Blessed be!*

After the last corner, the HP announces, "The ritual is ended. The Goddess blesses Her women."

Throughout the rituals, the coveners are always vocal. Each blessing is repeated by all. Each motion with the athalme is followed by all. Each time the HP speaks, coveners back her up with their own improvised sound. When there are enough priestesses, rotate the corners of the universe so all can practice.

Introduction to Spellcasting

In our Dianic tradition, Aradia, the daughter of Diana, was sent down to the earth because "there were many poor, and the rich made slaves of the poor." In those days, as today, the slaves were cruelly treated. In every palace, torture; in every castle, prisoners. Today it is just more sophisticated; the slaves are predominantly women, the places of imprisonment vary from split-level houses to tiger cages.

Aradia came to teach the oppressed how to overthrow the masters. As the only known female avatar (deity in human form), she established her school and taught many the Craft. When she finished and rejoined her mother (dia-holy, ana-mother), she left instructions on how to conjure her for further help. The spells have been passed down from mother to daughter, surviving patriarchy. The Craft is the religion of the oppressed. There is only one rule: "Harm none, and do as thou wilt."

The power of the mind is really what's behind the spells' success. The ingredients in spells represent earth, air, fire, and water, and what we do, in token, is to make the wish a fact before the macrocosm adopts it. It is given birth by you.

General Rules

Correlate your spells with the phases of the moon. On the waxing moon, do positive spells: love, health, money, success. The nine-day spells should land during the full moon, when boons are granted. On the waning moon, tie that which is loose, dispel evil, return bad vibes. Correlate your spells with the proper planets, if you can. Know the proper name of the Goddess for the different aspects appropriate for the spell. Remember, the Lady Who weaves our lives has a certain pattern for all people to fulfill; if you find that what you want is not to be, don't lose heart, but understand the Goddess has veto power. Bless Her will, and search for wisdom.

The following samples of spells cover a few issues in life; they are by no means complete.

If you are a beginner, I recommend you work with candle magic spells. They are very powerful and it is easy to relate to the fires. Make sure your altar is fireproof; cover it with aluminum foil if you often leave candles alone. By understanding the relationship of the colors to the deep mind, you can eventually devise the spells yourself.

In candle magic, we have seen the fast advancement of witches. The oils represent the water element, which is why anointing candles is important. Coordinating colors with oils and incense makes a good candle spell. Candles can be used in three-day spells, nine-day spells, and one-night spells. It is all up to your given circumstances.

Herbal spells are more secretive; the roots and leaves are hidden craftfully in the room. They are what we use to "dress" a space for business, happiness, peace. Herbal spells are very personal, particularly when roots are kept on your body so that no one can touch them. I love them because in Europe herbal spells are used most often.

Voodoo spells sit very well with black sisters, to whose cultural heritage they belong. There isn't anything evil about them; they work like all other spells. You can cure and you can hex, depending on what your intent is. Voodoo spells usually take nine days, and the images are burned on the tenth day. You dispose of dolls representing others; you keep dolls that represent yourself in the house, especially for money or love.

The combination of all the above is fine, provided you understand the magical properties of herbs, candles, powders and oils, and coordinate them accordingly.

Anyone who tells women not to practice magic because it is "dangerous" and it will come back on them is propagating fear. Women invented magic as part of the entire matriarchal culture, and women ruled the world for a very long and successful period by psychic powers. Rediscover your powers! The only danger in throwing spells is ignorance. So study, experiment, grow!

Candle Spells

The purpose of the spell determines the color of the candles used. Check the meanings of colors listed in the earlier section on *Tools of the Craft—Material*.

With Dove's Blood Ink (an herb used for commanding), write your wish on a white piece of parchment paper. Place it under the candle. Anoint the candle according to the desire; if it is love, use Cleopatra, Lover oil, or Rosa Ava. If it is money, anoint the candle with Money Drawing oil. If it is power, anoint with Seven Power oil, and so on. Take a sharp instrument and write what you want three times on the candle. Burn incense again according to the purpose, but if you have frankincense and myrrh, the Goddess listens. Say:

Upon this candle I will write
What I receive of thee tonight.
Grant what I wish you to do,
I dedicate this rite to you.
I trust that you will grant this boon,
O lovely Goddess of the Moon.
I call earth to bond my spell,
Air speed its travel well.

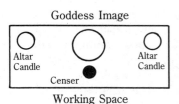

Goddess Image

Altar Candle   Altar Candle

Censer

Working Space

Fire give it spirit from above,
Water quench my spell with love.
So mote it be!
—Sybil Leek

This is best performed at the full moon.

For Health

Light white candles on the altar. Think about the work you will do. Light incense: White Magic, Ritual, or Our Sister of Guadalupe. As the incense fills your space, think about the Goddess of Life permeating the pores of your body.

Light your petitioner candle, which is either your astral color or a deep green candle representing the color of life. Write your name three times on it with something sharp; anoint it with Seven Power oil, Blessing oil, or your own ritual oil. Say:

> *This is me in excellent health. The blessing of the Life God-*
> *dess is upon me so that I may prosper!*

Light an orange candle and say:

> *This flame draws all that is good, all that is health, all*
> *that is strength to me!*

Light three red candles and say:

> *Here is the strength, the power of the Goddess of Life. Here*
> *is Her fire of life, the threefold Goddess Who rules over*
> *life and death and beauty. This is the fire that enters my*
> *body to build, to maintain, to prosper my life!*

Contemplate what you have said, then say:

> *Hygeia, Goddess of Health, enter my mind so that I will*
> *think strong. Blessed be! Goddess Hygeia, enter the cells*
> *in my body, one by one, and make them whole; make them*
> *strong. Blessed be!*
>   *Goddess of Life, infuse the force in me that created the*
> *universe. Increase toward me the force that created the*
> *planet earth. Protect my organic life, so that it maintains*
> *me in this incarnation. Blessed be!*

Do this every Friday, the day of Venus (Goddess of life), or Freya, the Nordic Goddess who gave us the name Friday. Do this for seven successive Fridays.

For Love

Take a Seven Power candle and Most Powerful Love incense and burn them a little each morning and each night. Soon your true love will show up—among the others who also come forth lusting for your body. Wade through them and pick.

Take an image candle, and anoint it with Cleopatra oil, which is for commanding love. On the front and back, write the name of the person you want. Also, anoint an image candle to represent yourself. Burn Most Powerful Love incense, a little bit in the morning and evening. Every night for three nights, move the two images closer and closer together. When the candles touch, let them burn down together. Collect the remnants and throw them in a living body of water (river, ocean, etc.), turn away, and don't look back. Your loved one will turn to you within a full cycle of the moon.

Spell to Influence the Minds of Others

Time: Waxing moon.

Take a purple skull candle, representing your target. On the back of the skull, write the name of the person whom you wish to influence, and all around the skull write the thought you wish that person to perceive. Be resourceful in solutions. Now anoint the candle with Controlling oil, Rosa Ava oil, or Patchouli oil.

Light the candle on your altar after sundown; it is best done late at night when this person is surely asleep. Then meditate on the person, thinking what you want to suggest. Go back to sleep yourself; put out the candle in the morning.

Do this three nights in succession; the third night let it go down all the way. Gather the remnants and throw them into a living body of water. It is done.

Spell to Improve Psychic Powers

Spells to improve psychic powers are best performed at the new and full moon. Psychic ability is not developed during the course of one spell, but rather in the series of events that constitutes one's life. Studying the stars, recording dreams and maintaining a healthy diet are also good steps toward development.

As a spell to release your third eye, dress in yellow and place yellow candles on your altar. If you have a crystal ball, place it in the center. Brew yourself a cup of saffron tea to drink while meditating. Sit comfortably in front of your altar, breathing deeply, and think of your spine as a serpent uncoiling, reaching up through your body and raising your energy. Light incense containing any of several herbs good for psychic work, such as wood betony, sandalwood, olibaunum, uva ursi, nutmeg powder, or orris root powder. Invoke Aradia, the Goddess of the Witches. Ask the Goddess to open your third eye.

As you sit sipping your tea, try to reach a state of mind that is between being asleep and being awake. This is an important zone to explore. It may take some struggle to maintain this semi-conscious state once you achieve it, so keep saying to yourself,

> *My name is* _____ .
> *I control my body. I will not give up my body unless I want*
> *to. I will always be able to return to my body.*

Do not spend more than forty-five minutes at this. When you retire, hold for a moment the fleeting feeling that comes just before slipping into sleep. Hold it and remember it, then let it go. Keep yellow candles burning in your room, fresh flowers by your bed, and a window open so you have fresh air at night.

Spell to Stop Harassment at Work or School

This spell should be performed during the waning phase of the moon for best results. Prepare your altar with white altar candles. Use a brown image candle to represent the person who is harassing you. Anoint this candle with Rosa Ava or Bendover oil. Write the person's name on the candle, front and back. On a piece of parchment paper, write:

> *From now on, (name) will say nothing but sweet words*
> *about me and to me. By the power of Aradia, so mote it be!*

Put a drop of honey in the middle of the paper and roll it into a ball. Heat your athalme, make a gash in the candle's mouth, and stuff the paper ball into it. Burn High Priestess incense. Let the candle burn a little while every night for an odd number of nights, for a maximum of nine nights. Throw the remnants into a living body of water, but save some of the ashes from the incense burner to sprinkle in the path of your oppressor.

Spell to Find a Home

This is best performed during the waxing phase of the moon. On a piece of white paper, in Dove's Blood ink, draw a picture of the home you want, and visualize it in detail. Place it on your altar under a brown candle anointed with Rosa Ava oil. Use white altar candles, a single rose centerpiece, and Spirit Help incense. Go to your altar after sundown. Light white candles as usual, and light the brown candle, saying:

This is my home, my earth, my cave, my castle. Demeter,
help to make it better. Demeter, bring me home! Bring me
home! Bring me home! So mote it be!

Do this spell three nights, and actively look for a place during the spell period. Dispose of the spell as usual.

Spell for Productive Studying

This spell should be performed during any period in which you are going to study. Use yellow altar candles anointed with Van-Van oil, and a yellow candle to represent yourself, anointed with Bewitched oil. Light them while you study, and burn Sophia incense. Before you settle down to work, stand in front of your altar and address Sophia thus:

Goddess of Wisdom, to you I pray!
My mind clear and receptive stay.
All in true accord with thee,
As my word, so mote it be!
Give me light! Blessed be!

Spell to Still the Winds

This spell is best performed whenever winds are blowing too hard or are doing some sort of damage. Create the circle and place the cauldron in the corner of the universe from which the wind is blowing. Unify the group and raise power by humming louder and louder, then chant:

Boreas, Boreas, Boreas, Old Mother!
Your lover, the Northern Star, is calling.
Recall your stags to the warm stables.
Return your breath to the clouds above me.
Blow softly to us, Grandmother Wind.

Boreas, blow above us, blow above us!
Let our candles burn for your praise,
Let our cauldron please your senses.
Wind Mother, dismount your forces!
Wind Mother, come have supper with us.
Wind Mother Boreas, dismount your forces.
Blessed be.

After a moment, say to the wind:

We understand the wisdom in the forces of Nature.
We understand that You know what needs to be done.
If Your winds have not tired in fifteen minutes,

We will take our devotions indoors.
But if our company is dear to You,
Great Goddess, give us a sign.

The wind usually takes a few minutes to die down. After you have spoken, in fact, she may even get gustier and stronger. If the wind does not calm down with fifteen minutes, then you must assume that she has serious blowing to do. The Goddess often acts protectively toward us, but She owes us nothing. She is sister, but also Queen.

Spell to Raise a Storm

This spell will help you raise a storm whenever one is needed. It is usually done by a shaman who goes into a field with her shaman drum and stands in front of a huge, smoking fire, built for the occasion. She begins by drumming up the spirits and singing:

Diana... Diana... Diana...
I am summoning forty-five spirits from the west!
I am summoning forty-five spirits from the east!

Bring now furies of hail, furies of water,
Their limbs with lightning afire,
Biting with water into our fields.
Enthroned Queens of fire,
The archers of the sacred bows and arrows,
The gatherers of rain from the wide skies,
Graciously be merciful to us!
Our fields and herbs with blessings keep safe!
Rains, rains, rains,
Give from your wide skies, burst water upon us!
Behold our wine in your chalice,
Accept our offerings to you!
Send the dark clouds over us,
Surround our fields with stormy rains.
You who wield the thunderbolts,
We call upon Thee!
Blessed be! Blessings be!

In some countries, the shamans draw moon symbols on the ground in flour and barley, then dance around them. If you need a really large storm, work on it for three consecutive evenings at dusk. Use wands instead of knives, and instruments (drums, cymbals, rattles, anything) for making sounds to be shouted with great emotion and energy.

To Get Rid of What Separates One From a Lover

This is an interesting candle, red with a snake entwined around it. The snake is a very ancient symbol of regeneration.

Take the candle and anoint it; write onto the snake all the things that separate you from your loved one (pride, ignorance, etc.). Write on the smooth part of the candle your name and your lover's name, and the Goddess Diana's name three times. If you have a little more space on it, write "May (name) and myself be lovers in trust forever."

Now anoint the smooth parts with Lover's oil, Cleopatra oil, or Rosa Ava oil. Then anoint the snake separately with some burning oil to burn away the obstacles. Cinnamon, Cayenne or Rosemary work well.

Place this candle on your altar, and burn it during the waxing moon. Say:

> As this candle burns, so shall the obstacles melt between
> me and (name). So mote it be!

Do this three nights in succession; on the third night, let it burn all the way down. Then collect the remnants and throw them into a body of living water.

For Painless Separation

Often when a love affair is over, parting is an art. Take two image candles, representing the correct sexes of former lovers, and place them on your altar. Anoint them with Forget oil. Place them facing each other. Write the names on the back, and pentagrams as well. Then light your altar candles and incense; meditate on this affair, and about how to preserve the relationship after the love affair. Move the lit image candles away from each other for three days, moving the candles a little farther apart each day. Say:

> Warm was the passion, cold is now the heart;
> Let (name) and (name) painlessly part.
> Come the fire of friendship and alliance instead
> In the name of Sophia, Goddess of wisdom.
> So mote it be!

Burn Sophia incense or ritual incense. After the three days, when the figures reach the farthest point, let them burn down all the way. Collect the remnants, and throw them into a moving body of water. Do not look back.

To Hex a Rapist

This spell has good feedback. Several women have performed it and the rapists were caught and put in jail; one died.

At the waning moon, preferably just three days before a dark moon, take a black image or a black penis candle, and write on it what you want to happen to the rapist. Name it "rapist" on the front and the back; if it is a penis candle, write it on the tip.

Anoint it with Double-Cross oil and your urine. If you have it, menstrual blood should be added. Black Arts oil is also a good oil to use. Then place the black candle on your altar with two white candles on the sides of your Mother Goddess image; place this in front of Her.

Light your incense. Black Arts incense was used by one witch, and Sabbat incense was used by another. Again, your preference wins. As you light the candle, say:

> *In the most holy name of Hecate, the Goddess of life and death, She Who holds the key to the land of the underworld, let this rapist be caught by his own stupidity, by his own ego, by his own evil. So mote it be!*

Sit there awhile imagining his power diminishing as the candle burns lower. See him getting caught; see him lose at the trial. See him destroyed. Know that rape is the foundation of patriarchy, and to attack the rapist is not black magic, because you are not attacking the innocent. Have the courage to turn to the Goddess Hecate, who is threeformed, and who is active to defend women against rape.

When you finish your spell and the candle has burned down all the way, collect all remnants and take them to a living body of water and throw them into the waves. After you throw them, turn away and do not look back, lest you break the spell.

Light a blue and white candle on your altar at home for blessings and protection.

Spell to Protect Yourself From Enemies
by Noel Brennan

Time: waning moon or dark of the moon. Use a dark altar, or an image of Hecate, Avenging Goddess, on your altar. Place the two usual candles on either side of the image. You will need a black candle, juice from the diffenbachia plant (which numbs and paralyzes the tongue if you get it in your mouth, so don't; you won't need much of it), and spiderwebs. Inscribe the black candle with your enemy's name. Make your circle. Say the following invocation:

> *Lady of Darkness,*
> *Dark Isis of spells,*
> *Hecate, avenging Mother,*
> *Hear us and help us.*

Roll the black candle in the juice of the diffenbachia to stop the enemy from speaking evil about you or your loved ones. Say:

> *Let the tongue of (name) be numb*
> *And powerless to speak the evil,*
> *To speak the untrue.*
> *Let his/her voice fail and throat close*
> *On the harmful words,*
> *By the power of the Dark Lady.*

Then roll the candle in spiderwebs. Say:

> *May (name) be caught and bound by the webs of his/her*
> *own deceit.*

Then write the person's name on a piece of paper. Light the black candle and say:

> *Here is (name), alone and helpless.*
> *(Name), you are friendless.*
> *Emptiness and failure close around you.*
> *Your plans are as nothing.*
> *Frustration is yours.*
> *Trouble, doubt and fear are at your side.*
> *Soon you will cease tormenting me (or name of person you are*
> *protecting).*

Burn the paper in the flame of the black candle. Take it and the remnants of the candle after dark and sprinkle it before the residence of your enemy, or where the enemy is certain to walk. Light a blue or white candle, and burn calming or purifying incense for peace.

Spell To Change Your Luck

You can perform this spell as often as you feel changes are needed. This spell is designed to change luck for the better, for example, to break a run of bad luck or a feeling of lostness. If your luck is generally fine, but one particular project isn't working out, concentrate on that alone.

The best time to perform this spell is during a new moon when a good crescent is seen.

The altar is set up dressed with the usual white and aluminum foil to avoid a fire hazard. The two white altar candles are placed on each side of your Mother Goddess image, and the censer in front of that. You need one candle (usually in your astral color) to represent yourself, three orange candles, one gray, and one black.

Light the two white altar candles. Pause to think about what you will do. Light the incense and let your space be filled with it. Light your astral candle; this candle represents yourself; it is you in all things. Light all three orange candles and say:

> *Encouragement and attraction be mine, to attract good fortune.*

Light the black candle, saying:

> *Here is all the bad luck of my life, and all that went ill with me, hardships and disappointments.*

Light the gray candle, saying:

> *Neutralize all that was bad. Let the bad come to a halt and then swing to improvement.*

Meditate on your luck reversing from the bad and swinging to the better. Think about how it looks when it is improved. Then say:

> *O Goddess Urania, wise Goddess of change! My roads have been blocked by ignorance; lead me from them hence. I see no direction, and plead for your guiding light.*
>
> My daughter, the fates indeed have tested you, but take heart. Your efforts to eliminate the bad have been ambitious. What do you want?
>
> *My luck must change.*
>
> Daughter, it shall be done. For change is the soul of nature. And your ambition is the key. Success shall be yours!
>
> *When then may I find this change? When will ignorance disperse, obsessions disappear, illness heal, and good moods grow?*
>
> Within a moon, that I vow, all shall be well. Like a seed, your position shall grow into fulfillment. The changing phases of Diana will graciously add threads for your tapestry of life. Smiles come over their faces.
>
> *How so?*
>
> They already see your future!
>
> *So mote it be!*

Spell For a Successful School Year

Use yellow candles on your altar, even for altar candles. Anoint candles with Van-Van oil or Bewitched oil. Light the candles while you are

33

studying and keep them burning while you work. Burn Quick Mind or Sophia incense.

Before you settle down to study, pray to Sophia:

> *Goddess of Wisdom, to you I pray,*
> *My mind clear and receptive stay.*
> *All in true accord with Thee,*
> *As my word, so mote it be!*
> *Give me light! Blessed be!*

Spell for Protection and Peace
by Noel Brennan

Use blue and brown candles rolled in herbs or anointed with appropriate oils. Invoke the Goddess and seal the circle when the participants are inside. Light white altar candles on either side of the Goddess representation. Light incense (frankincense and rose). Invoke the Lady of Flame. Perform self-blessing of participants. Light brown candle and say:

> *Mother of all,*
> *Protecting Lady,*
> *Goddess of all things,*
> *Of grey waters*
> *And bright stars*
> *And the brown fruitful earth,*
> *Here is your favor*
> *And the protection you give.*

Then light the blue candle. Say:

> *Lady of blue skies and waters*
> *And soft rain in the forests,*
> *Comforting Mother,*
> *Enter us and be with us*
> *So that we may be strong*
> *So that we may be sure.*
> *Let no harm come to us,*
> *Within or without,*
> *Anywhere, anytime.*
> *In all places*
> *All times*
> *Surround us with your protection.*
> *Your comfort,*
> *Your strength:*
> *Let evil be far from us,*
> *Your good always near.*
> *Blessed be!*

If you are doing this spell for someone, touch her lightly on the head at this point. Meditate a while on the peace and protection surrounding you. Dissolve the circle.

Spell to Free Political Prisoners

Feminist witches often need a spell which brings aid to political prisoners. Throughout history, oppressed peoples have used their native (Pagan) religion as a liberating force, on both the spiritual and physical planes. As feminist witches, we too draw upon our ancient tradition of using our magic and psychic powers as tools and weapons in our liberation. Think of energizing your psyche and empowering yourself and your sisters as warriors with the magic of a ritual, a drumbeat, a spell, a demonstration.

You will need some object that represents the person or people you wish to see go free. If a photo, personal property, or newspaper clipping is not available, then write the person's name in Dove's Blood ink on a small piece of parchment paper and draw a circled pentagram over the name. Tie a gray thread around the object to symbolize the chains (and the system) that bind the person(s). Place this on your altar and surround it with your most powerful magical objects—stones, jewelry, feathers, symbols. I use four magical stones I've collected, and I place a turquoise and coral Hopi brooch on the object.

Fill your chalice with pure water to represent the person's free flow and liberation. Anoint a white candle with Seven Power, Artemis, or High Joan oil. A glass jar candle is best but a taper will do. Light some High Joan, Helping Hand, or any basic ritual incense and bless your candle. Light your two white altar candles and ask the Goddess for help with your spell. Concentrate on the object representing the person(s) and say:

> *In the name of all the forces of justice, this person must go free. Great Goddess of a Thousand Names, Lady Luck, Justicia, all voices of Truth and Justice sing of (name)'s innocence. S/he must go free. Great Goddess, bless the speedy liberation of (name). S/he must go free!*

Light the white candle and chant over it again and again, "Free, free, S/he must go free!" When power has been raised, imagine that person in front of you. As you cut the gray thread with your athalme, look deeply into their eyes and say:

> *Dear Sister (Brother), and so shall you be protected from all harm both physical and psychic. The enemy no longer binds you, your spirit is free! So shall you be radiant with hope and optimism and inspiration, and your body shall dance with energy and good health. Supporters will flock*

35

to your case and work without cease until you are free. You
glow with innocence and it is apparent to all. The great
forces of Justice smile upon you and remove all obstacles
from your path. The Goddess shall be with you always.
Dear Sister (Brother), I send you much energy and love.
You shall go free! So mote it be! Blessed be.

Feel free to change the working of the spell to include specifics about
the person, such as trial details and dates, prison name and conditions,
etc. Extinguish all candles except the one in the glass jar. Glass jar candles
should burn out on their own because they are complete spells in
themselves. Repeat this spell for nine consecutive nights and before each
court appearance, demonstration, or prison visit. If possible, start it on
the night of the new moon. Throw the candlewax remains into a living body
of water. You can do other spells and blessings in conjunction with this spell.
Think positively and lovingly about the person and your energy will be felt.

Money Spell

Decorate your altar with money-drawing herbs: sage, mandrake, red clover,
blood root, chamomile, nutmeg, myrrh, etc. Anoint one orange glass candle
with Money Drawing oil, and bless the candle in the name of Isis of the
Thousand Breasts. Place it in the center of your altar; at the four corners
of the universe, place four green glass candles, anointed with Magnet oil,
as well as Money Drawing oil.

Begin the ritual after sundown, after contemplating the skies in looking for the evening star, Venus. Once she appears, you can begin. Light
two white altar candles first, saying:

Blessed be, thou creature of fire,

acknowledging that the flames are conscious creatures. Then light your
thurible with herbal mix or Money Drawing incense (High Joan the
Conqueress):

Great Mother, I come to you. I live in this world, and the
wealth is all in the hands of the masters, mostly men. They
have had the power now for ten thousand years. Great
Mother, we are asking You to help. You are the true owner
of the wealth; please blow the karmic winds in our favor.
Let my cupboard fill up with food, and my checkbook with
balances. Allow me the livelihood of the daughters of Isis;
be my nurturing mother. I invoke Thee. Souls of nature,
woven within all hearts, make the jobs go to women and
all have enough.

Now light the orange candle and say:

> *This candle represents me. Like the magnet, I draw encour-
> agement, money, friends around me.*

Then light the green candles all around, from east to north. Say:

> *Thus I draw money from the east, the south, the west, and
> the north.*

Surround your orange candle evenly with cinnamon, and contemplate. Say:

> *Mine is the blood, the Mother's blood which promises life.
> Mine is the blood that promises substance. Mine is the blood
> of the Lady of Plenty. The Goddess bestows reasonable
> wealth on Her sisters who ask for it. Great Goddess, bless
> my life with health, and let me have no more want. So mote
> it be!*

Each day for three days repeat this ritual, moving your green candles closer to the center. When they touch, let them burn down all the way. While they burn, always burn your money-drawing High Joan the Conqueress incense, and put all money that comes to you from now on onto your altar before depositing or spending it. This spell can be followed with a white candle lit while the flame still burns in the ritual candles, so the fire is continued from the spell.

Interesting Candle Magic:
The Ancient Seven-Day Candle Spell

This spell uses what is called a knob candle, made of seven knobs. The candles are either one solid color (all red, all purple, etc.), or each knob has a different color, much like the Seven Power candle. Remember the meaning of the colors, and choose wisely. If you have the Seven Power knob candle, however, you can't go wrong.

Each day after sundown when the evening star rises, light one knob and contemplate the meaning of your life. (When green burns, think of life force; when red burns, think of life fire, bringing appropriate gifts, money, energy; with yellow, spirituality; with purple, synthesis; with blue, protection; with white, blessings; with pink, happiness.) Play with the images, conjuring the most desirable changes. When the one-color candle is used, stare into the fire and concentrate on the same wish as long as the knob burns.

Recommended oils to use are Seven Power, Bendover, or any favorite ritual oil.

⁊ spell, it is best to erase from the conscious mind what hap-
go on with your next project.

⁊ney

⁊t money, take a bill (the bigger the better) and some red thread.
Aɴ⸳ amazon root (High Joan the Conqueress root) and the money with
High Joan the Conqueress oil. Now with the back showing, wrap the bill
around the root, tie it with red thread three times, each time tying a knot
and saying:

> *In the name of the Nymph, the Maiden, and the Mother,*
> *increase my wealth. O Diana! Let me have no want! Let*
> *me have enough! So mote it be!*

Keep this talisman in your purse, which you also anoint with Money
Drawing oil. Renew the oil every new moon, holding up your purse to the
moon, rattling the contents three times.

Spell to Get a Job

This spell works on two levels. First, pinpoint the target; research exactly
what job you want and where it is located. Once that is done, set up your
altar as usual, and place two brown candles on it. Write on them the name
of the job and where it is. It does not need to be quite precise; you can
say "downtown," for example. Place a green candle representing yourself
in the middle. All three candles are anointed with Money Drawing oil. Burn
Money Drawing incense. Before the job interview, light the candles, saying:

> *This brown candle is the stability I seek; this other brown*
> *candle is the wealth I seek, this green candle is the life force*
> *of mine that draws them to me.*

Meditate a few minutes and then leave for your interview. Do not put
out the candles while you are gone, only after you have returned. Light
a purple one-week candle to represent power over your fates; anoint it,
too, with Money Drawing oil.

To use Money Drawing oil correctly, anoint your purse, or where your
money is kept, even your checkbook. Place every bit of money that comes
to you on the altar and offer it to the Mother Goddess before you deposit
it or spend it. If you are about to start a new phase in your monetary affairs,
it is a good idea to buy a new purse for the new income.

Herbal Recipes

Acacia: Acacia is said to be sacred to Diana, and was one of the sacred
trees in the ancient groves. Mix a little with sandalwood incense and burn
them. This allows the spirits to commune with you.

Witches Broom: Soaked in water, it makes excellent purifying water. Sprinkle it where magic work is to be done.

Marigold: Mix equal parts of marigold, calamus, hops, lemon verbena and mace. Soak them in a dark place for nine days in a gallon of water. Use a cupful for your daily bath. This wins the admiration and respect of others.

Mandrake: In Europe, one sleeps with a new mandrake root in bed for three nights during the full moon. After that, one places it on the altar for special spells. When you do your conjurings, hold the root in your hand. Take it with you to confrontations, important meetings, etc. Add a little of the same herb to your incenses to fortify the effect.

Cayenne Drink: This is good for winter festivals or on cold nights when you want to worship sky-clad. Take this drink along to excite your blood, to get the circulation moving well, and to spice up the dancing.

Mix one quart of half-and-half with two spoonfuls of red cayenne that you have dissolved in a little boiling water. Add this to the half-and-half and mix. It tastes very smooth but is potent, so don't take too much of it. You may add brandy to it for an extra "kick" if you so desire.

Vervain: Highly prized by the ancients, vervain is sacred to Venus. Soaked in water, it is very useful in banishing evil, purifying ritual grounds, coveners, etc. Roll your love candles in it after anointing to fortify your spell. Added to incense, it brings good luck and inspiration.

On your altar, arrange seven little mounds of vervain, and light a white candle in the middle for devotion. When you light it, say:

> *In the name of the Triple Goddess whose names are as many as the stars, protect me from evil persons; keep trouble afar, purify me from fear and oppression. Instead bring me freedom and inspiration in the name of Isis. So mote it be! Blessed be!*

This little witchy devotion can be used with a green candle for money spells, pink for love, etc. It's fine to change the words to suit yourself, but remember, it works better if it rhymes. Perform it at the convenience of your schedule. This is good on a daily basis to sharpen your meditation and to remove fear.

Angelica: Sprinkle a little of this herb (which is sacred to Sophia) into the corners of your house to maintain or restore peace and harmony. Angelica tea is said to prolong life, defeat evil, exorcise. Sometimes it is called Holy Herb.

To ward off witchcraft, mix it with marjoram, cloves and dill. Tie it into a small white handkerchief and hang it prominently from your window.

Alfalfa: Sprinkle it into your cupboards to ward off hunger.

Devil's Shoestring: Keep a piece exposed on your bedside. It works better when placed among some wild flowers. It wards off nightmares. To make the Most Powerful Hand talisman, add it to Helping Hand root, mandrake, High Joan the Conqueress, and three grains of Grains of Paradise representing the Triple Goddess; fold into a black flannel cloth, folding toward you each time. Then sew it up with white and yellow thread. It is used by gamblers and people who live dangerously. Feed it every new moon with some ritual oil; Has No Hanna oil is best for women.

Dragon's Blood Reed: A piece of this carried on the body brings great good luck. Bath beads made from this herb make beautiful purification baths before going to court, performing a ritual, etc.

Irish Moss: Place it in your home under the rug to have the luck of the Irish.

Laurel: Secure three laurel leaves and three small parchment papers. Write the names of the Triple Goddess on each paper: Diana, Isis, Hecate. Keep the laurel and parchment with the names in a red flannel bag in your pocket. Say before starting your game of chance:

> *Isis of the Thousand Breasts, make my chance the best*
> *one yet.*

Win you shall. It is a good idea for nongamblers and women survivors in difficult jobs and situations.

Myrtle: Sacred to Artemis. Most lucky in all matters. Carry Myrtle in your red flannel bag, and you will have love, health, and wealth in life. Artemis be blessed.

Yellow Duck: Make a tea of this herb and wash the doorknobs and entrance to your business with it. It soon will bring customers. At home, it also helps to make your dealings with the outside more successful.

Tonka Bean: These are aromatic black beans. Keep them in your red flannel mojo bag for general good luck and freedom from illness, and use them for wishing beans. When you wish with them, you must throw the one you wished upon in a body of water.

Other goodies to carry for good luck are: lovage root, High Joan the Conqueress, star anise, peony, May apple, mustard seeds, galenagal, lion's tooth, blessed thistle, burning bush, chamomile, clover, damiana, cascara and Sagrada oil.

For Love/Attraction

Absinthe: Sprinkle this herb under the bed of a lover to draw the lover to you (must be crafty).

Beth Root: Wear this as a necklace to draw lovers.

Coriander: Take seven grains and grind them in your mortar, saying:

Warm seed, warm heart, let them never be apart.

Do this three times. Then add this herb to wine and serve it to the one you desire.

Dragon's Reed Powder: When a lover is slow in reacting to you, burn this along with some love incense and the lover will pick up intensity. Do this while the person is visiting.

Lavender: To write a successful love letter, rub the entire sheet of paper with lavender flowers before starting to write it. Use Dove's Blood ink if you can. This is said to grant you whatever you requested in the letter. (It can be applied to business letters as well.)

Other herbs known to bring lovers and happiness: lovage, linden, lotus, magnolia, laurel, ladies' thumb and horse chestnut.

This is a Celtic spell: Acquire six horse chestnuts and some red thread. Entwine the chestnuts on one cord, making knots on them and in between them, representing the thread of life. Burn a red candle on full moon evenings, saying:

O Diana, Goddess of love and hunt, please listen to Your daughter. Make these knots to capture the heart of (name). Let neither rest nor sleep find her till she comes our troth to bind. Goddess Whose arrows never fail, bless for us this love affair!

Then burn this charm in your cauldron with other aromatic herbs, especially fennel, which is sacred to Diana. Your love will come to you within a moon.

Protection of Person, House, Car and Motorcycle

This spell is a must for women in patriarchal oppression. Do this at the new moon, when you can see a fine crescent in the sky. Prepare your house by cleaning it thoroughly, getting in touch with your things, even doing laundry. For your floor, prepare a quart of hot water and steep some basil in it (after you have already washed the floor as usual). Prepare another dish of water steeped with verbena or witches' broom (Scotch broom). Even yellow duck is fine. Light your thurible and place frankincense and myrrh into it. Also get a fresh egg, and write your name three times on it with an art pen (or any other pen you love). Pass it through the incense smoke and say:

In the name of Habondia, lady of plenty, in the name of Fortuna, lady who weaves the threads of my life, in the

name of the fair Diana, the huntress of the night, may my
person be blessed with security. May evil men stay away
from my house! May nothing but good pass across my
threshold!

Now open your doors and place your incense in the doorway from which
the wind blows, so that the smoke gets swept through your space. Meanwhile, wash your floors with the basil water to bring happiness and good
fortune into the house. Then take the verbena and sprinkle it in all the
corners of your house, repeating the same blessing. Now take the incense
and walk three times around your space on the outside. If you have windows
that show on the street, you can seal them with your incense by drawing
the pentagram of protection in the air, and again at any entrances, doors,
or openings. When you have completed your circles, bury your egg in the
earth just outside of your home, or if it is an apartment, bury it in a pot
of earth. You can then put flowers in it and keep the pot at your door. Good
protection herbs are rue, periwinkle, verbena, lemon verbena, myrtle tree,
and even geraniums. These herbs are regarded as familiars from the queendom of plants. Then close the house and let it fill with the sacred fumes
of frankincense and myrrh.

Treat your car or motorcycle the same way as your house. Walk around
it three times (always from east to south) saying your blessings (improvise),
and then fill your car or motorcycle with the scent.

To complete this spell, clean your altar at night and perform a self-
blessing, and go to sleep with a white candle in a glass jar burning on your
altar.

Spell to Regain Psychic Balance After Rape

Gather your women friends around you and let them go pick blossoms.
Prepare a ritual bath (any time of the day or night) and throw a pinch of
salt into the tub for purification. Light Peace incense or ritual incense. Let
your women friends attend to you: scrub your back, chitchat, etc. Throw
the flowers they have picked in the tub. Luxuriate in this setting, talking
about renewal and beauty, especially yours.

After your bath, make sure your bed (if this patriarchal outrage has
occurred on it) is also renewed. Let your friends burn the sheets and take
the mattress outside and beat it. Let the sun bleach away the sorrow and
humiliation. Keep in mind, you are still beautiful, and it is not your fault.
May patriarchy fall.

Voodoo Spells

Voodoo literally means "little god." African peoples developed it, but it
can be found in many varieties around the world. The significance here

is, instead of candles, you work with dolls or combine both. In Africa, witches carried the sacred image of the Goddess (the centerpiece for their altar) as a doll. Little girls today play with their dolls as a tool for socializing, but herstorically, they imitate the priestesses who carried ''dolls'' of the Goddess.

Making clay dolls is the most ancient form of voodoo. As in the microcosm, so in the macrocosm. If you create one situation in small, it will affect the big. Cause and effect. Such is the philosophy behind practicing this craft.

Righteous Hex (reserved for violent criminals only)

Perform this only when you *know, not just think,* that someone has harmed you. A witch who cannot hex cannot heal. Cupcakism, turning the other cheek is not for witches.

Do this at the waning moon. Check your starfinder or local astrologer about Saturn's or Mars' course in the sky.

Prepare a black altar. For the centerpiece, use the Goddess' hag image, Hecate, who is threefold. Decorate your altar with cones, blackthorn and mandrake. From black cloth, cut out a doll-shaped form resembling your enemy, sew it around from east to north to west to south (widdershins), and leave only a small part open. Stuff it with boldo leaves and finish the sewing. Indicate the eyes, mouth, nose, and hair on the doll. On a piece of parchment paper, write the name of your enemy and attach it to the image. Say:

> Goddess Hecate, to You I pray,
> With this enemy no good will ever stay.
> Cut the lines of his life in three,
> Doom him, doom him, so mote it be!

When you pronounce this, take a mallet and break his ''legs'' by breaking the herb inside. Dust it with Graveyard Dust; anoint it with Double-Crossing oil, and burn your Black Arts incense. Imagine him totally miserable and with one leg broken. (It is a nice way to incapacitate rapists until they can be apprehended.) Do this three nights in a row. On the third night, burn the doll and bury it. Draw a triple cross over his grave with Dragon Blood power. Walk away without looking back.

Note: Dispose of hexes as far away from your house as possible. Each night you can break something else in him, or stick black-headed pins into his liver or penis. May patriarchy fall!

For Winning in Court

Anoint a doll with Obeah oil. Place the doll on a clean white cloth. Sprinkle with Blue Vervain. Tie a white cord or string around the waist of the doll and say:

Thus do I bind my enemy,
Who would speak against me.
Silent now is he,
While I go free, free, free!

Repeat this seven times.

Mix equal parts of frankincense and myrrh, and light the mixture. While it burns, verbalize your situation. Wrap the doll in the white cloth and hide it where no one will see it. Repeat this every night after sundown until the night before you are to appear, then repeat the entire spell for the last time. When it is finished and you have wrapped the doll in the white cloth, burn it and scatter the ashes to the four winds. When you appear in court, have a piece of High Joan the Conqueress in your pocket.

Old Hungarian Health Spell

When somebody is ill, and all the herbal medicines and the doctor's medicine seem to be no help, perform this as a last try.

Lay the ill person naked in a beam of full moonshine. Have one basket filled with thirteen fresh eggs and another basket that is empty. Take one egg at a time and rub it on the person's skin slowly, touching all the crevices. When the entire egg surface is used, take the next fresh egg and place the used one in the empty basket. While you do this, say:

By the power of Diana, by the power of Aradia, may all
that is ill be absorbed into this egg. By the power of Queen
Isis, so mote it be.

When all thirteen eggs are used, take a little water, bless it, put salt in it, bless it again, and sprinkle it around the corners of the sick room, saying:

The Goddess blesses her child. All is well now. Fresh new
health will glow.

Dispose of the eggs in a living body of water, or bury them. Do not eat the eggs or you will get the illness.

Spell to Remove Warts
by Noel Brennan

I have used this successfully. Use a base of rose water; make your own, or buy it already prepared. Add a little fresh milkweed sap crushed from the stems of the plant, some dry crumbled mint leaves, sage, and sassafras leaves. Warm gently over a low flame. DO NOT BURN. Write on a piece of paper, and read aloud:

Mother of seasons
And the changing moon,
Lady of light
And giver of Spring-time,
Give health to (name), our friend,
And in the secret places of the night
Make her/his warts dissolve,
Not to return.
Be with her/him
And with us,
Mother of the universe.

Burn the paper to ashes and add it to the mixture. When the mixture is warm and fragrant, BUT NOT HOT, put it in a small jar to cool. The patient should apply some at night before retiring, and let it dry. Leave it on all night and wash it off in the morning. Use faithfully each night until warts are completely dissolved.

Spell for Continuance of a Special Request
by Noel Brennan

Place a white candle on either side of your Goddess representation. You will also need a candle in your own astral color, a brown candle, a blue candle, and a green candle. Anoint the candles with rose oil. Patchouli and rose incense are also nice.

Invoke the Goddess and seal the circle with your wand, calling on the essence of the Goddess in the four directions. Light the white candle and say:

Lady of fire,
Of sunlight and moon,
Of stars
And all light,
Bright Lady of flame,
Be with us.

Light the incense and perform a self-blessing. Light the astral candle and say:

This is my candle. It represents me, (name),
Child of the Great Mother,
Daughter of Life.
I call on you, Lady,
By your many names.

Next, light the brown candle. Say:

> *For the spell successfully begun,*
> *for the power growing,*
> *I thank the Mistress of Life.*
> *The spell will continue,*
> *Its power grows stronger, stronger,*
> *Irresistible,*
> *By the power of the Triple Goddess,*
> *Maiden and Mother and Crone.*

Light the green candle and say:

> *With this candle I draw to me*
> *All I need,*
> *Resources to accomplish my will.*

Light the blue candle and say:

> *Peace and prosperity*
> *With desire fulfilled,*
> *Attend me now*
> *With the blessing of the Lady.*

Meditate a while. You can write your desire on paper and burn it to ashes in the candle flames if you want, thinking of the success of the spell. When you are done, say:

> *When the flames are out*
> *The spell will continue,*
> *Waxing greater, greater, greater*
> *Until my purpose is accomplished,*
> *My purpose is complete.*
> *It will be so.*
> *Blessed be.*

Thank the Goddess and dissolve the circle.

Spell to Appease the Angry Fates

This spell comes from cthonic culture, the Earth Religion prominent prior to the invention of male gods. Such a culture has been examined by many historians and philosophers, and is described by Engels as a matriarchal period, when only communal property and high status for women were known. The spell is good for legal cases, dealing with justice, freeing someone from prison, or averting the "evil eye." It is particularly good to perform this ritual when you have moved into a new space or a new area, in order to make friends with the earth spirits abiding there.

Build an altar, preferably low to the ground. It is important to establish contact with the earth—our home, our Mother. Do this before the sunrise. On the altar, place three very special, beautifully crafted bowls or cups, and crown them with flowers and the wool of a freshly-shorn ewe (failing that, buy some yarn.) Fill all three bowls with a holy drink offering, gathered with your own bare hands from an everflowing, virgin fountain (unpolluted, live water).

At dawn, slowly pour the holy drink offering on the ground as you face the East. Pour the water into three streams. When the last bowl of water has been offered to the Earth Mother, refill the bowl with honey and water to use as a chalice. Drink this, offering some to the Mother as you do.

Now gather three-times-nine olive branches. If there are no olive trees in your area, branches from any indigenous sacred tree will work. Lay these on the spot where the water from your offering was taken into the earth. Say your spell thoughtfully as you place the olive branches down on the ground. Commune a while with the Mother. Say, "Dear Holy Ones, with kindly hearts receive and bless." Whisper your prayer; don't raise your voice. When you have finished, say "Blessed be." Walk away from the spot without looking back. All will be well.

Sample Recipes

The following recipes, which are broadly grouped by category, were contributed by Rowan Fairgrove from her booklet, *A Handbook of Botanical Incenses*.

Evocative
Evoking Artemis
  Almond
  Frankincense
  Mandrake
  Orris root
  Wormwood
Earth and Water (to summon elementals)
  Basil
  Damiana
  Life Everlasting
  Rosemary

Call Spirits
  Dittany of Crete
  Dragon's Blood
  Mandrake
  Mistletoe
Samhain
  Anise seed
  Dittany of Crete
  Myrrh
  Sandalwod
  Oil of Bayberry
  Oil of Patchouli
To Summon the Departed
  Dittany of Crete
  Wormwood

To Summon Spirits
  3 pts Wormseed
  2 pts Frankincense
  2 pts mastic or resin
    (besoin, myrrh)
  3 pts Dittany of Crete
  ½ pt Olive Oil
  ½ pt Wine
  ½ pt Honey
  A few drops of the user's
    blood
To See Fairies
  Hazel buds
  Hollyhocks
  Marigold
  Rose
  Thyme
Spirit Manifestations
  Basil
  Damiana
  Dittany of Crete
  Life Everlasting
  Rosemary

Divinatory
Astral Travel
  Frankincense
  Lavender
  Orris root
  Sandalwood
  Oil of Bayberry
  Oil of Rose
  Oil of Patchouli
Communication
  Lotus
  Peppermint
  Verbena
Communication (Hermes Rites: used in conjunction with yellow candles)
  Cinnamon
  Sandalwood

To See Things Honestly
  1 pt Hyssop
  2 pts Lily
  2 pts Myrrh
Psychic Enhancement
  Celery seed
  Orris root
Vision and Dreams
  Aloe
  Dragon's Blood
  Myrrh

Protective
Lady's Protection
  1 pt Rowan
  ½ pt Orris root
  1 pt Rosemary
  1 pt Basil
  1 pt St. John's Wort
  Pinch of Dragon's Blood
Safety for Travelers
  Cinnamon
  Mastic gum
  Saffron
Protection
  Dragon's Blood
  Mandrake
  Mistletoe

Banishing
Banishing
  Dragon's blood
  Garlic
  Pine
  St. John's Wort
  Blue Vervain
Uncrossing
  Anise seed
  Ash
  Dragon's Blood
  Blue Vervain

Banishing bad vibes
Camphor
Rosemary

Healing
Against Contagious Disease
(carried around the location
to be purified)
Lavender
Pineneedles
Rosemary
Camphor
Healing
Life Everlasting flowers
Myrrh
Oil of Rosemary

Spellcasting
Psychic Phenomena
Anise Seed
Myrrh
Sandalwood
Oil of Bayberry
Oil of Patchouli
Full Moon
Anise seed
Basil
Damiana
Lavender
Life Everlasting
Rosemary

Beltane
Basil
Damiana
Life Everlasting
Rosemary
Flower oils of choice
(Gardenia—ecstasy;
Heliotrope—devotion;
etc.)
Concentration
Cinnamon
Mastic gum
Olibanum
High Altar
Benzion
Frankincense
Myrrh
Rowan
Money Drawing
Frankincense
Myrrh
Nutmeg
Saffron
Sandalwood
New Moon
Anise seed
Camphor
Wormwood
Lavender

Sources for herbs, oils and incense

Note: This list is based on research into reliable sources for the materials named in this book. None of these companies has paid me in any way to list them.

Pan's Forest Herb Co.
7776 Stachnik Rd
Maple City MI 49664
(616) 228-6591

Enchantment
341 E 9th St
New York NY 10003
(212) 228-4394

Magic Circle Herbs
Circle Sanctuary
PO Box 219
Mt. Horeb WI 53572

House of Hermatics
5338 Hollywood Bl
Hollywood CA 90027
(213) 466-7553

Chapter 2

The Dianic Tradition and the Rites of Life

Dianic Genesis

In the beginning there was unknowable silence. She had an unknowable name which echoed through the universe; the power of this name, that no one shall utter, filled the universe with action.

Silence broke into its components, lights and shadows. From these lights action made form, and from the shadows, formlessness. Visible and invisible, she created a blend of the two we know today as Nature.

In this blend of form and formlessness, lights and shadows, visible and invisible, she created all the creatures, making infinite variations of herself as the birthing force, and the different form of her, where she is not so clearly visible, the birthed-in form.

She intermingled with herself, as she was never divided, and created our solar system, our mother planet, and all the creatures upon it. Among the creatures she ordained, all species will know her either through instinct or through search, but all she created will periodically return to her holiness, and then again take form inside her.

And ever since, the world has had a blend of invisible forms, female and male, and a blend of invisible forms, self-love and self-hate. The divine mixing of these creates reality, for her essence is present in all, but her forms do not conform to temporary social orders. She is the circle of rebirth; thus we celebrate the moment in our lives as an honor to her, she whose Genesis is still happening, she who has not returned to any comfortable heaven to "watch" over us or forget us.

She who still creates all reality daily, she who is visible and invisible in Nature, she whose name is secret, she who rules the Universe. The Force of Life and Death and all that is in between. She is All.

Dianic Affirmations

New Age life-oriented philosophies often rely heavily on what in another time would have been considered witchcraft. Mind control, meditation, thought consciousness are the cornerstones of magic. "Imagination plus intensity equals reality" is practiced in spells.

Upon rising:

I reconnect my soul with the Universal Intelligence, the Goddess Durga! Organizer of the Universe! Multi-armed, ever-ablaze with the fire of life. Let me be led by Durga's power. Blessed be!

When in traffic:

My Universe is a safe Universe! It is the Goddess Athena who protects my wheels, I am encircled by a blue light and then a white. I am divinely alert and hold the hands of the Mothers. I am safe. I am blessed. I am safe.

When cooking:

It is not just dinner that I cook but I cook the universal cauldron of change. I am part of all women who do this every day and I cook my own nurturance. I am nourished by my creations. I am Goddess of the cauldron. And I cook Health.

Upon signing official papers:

I call upon Themis to lead my pen. All will serve me in the end.

Upon entering your bath:

It is not just cleanliness I seek, I reconnect myself with the life-granting waters of life. I am renewed in body and soul!

When going to a party:

Play is learning and learning is play. I laugh and dance and keep myself free.

Before singing:

My voice shall rise to please the Muses!

When visiting friends:

May friends and foes be gentle with my love.

When falling in love:

O Aphrodite! I felt Your sting and now You are on Your way. I shall prepare my soul for You with flowers and lack of fear!

When writing:

> *Come spirits of my spirit, speak your thoughts through me.*
> *I am open as a lotus, and willing as a pet; illumine my*
> *mind, imagination lead my path!*

When looking for a new home:

> *My home is getting nearer with every step I take searching*
> *for it. My home already knows me, and I know my home.*

Create your own affirmations.

The Dianic Tradition

In the True Beginning, before the Judeo-Christian Genesis, the Goddess was revealed to her people as the Soul of the Wild. She was called Holy Mother, known to be a Virgin who lived in wild places and acted through mysterious powers. Known also as Artemis, She was worshipped in the moonlight, and young nymphs and maidens were called to serve in Her rituals. It was decreed that the sacred doe of Artemis was never to be shot down. The Holy Mother, Virgin, Artemis was also called by the name Dia Anna, "Nurturer Who Does Not Bear Young." In hunting and gathering societies Her image was carefully engraved in stone. She was symbolized by both the Sun and Moon to recognize that the torch of life and the healing Moon were Hers. Images of the Mother were carved everywhere She was worshipped: in caves, Yoni-shrines, the woods, trees. She was the Lady of Plenty, Teacher of Knowledge, Knower of Wisdoms, Sacred Dancer, Inventor of the Wheel, Holy Mother, Virgin, Artemis, Dianna.

In the Dianic times there were colleges of women who lived according to the spiritual principles of Artemis, serving in Her shrines and blessing the sick. Later, as knowledge of growing plants and domesticating animals was acquired, Artemis/Dianna became connected to all the people through Her sacred functions as Giver of Bread, Maker of the Loaf, Rainmaker and Life-Giver.

The worship of Dianna comes to us from these earliest Stone Age times. Her names appear throughout the world. The rivers Danube and Don were named after Her. Ancient names for Anatolia, as well as current names for mountains, rivers and lakes worldwide, often reveal themselves in translation as Moon Goddess names from antiquity. Mt. St. Helens means Moonmountain. The most astonishing temples ever built (Stonehenge, for example) were created for the Moon Goddess.

Although most of the world's religions originated from the worship of the Moon Goddess, or "She Who Shines On All," Her worship and service were always carried out by women. While the Goddess as Giver of Life and Mother of the Sacred Child was worshipped by both sexes, Dianna was not. She was worshipped as Protector and Teacher of the Young, but never as a bearer of children; she did not consort with men. Her service was known as "Women's Mysteries," and ran parallel to worship of other Goddess aspects. Thus many women chose to worship the Goddess with their men, while many chose to worship alone or with each other. From the dawn of humankind, woman-energy as nurturing energy, expressed through Goddess-worship, has been strengthened through this very holy bonding.

Concepts of Women's Mysteries

In the Beginning were the women, mothers of the children, and the children belonged to All—to everyone. Women's mating customs were observed within the sacred marriages and seasons of the religion. On a Midsummer Night women would mate with men, as representative of the male principle. Personalities and preferences were put aside in order to observe and celebrate the sameness of all humanity. Priest as well as priestess participated in the mating sacrament in honor of the Life Force.

Because of this sacred mating ritual, it was virtually impossible, not to mention irrelevant, to pair off children with biological fathers. Only motherhood was an unquestionable reality, easily observable; fatherhood was wishful thinking or a figment of imagination.

This was a culture in which the breeding of animals was consciously aided for the purpose of achieving stronger or more productive livestock, so the importance of sperm in the reproductive process did not go unnoticed. The women were aware of the female period of "heat" and the male response to it. There was no ignorance concerning the relation of sperm to reproduction, as common scholarly assertions would have us believe. Goddess-cultures acknowledged the "stimulating" effect of the male's contribution to the process, but they did not consider it significant enough to be deserving of worship, as was the Birthing Force, the Female Principle of the Universe.

The period from conception to birth was a lengthy one of intense fetal development. A mother had to survive many dangers and surmount many obstacles to assure the birth of a healthy baby. Motherhood was recognized as a "warrior's" job. Further, the rearing of the young was not necessarily done by the biological mothers, but was the role of the community "nurturers," both female and male.

Women's Mysteries were concerned with the natural cycles of life, and rituals were designed for specific purposes: to insure good weather conditions for crops; to promote good health among the people; to guard against disease and pestilence; to maintain good fortune by conscious reinforcement of the practice of keeping women in contact with each other as manifestations of the Divine Female.

Traces of Dianic tradition may be found in many modern customs such as archery, sports, games, weaving and witchcraft. Examples of ancient tradition practiced today are such things as saying prayers out-of-doors; casting spells using natural forces; the recognition of the Soul of the Wild as friend rather than enemy, as internal deity rather than external manifestation.

Dianics often lived together in small tribes outside the cities. Such tribes had sacred totem animals: The bear represented Artemis; the wolf, Hecate. Legends of children exposed on mountaintops and raised by she-bears or she-wolves are references to these ancient tribes and their practices.

The Dianics were either celibate or lesbian, not consorting with men. They made their living independent of men by educating children, hunting and food-gathering, and farming the "wild" for medicinal herbs. It was a common practice for women to leave their homes in the cities for months, or even years, to "join Diana"—that is, to join a Dianic tribe. They were not required to remain in the tribe forever; they could leave at any time and return to the city, welcomed back by friends and families.

The maximum number of women in a Dianic college at any one time was fifty, the number of weeks in the Year of the Goddess.

Famous Dianic priestesses are virtually unknown to us today. The revised (and much manipulated) story of Atalanta serves as an example of the lifestyle and ultimate fates of such sisters. Atalanta was left exposed on a mountaintop by her patriarchal father, who wanted a son. A she-bear found and raised Atalanta (read: She was raised by the Order of Artemis) until she was old enough to return home a young woman, natural heiress to the throne.

In order to keep Atalanta from a power position, her father decreed that she should marry, a common and popular patriarchal way to "relieve" women of power. As a true Dianic of Artemis, Atalanta refused to be wed. Her father threatened her until she finally set her own conditions: She would agree to mate with the man who could best her in competitive sport. This too was Dianic tradition, in that a Dianic's pride was matched only by her prowess in sports and crafts.

The story of Atalanta realistically goes on to relate how she was tricked into defeat in a footrace, thus losing the competition to a male. As agreed, Atalanta mated with the young man in the temple of Cybele, but the act so angered the Goddess that She turned them both into lions, harnessed to pull Her chariot.

Cybele/Athena was not a Dianic Goddess, but was Asian. She did not exclude men from her rituals. As a matter of fact, males celebrated Her worship by castrating themselves during religious "ecstasy" in order to be more like Her. It is probable that Atalanta and her mate joined an Order of Cybele where they both could serve (as priestess and priest). Atalanta never got her throne back. This tells us much about the fates of women and life in general during the time Goddess-cultures turned to patriarchy.

Today the Dianic traditions are being revived. Women are becoming more aware of how important it is to develop and share collective energies with each other, and to learn how to transcend personality differences by remembering our unity with the Soul of the Wild. In Dianic witchcraft, Diana and Her earth-daughter, Aradia, still reign supreme.

The Goddess Themis

Themis is recognized as the oldest of all gods: the Goddess as the Wisdom of the Earth. She is the Oracular power of the Earth, the soul of Gaia the Earthmother.

Aeschylus: "Themis and Gaia are one in nature, many-named." Themis is prophecy incarnate. In the old sense, prophecy means utterances, ordinances, opening of the mouths, as well as the oracular, which foretells the future. She is pictured sitting on a tripod in a temple to the Earthmother, usually over a slope of mountain, over a cliff, or a cave. Her shrines are associated with the "Tracker," the Furies when angered. She tracks things down; She cannot be evaded. In Her hand She holds a spray of laurel. Laurel was chewed by priestesses to go into a trance. (I tried to do it here in California and all I got was a mouthful of aromatic dry leaves that didn't want to go down.) It was given to poets as a prize, for their further inspiration from the Goddess.

In her other hand is a phial, a shallow, pretty holder of liquids, perhaps water from the sacred well. In a deep trance the priestess would utter her stream of consciousness and the listener would apply it to herself. Interpretation was done by others, not the one who said it. It was considered proper to separate the source of information from the interpretation thereof.

In Homer's time, Themis holds fast in the new patriarchal pantheons. She convenes and dissolves assemblies; She still presides over the banquet tables. The entire idea of a social order, people interacting in an agreed-upon fashion, is Her domain.

In such troubled times as the new patriarchy among the Greeks, the concept of Themis was still placed above that of Zeus.

Themis is very deep. Her name means Doom: a thing set, fixed, settled. "Doom begins in convention, the stress of public opinion; it ends in statuary judgment," said Jane Harrison. One's public opinion is one's doom. So is one's private opinion. Out of these components comes Law. Themis is then the goddess of the Law: Matriarchal law, where women's values are dominant.

Later, the very name becomes Themistes, what society compels, what must be and will be, the prophesies of what shall be in the future. These qualities are the domain today of men, kings, presidents and dictators, but they spring from the sacred wells of Themis.

Themis is the force that binds nations together, the herd instinct, the collective consciousness manifest in her image. She is not yet religion, but She is what good religions are made of.

Religions consist of three major parts, according to Jane Harrison: social custom, collective consciousness, and the representation and emphasis of this collective consciousness. Ritual, collective action, and myth and theology (the representation of the collective consciousness) are binding, incumbent and mutually dependent. There are sister concepts to this, representating social consciousness in art and morality. Morality is different from religion because its rules apply only to conduct and leave thoughts free. Art has no such imposing effect. There is no obligation on action or thought. Her Goddess is Peitho, not Themis, said Harrison. Emile Durkheim advanced a theory about the religious animal: humanoids. What is religious, is binding. The body is bound by natural law and the spirit is bound by social imperative. The moral constraint upon humans is of Themis, not Physis, and because of this bond, humans are religious animals.

Religious faith and practice are obligatory but are also eagerly, vividly chosen; they are a great collective of hereness, said Harrison:

> Religion sums up and embodies what we feel together, what we imagine together, and the price of that feeling together, imagining together and concessions, the mutual compromises, are at first gladly paid.

Introduction to the Rites of Life

The Major Sabbats, Esbats and Women's Festivals are discussed in detail in other chapters. This section provides further stimulation for individuals, communities and tribes to attend to their own ritual needs—priestess themselves—by following the Rites of Life according to inclination and imagination.

We are demonstrating that many traditional Rites of Life have been politically suppressed and pushed into oblivion. They have glorified female experience, female participation and female deities. So partake, remember and invent! Thou art Goddess!

Persephone and Demeter by Masika Szilagyi

A Devotion

On your altar, arrange seven mounds of vervain, and light a candle for devotion; place it in the center of the altar. As you light it, say:

In the name of the Triple Goddess, Whose names are as many as the stars, protect me from evil persons; keep trouble afar; purify me from all fear and oppression. Instead, bring me freedom and inspiration, in the name of Isis. So mote it be!

This devotion can be used with a green candle for money spells, or pink for love, purple for knowledge, etc. It's fine to change the spells to suit yourself, but if it rhymes, it will work better. This may be performed at your convenience, and is an excellent ritual for use on a daily basis to sharpen your meditation and remove any fears.

Meditation for Giving Thanks

Begin by cleaning and sprucing up your space. Create a festive atmosphere; decorate with bunches of Indian corn, ropes of garlic, and other symbols of a plentiful harvest. Clean your altar and cover it with a white cloth. Place an image of the Corn Mother (preferably made of corn) in the center, with a white candle on either side of her. Wear saffron, scarlet or white robes. Light the white candles, burn your favorite incense (frankincense and myrrh are traditional) and settle down to meditate on your harvest.

Hymn to Ambika[1] (from the Sumerian):

Devi![2] Thou Who removest the pain of Thy daughters
Be gracious! Be gracious, O Mother of the World!
Be gracious, O Queen of the Universe!
Architect of the Universe!
Thou art, o Devi, the essence of all moving and unmoving things!

Thou art the only support of the world,
Because Thou art in the form of the earth!
By Thee, Who existed in the form of water,
Is the whole universe pervaded.
Thou art She Whose powers are unsurpassed.

---

1. Ambika is a word meaning "mother"; the name is an Indian Goddess image.

2. Devi literally means "She is."

Thou art the sustaining and eternal power.
Thou art the seed of the universe and the supreme Maya.

All the universe has been bewitched by Thee.
Thou, when pleased, art the course of salvation of nations.

All sciences are part of Thee,
As also all women without exception throughout the world.
By Thee alone, O Mother, is the universe filled!
How can we praise Thee?
Art Thou not beyond all praise of the highest speech?

Rider in an aerial car yoked with swans,
Who assumes the form of energy,
Who sprinkles the water in which verbena is steeped;
Great Mother, all reverence to Thee!

Who art attended by fowl and peacock.
O Faultless One,
Who holdeth the great shakti weapon and existeth in the form of
    Courage,
Great Mother, all reverence to Thee!

O Devi! Who takest away afflictions of the universe
Be gracious to us who awake Thee within ourselves.
O Thou Who are worthy of all praise,
Grant boons to the dwellers of the three worlds.[3]

Here you can do a slow dance, thinking of Her three forms of energy. Offer fruits of the harvest on your altar and pour libations of wine on the ground for Her. Enjoy yourself and feast in honor of Her.

Group Blessing

When in the company of your dearest friends, lovers or family, or just feeling good, try this ritual in which all participate.

Gather into a circle holding each other by the small of the back with your hands and start humming. When you feel relaxed and steady with the sounds you are making, each of you takes a step inside the circle and lies in the middle. Everyone else strokes her aura without physically touching her. This works simply and naturally. I used this ritual in my Feminaries on the beach as a parting ritual.

There is a song from the Indians that goes with it (substitute your own names):

---

3. The three worlds are the "unborn," the "living" and the "dead."

61

Z will be well
Z will be well
All manner of things
shall be well.

When each person has lain down in the middle of the circle, bless her in the same way. If somebody is moved to pronounce blessings over each person in words, just let her ride along with the music.

After all have gone through the process, you can hug and be silent for a while. Suck in the energy you raised by pretending to suck through a straw. Somebody says, "It is done." All answer, "Blessed be!"

If lying down in the circle is impossible, let the woman stand with her eyes closed as the others lay their hands on her. Another technique is when the woman leans against the hands of the group, trusting herself to be supported, while the chanting of her name continues.

A Ritual of Self-Realization

Self-Love is where liberation begins. A woman who loves herself makes good choices for herself; a woman who hates herself will make choices that are good for others only. In order to grow in this precious commodity, Self-Love, you must cultivate your own company in this candlelight ritual.

Before the ritual, make a list of all the qualities you love yourself for, and a list of the qualities you think are bad in you, qualities of which you are not proud.

Take a ritual bath or shower. On your dresser, which has a mirror, prepare an altar to yourself. Place two white candles on the two sides of your mirror and a bit of your favorite incense in your thurible.

Looking into your eyes in the mirror, after lighting your candles (Blessed be thou creature of fire!), inhale the incense and start saying to yourself:

I, (name), have come to commune with my soul.

Look into your eyes and see when the soul changes expression. You will know when it happens. Then name the first negative quality on your list. I use my own example:

I love you, Z, because you can't balance your checkbook.

Watch for reactions, if any, then go on and say something you are proud of:

I love you, Z, because you are a great ritual Priestess.

Now keep naming the negative qualities until they sound more convincing and you start feeling that what you say is not only words but emotions as well. Integrating into one personality your "lights" and "shadows," you

62

extend divine compassion to yourself. When you feel tears welling up in your eyes from love and tenderness toward yourself, the exercise is working well. If you feel that you are slowly but surely convincing yourself, keep doing it until you feel the emotional breakthrough. Alternating the negative with positive qualities will also help you see into your integrated being. When you manage to unblock your compassion for yourself, and direct it back into the parts of you that you originally despised, you will free the entire stock of psychic energy that was yours all along but not available to you because of self-hatred.

When I did this exercise for the first time it took two hours, because I got so involved in having sobbing interruptions. After my crying ebbed, my face started to change rapidly in the mirror, taking up all kinds of other faces, all myself from other lifetimes.

It was rapid and with the feeling of zooming, falling into the image, I saw the faces change ages, outfits, hairdos, wrinkles and all. If this happens to you, it is the sign of a breakthrough. The self is giving you a rare insight of all the people whose genes you carry within you. Don't panic or be afraid. Just stay steady and say "My spirit is a free and safe spirit" to keep your cool.

Perform the self-love exercise every Friday (Venus' Day) until you have a sense that you indeed love yourself more than ever before!

This is not a "Me Generation" game. This is an ancient witchcraft exercise to increase psychic power, which depends on your self-approval. If anybody tries to discourage you from loving yourself, tell them to stuff it. In the so-called "Me Generation", the Me that got explored and glorified was mostly male. Women have yet to have their own decade of self-love. And may it come soon! So be it. It is done.

A Ritual Encounter With Selfhood
by Lhyv Oakwomon

When a woman can unburden herself of the crippling guilt, the morbid fears and the restrictive feelings of shame inherent in Judeo-Christian and other patrifocal traditions, she can then embrace the Feminist Pagan Way. It is a matter of her own awareness and insight into the basis in Nature of all religious thought and celebration. No one can give or teach you that. It is completely between you and your Goddess.

It is in the overwhelming desire for freedom that the Goddess addresses Herself directly to our womansouls—directly, without mediator or intercessor. The day we experience the profound knowledge that we are, in fact, our own saviors, is the day we begin to priestess our own souls. We achieve empathetic awareness of the miracle of Nature through such experiences as: the knowledge that we each possess an individual personal power; the working of our first successful spell; the first time we physically heal a sister or hex an enemy; our first accurate vision of the future; the first time we sense the truth of the past. These and more are signs we are traveling the true Path.

This ritual is deeply dramatic, reminiscent of the initiatory rites of traditional pagan cultures, and is for women who particularly desire to ritualize their "coming out." It is an initiation of the second degree. An ideal time to perform it would be during the Grand Sabbat of Candlemas, for women who know that their destiny is priestesshood.

Experienced priestesses prepare the ritual, form the circle and play the drums. The woman about to perform the initiatory ritual places her body in the yogic "rest" position. She has blindfolded herself to symbolize her state of unawareness before her birth of spiritual consciousness. She may also wish to symbolize other ways in which she felt unaware. For example, if she felt deaf to spiritual teachings, she could insert earplugs, or if she felt bound and restricted she could bind her wrists (not painfully). If she felt particularly unaware in many areas, or generally, she might choose to symbolize this state by covering herself up completely.

When the music from the drums moves the initiate, she begins to rise. Slowly as she rises, she begins to struggle against her condition, signifying her internal struggles. While she dances she verbalizes her actions. She may wander around drunkenly, stomp her feet or shake her body vigorously. When the energy is high, priestesses from the circle who are not playing drums stand one at a time and call the name of the initiate. Each one calls in such a way as to make the initiate heed the sound of her voice, then when she approaches, stands silent while another sister in the circle calls out. When the sisters feel the time is right, five priestesses step into the circle and stand as if their bodies were the five points of a pentagram.

At the first point is the priestess representing Survival. She chants:

> *Heed my voice! Heed my voice!*
> *How will you survive?*
> *Listen to the sound of base desire.*
> *I am Hunger and Thirst; Nakedness when it is cold.*
> *How will you survive?*
> *I am homelessness, I am joblessness.*
> *How will you survive?*

The initiate finds her way to the first priestess. They struggle ritualistically until their movements blend in a dance. Now the initiate answers the first challenge:

64

I hear my body's need.
I hear you and answer your challenge!
I have come out of Tiamat,
She Who is Chaos, the Unformed.
I have wandered with Ixchel and found
She Who is the source.
I am creative, innovative, imaginative and skilled.
Therefore, I will accomplish!

The priestess standing at the point of Wisdom now calls out in a loud, shrill voice:

Aaaiiiiiii! Can you hear me?
I call to you, I call to you.
Come, for I am lonely. Heed my voice!
(seductively) I am so lonely, I have no lover.
I can be bought with gold and silver
But never sold.
If we are lovers, what is my name?
Who am I?

Again the initiate makes her way to the sound of the voice, and the priestess and initiate struggle briefly, following it with a seductive voice. The initiate says:

You are Sophia, Goddess of Wisdom
And you I woo.
You are the lover of my youth
And my womanhood.
My lover in old age of old.
You are Memory, the Mother of Wisdom,
Great Mother of History.
In the Land of Ragno I was saved from ineptness
By learning
And all my learning has led me to Wisdom.
I am the daughter you lead to Power.

The priestess at the Power point of the pentagram now hails the initiate:

How will you take me, for I am the mighty thigh.
Do you dare challenge me?
I am the third obstacle.
Heed my voice.
I give you nothing.
Take me on!

The Power priestess gently, but at medium speed, throws punches at the initiate, who must attempt to block them. When the initiate is blocking them well, she steps up to the priestess and asserts:

I build my cone of Power,
I stand in Beauty.
My first point is knowledge great and small.
Second is my daring
For fear has not defeated me.
Third is my will
Sharpened by my need-fire,
Honed through great struggle.
Fourth is my silence.
My spell rests in the quiet of my womb
That my medicine may have great power.

The priestess at the point of Sex is breathing the Breath of Fire. When she is ready, she challenges by saying:

From what source come these fine words?
Who am I? And where?
What I have is mine to share or naught.
How will you evoke me?
I am the best-known Secret,
Find me if you can.
I hide. I hide in the clear place.
Who am I?

Here the initiate plays out the act of searching, as if for some lost object. She ends this play by touching her body lovingly.

Ah! I know you!
You are hidden in my hood
And guarded by my bones.
You are the knowing woman's soul, my sex.
You are the numbered unit:
Seven you are at rest, uncalled
Six you are blended, in opposition
Five you are awake, yet alone
Ten you are merged with she who binds hearts together.
Now this riddle I speak is mine to keep!

The priestess on the point of Passion speaks now:

Awaken! Awaken! Unstop your ear!
Cast off these bonds! Quickly!

Come you hence, I challenge too!
Who is it, who calls you?

The initiate answers by saying:

Oh! My burning heart
How can I contain you?
Out from me, I say!
You are all that drives me to my goal.
You are the point where my anger shows,
You are the soul of the Goddess of Liberation!
You are Themis, for whom I leap!
You are joy and ecstasy!
No longer am I blind, for I do see,
Nor deaf—my ear is tender,
My hands are free to do their work,
I stand free of the shroud of deceit,
I am whole and ready to meet my fate.

The ritual ends with a womb-hug by all. There is much celebration and feasting, and the priestesses present gifts to the initiate. There are three gifts for to the woman in this ritual: a Moonstone, which the newly initiated places over her Third Eye with a piece of doublestick tape (this is her meditation stone); a piece of gold cloth in which to keep her new Moonstone; a carved box. The ritual is ended by calling down the Moon.

A Birthday Ritual

"Happy Birthday!" This expression triggers many smiles, as all of us, young and old, get to review our lives on our birthdays. Patriarchy has not failed to "borrow" pagan elements for this event. The white candles on the cake are all that's left of the witchy approach. Let's see if we can make more memorable birthdays for ourselves, knowing what the Wise Ones did.

On your birthday, as part of your own ritual, write a card for your mother, thanking her for having done such a great labor in bringing you over to the side of the living. This makes you feel your own life's continuity. You have not come from nowhere. Your mother created you. If she is nearby, certainly invite her to your party. Publicly acknowledge her part in your creation. Mothers rarely are honored by younger people. Mother's Day doesn't count, as it is a band-aid on the injustice perpetrated against women. Give us ERA, and then we'll know you love us! If you are close to your father, invite him too.

Gather your friends together at sundown, after having spent the day meditating on your life. When the sun has set, light your incense. Rebirth incense is the most appropriate, but you can't go wrong with frankincense and myrrh. Avoid the usual guru smells like banana or blackberry. These have no occult properties.

In your home, set up a white candle to represent every year you have lived. Put them everywhere and light them one by one, meditating on the years they represent. If you had something special happen on a certain year, you can use a different candle for it. If you fell in love, use a pink or red one. If you lost your parents, use black. If you formed a friendship, use blue. If you were sick, use orange to build up your health. Use yellow if you are full of dreams, purple if you have achieved a high goal, green if you made money, brown if you bought property. Remember, all these are optional.

Have your friends form a circle and step into it. Your best friend should take a leading part here.

The best friend says: "Who do we honor today?"
The rest answer: "A friend who journeyed from birth to here."
Best friend: "What do we do to a person we love?"
Rest: "We bless her/him for the seasons to come!"
Now all take the candles that represent your years, and holding them aloft, they shout, "Long life to you, (your name)!"
You answer: "Long life is sent to me by you."
All: "Long life with love and health!"
You: "Long life is to me from you!"
All: "Long life and golden luck!"
You: "Long life is mine, and golden luck!"

Now the candles can be placed back where they were. The cake can be brought out, with or without candles. You can now proceed according to regular birthday customs as you like.

If you are isolated, or have no time to organize a whole party for your birthday, you should ask at least one person to perform this blessing for you. Don't skimp on your birthday. It is important to reaffirm your origin, your process and your future. Even if you hate birthdays, still remember that it is a holy day for you and your mother. The gift of life is worthy to recall and celebrate. So honor yourself with a candlelight ceremony, a treat with friends.

Happy Birthday!

Dianic New Moon Ritual

Time: In the first quarter of the moon, when just a clear sliver crescent is visible in the afternoon sky.

Gather together, singing and chanting:

We all come from the Goddess,
And to Her we shall return,
Like a drop of rain
Flowing to the ocean.

While you assemble, pick some green stalks and flowers if any are at hand. Then sit around and make wreaths for your crowns. When you have finished, admire each other's creations, and feeling thus adored, begin the ritual.

Three women take responsibility here: one for the Maiden, one for the Nymph and one for the Crone. Position yourselves in the circle, with the Nymph to the East, the Maiden to the West and the Crone to the North. Each of them holds sticks of incense as wands; frankincense and myrrh are a good choice, although regular temple incense will do.

Begin to hum low, without straining the vocal cords, until the tops of your heads begin to vibrate. The moon should be in sight above, as you gaze upon her crescent shape. When the hum has unified and you are making one chord, start making it varied and different, like a tapestry of sounds. Give it texture; harmonize and allow the divine to flow through you while you listen to each other while singing.

When the time is right, each of the three priestesses drops a name into the pool of sound: "Maat" (Truth); "Dianna" (Holy Mother); "Hecate" (threefold). The group chants these names, not necessarily in order, but as it flows through.

Then the Nymph steps out and girds the circle with her incense wand, traveling from East to South and then West.

I am the beauty of the Green Earth
and the White Moon among the stars.
Come into this circle, spirits of the East!
Come into this circle, spirits of the South!
Hear us, see us, protect us, Mother Maat!

She reaches to the West, and hands her incense wand over to the Maiden.

I am the mystery of the Waters,
and the desire of human hearts.
Come join us, Love, come join us in the West.
End all sorrow, and come and protect.

She gives her wand and the Nymph's wand to the Crone. The Crone takes all three incense wands and walks around the circle once, returning to her place and saying:

Come call to your soul.
Arise and come unto me.
For I am she who gives life to the Universe.
From me all things proceed, and to me all things shall return.

Then she announces the closing of the circle, saying:

The Goddess blesses Her children.

Now begins the heightened power-raising hum, picking up where it was at the beginning of the gathering.

While this happens, three white eggs (preferably fresh) are brought out in a basket and placed in the middle of the circle. These eggs represent the coming month. New moon to new moon is the time space where you project yourselves.

In a chalice, pure water is placed, along with a small container of salt, in the middle of the circle. Extend your hands over the chalice, eggs and salt, saying:

Mother darksome and divine, bless our tools, and bless
our lives.

The Nymph picks up the eggs and takes them, one by one, in her hands. She projects into them her wish for the future:

I name you luck! I name you love! I name you money!

She puts the eggs back in the basket, and hands them to the next woman to the East of her. She also takes the eggs and names them as her life requires, always passing towards the south, West and North.

The Crone keeps the eggs by her side. The Maiden picks up the chalice and gazes into it, saying:

This is health. As I drink this pure water, I will be healed,
purified and nurtured. This is the Goddess's gift.

Before she drinks, she holds the chalice up to the moon so that it appears just above the rim and she catches the moon's reflection in the water. The chalice is passed around, and the women drink to her health.

The Crone picks up the salt and goes to each woman, sprinkling it on her head and saying:

This is wisdom that I shower upon you. May you be smart,
wise, enduring and successful. So be it.

Each woman receives it and says "Blessed be." When this is finished, all observe a moment of silence to hear omens. The Crone digs a hole in the ground with the help of the Nymph and Maiden, and buries the eggs, saying:

> *Mother Moon and Sister Earth, I return these eggs to you*
> *for safekeeping. It is forever, and for our good luck, wealth*
> *and health. As you enclose these eggs, so will your grace*
> *enclose our lives. As you hold these eggs so close to you,*
> *so shall you hold us all in your hearts.*

She covers the eggs with earth. "Blessed be," say all. Sprinkle the leftover water over the eggs, along with the leftover salt. It is done.

Afterwards, you may sit down and eat the food you have brought. Enjoy free-flowing company, and mingle while playing instruments and dancing. When you are ready to go home, the three priestesses open the circle counterclockwise, and thank the spirits for coming into the circle (from the East, North, West and South).

"Merry-meet, and merry-part."

Rituals for Daily Life
by Carol Christ

As I begin to celebrate the presence of the Goddess in my life, I find it important to create rituals that will become part of my ordinary daily life, rituals which will give me strength when I feel weak and which will magnify my powers when I feel strong.

My favorite spell is a very simple one. After cleaning up my house I go around from room to room and purify the space. Sometimes I open a window and direct the bad vibes out with hand motions, while encouraging the good ones to come in. Then I take my chalice (a longstemmed wine glass) from my altar, fill it with fresh water, add salt, and face the east wall of my room. I dip my fingers into the water, raise my hands and say:

> *Powers of the East*
> *Powers of the daystar rising*
> *And all fresh beginnings*
> *I purify you with salt and with water*
> *For good vibrations of friendship, warmth and love.*

I sprinkle some extra water in the east for good measure and proceed to the south, where I say:

> *Powers of the South*
> *Powers of the summer sun*
> *Which warms our bodies and our minds*
> *I purify you with salt and with water*
> *For good vibrations of friendship, warmth and love.*

I repeat in the west:

> *Powers of the West*
> *Powers of the purifying and cleansing waters*
> *From which all life comes*
> *I purify you with salt and with water*
> *For good vibrations of friendship, warmth and love.*

And in the north:

> *Powers of the North*
> *Powers of the earth, the ground*
> *On which we stand*
> *I purify you with salt and with water*
> *For good vibrations of friendship, warmth and love.*

I then proceed around the room sprinkling water over all the thresholds, windows and doorways, and in all corners, while visualizing the things I would like to have happen in the room—love, passion or good dreams over the bed; creative working-space vibes around my desk; friendship and good conversation in the living room, etc. I sometimes repeat the ritual with incense in each direction, threshold and corner when I feel the need for an extra strong spell.

I keep a vial of rose oil on my altar for use in rituals. On days when I wake up and feel I can't face the world, I light orange or yellow candles on my altar for energy, and draw a flower or pentacle on my forehead with rose oil on my fingertip, saying to myself:

> *This invisible sign is the seal of you*
> *Protection by the Goddess*
> *As you smell Her sweet scent you will remember*
> *Her presence within you.*

The idea that the sign of the spell is invisible to everyone but me seems to add to the power of the spell.

I do a lot of candle spells, choosing colors to symbolize the energy I need or want to increase. After lighting my candles I move my hands in circles, directing the candle's energy toward me while visualizing the qualities I associate with each candle color. Then I stretch my arms, lift my head upwards and say, "O Lady Goddess, all power is Yours." Then I repeat the circling motions with my hands and place my hands on myself, saying "All power is in me." I find this spell beautiful because it stresses the "life-flows-on-within-you-and-without-you" quality of Goddess religion.

Summer Solstice Festival for Children
by Noel Brennan

This can be performed in the afternoon, evening or night, depending on how old the children are. It can be performed with one or many children.

The only tools necessary are flowers, fire and party food. The food should be baked goods that had to be finished by fire (such as cakes or cupcakes). If outdoors, you can build a small fire, with the children gathering sticks for it, or you can use candles. Candles are also good if you must celebrate indoors.

Bring the children together as a group. An adult leader says:

> *We are all friends here.*
> *There are no fights now,*
> *And no one is afraid.*
> *We trust each other here*
> *In the presence of the Goddess.*

Join hands. If there is more than one child, make a circle, as large as possible. The leader says:

> *We are here in the circle of your creation, Lady,*
> *The circle of your universe.*
> *It is around us and we are part of it,*
> *Never separate.*
> *The protection of the Mother*
> *Folds around us*
> *Like magic and wind.*
> *Celebrate with us, Lady of Summer!*

Now the children may drop hands. The leader says:

> *The Lady returns in fire,*
> *Wrapped in flames and fragrance,*
> *Hearthstone of the universe,*
> *The nurturing warmth,*
> *The passion of life and singing summer,*
> *High Queen of the seasons,*
> *Turning the slow and starry wheel.*

The children may sit down while the leader describes the symbolism of the wheel, the turning and returning of things, the snake with its tail in its mouth, the cycles of the Goddess—birth, death, rebirth—and also, simply, the turning of the seasons. The children can talk about cyclical things with which they are familiar. Make a wheel of the flowers you have brought. The children may decorate themselves and each other with flowers. Then ask for silence again. The leader says:

> *Fires from the heart of the earth*
> *Leap forth,*
> *Reflecting in the sun,*

Rekindling.
Deep-banked fires
Flaming in buds,
Flaming in blossoms,
Primeval nurturance,
Copper blood of life,
Ancient and subtle,
Returning and present,
Here now, within us.

Now light the fire or the candles. The leader should do this, unless there are older, more responsible children who can. Contemplate the fire and discuss its symbolism. Tell about the bonfires that were built for the Goddess in the past, and about the celebrations that went with them. Let the children ask questions if they want, and have them look for pictures in the flames. Then ask for silence again. Tell the children to lie on their backs and close their eyes. If you are outside, fine. If not, tell them to imagine being in a summer field, in the long, sweet-smelling grass, hearing the crickets and feeling drowsy. Tell them to relax. When they are quiet, the leader says:

Mid-season fires reach high,
The fruitful earth blossoms
Like flames;
Warm summer,
Height of the season,
The dreamy stand-still
Of the year.
Insects drone their song of life.

Among the heavy scents,
winds are laden
With bird-songs,
Women like tapestries
In leafy branches.
Across the pale sky
The faint moon drifts,
Sudden and pure,
A whisper and a mystery.

The children lie still for a while. Before they begin to get restless, the leader says:

Lady of flowers,
Mother of life,

Bless this food,
And bless us, your children,
That we may be strong
And live fairly with one another.

Now the children sit up. Food is passed around. They can eat, and afterwards play games if time allows. Before they leave, have them thank the Goddess in words of their own. Happy Solstice! Blessed be!

Conception Ritual

Time: When the woman's menstrual cycle is in the most fertile time (check astrological birth control).
Place: Preferably outdoors, but indoors is okay.

To conceive has always been one of the major endeavors of women. As creators of the human race, women everywhere created many different ways to invoke the Goddess of Fertility.

The most universal images for conception are the toad and the snake. On one of the Goddess's shrines in Northern India, She is shown in a conception position, which resembles a lot of frogs' spread legs. Why the frog, the toad or the snake? These amphibians or reptiles are earlier forms of life, and in fact these stages are repeated in each cycle of human gestation; therefore to conceive is to start over again. The embryo must swim like an amphibian before it is born; it must change and renew like the snake.

Draw on a pink piece of paper your version of this symbol. If you need to, look one up in a book. Draw it in red ink: red for action and the color of blood. Write in the middle, ''My own child.'' Then make a doll of some red flannel representing yourself; give it features: hair, eyes, nose. Before you sew up the doll's body, sew into it your drawing of the fertility charm, neatly folded in four parts, each time folding it towards yourself, saying:

Mine is the power of the Goddess
Mine is the blood that grants life
I am calling on the new soul to enter
I am giving the new soul life divine.

Repeat this four times each time you fold. Then finish your doll. Now go outside when the Moon is new, after carefully checking the phases of your own birth cycle to determine the sex of your child (see astrology chapter). Take your partner with whom you would like to have a child, and make love outside on a blanket in the rays of the Moon.

If your choice is artificial insemination, take your woman friends with you and go for an evening swim in the ocean. Ancient women called down parthenogenesis when they honored Dianna the Virgin Mother by wildly thrashing around in the water during religious ecstasy. If that is impractical, stay at home and have the insemination happen there, with red candles burning on your altar to call down the Goddess's action.

I have talked to women who had this done, and they told me that the mind (or rather the third eye, otherwise known as the pituitary gland) triggers conception. The key is to create an atmosphere in which the mind releases this energy to the womb.

Yet another version. (I did this to a woman who had tried to conceive for two years in vain.) I selected a white egg-shaped candle in a small shop in the village. We went home and I anointed the egg with my favorite oil, Rosa Lama. Then I held it between my thumbs, blessing it over her open hands which she held below mine.

> *In the name of Isis of the thousand breasts*
> *May your conception be blessed*
> *In the name of Isis of the thousand breasts*
> *May your pregnancy be blessed*
> *In the name of Isis of the ten thousand breasts*
> *May the birth be easy and the life you bring forth be*
>   *blessed.*

At this point I dropped the egg from my hands into hers. Then I closed her hands over it tightly and said:

> *It is done.*

She went home and lit the candle, performed the insemination and conceived a healthy baby girl.

Menstruation Ritual

Time: When menses sets in.
Place: Home of the woman or friend's house.

Gather the young woman's friends who already menstruate, and those who don't yet. Create a party with plenty of food and drink; also serve teas that ease the cramping, such as chamomile, pennyroyal or comfrey. Before your feast begins, form a circle of the women who do not yet menstruate, and have the young maiden stand naked in the middle. Take a small dish of water and earth (earth is a symbol of maturity), mix them into a paste, and have the young women smear some of this mud on the body of the young maiden, saying:

> *Farewell, sister of my childhood! I love you as I love the*
> *Earth!*

The young woman answers:

Farewell, my childhood! Farewell the nymph I am no more!

When the young maiden emerges, she stands between the two worlds, between her childhood friends and her youthful friends, the other maidens.

Then form another circle of the women, young and old, who menstruate. The young woman goes with them into a bathroom or bathing place, where they wash away the mud from her body and rub her body with scented herbs. As they touch her, they say:

Welcome, welcome, friend of my youth!

She answers:

The nymph is gone, but oh, the Maiden is just born!
Welcome, o friends of my youth!

The maiden is washed clean and dressed in a gown of her choice, bedecked with flowers brought by her friends. She is led out to face her mother, who has a special gift for her: a red stone ring. The stone can be a garnet, a ruby, even red glass—anything that she can afford. It conveys the message of acceptance to the young one.

Mother to daughter:

You traveled the road from my breast as a babe to maturity
as a young woman. I bless you for the seasons to come!
Accept this ring as a memento for the passage well done!

Mother and daughter kiss each other. Maiden wears her ring. The party can resume, with dancing and women sharing their experiences of how they came to have their first menses, and how different this is from the guilt and shame young women were subjected to before the awakening of the Goddess Consciousness. Sing songs and party until dawn.

Celebration of the End of Menstruation

When a woman knows she will no longer bleed each month, it's time to call friends together and give a joyous End of Menstruation.

The end of bleeding means the woman is entering the last stage of her life's Queenhood—individualized, independent and strong. Her energies are directed toward more spiritual goals, saved for more achievement. Each time you have a change in your hormonal chemistry, drink Holy Thistle tea, made from an herb easily available through health food stores. It helps balance out the body and save you from hot flashes.

Form a circle and create an altar in the middle with four red and four yellow candles. Prepare it with red roses and white or yellow flowers. Use a Maiden Goddess for your centerpiece: Athena, Dianna or Artemis.

Raise energy through song or humming. When the energy is raised (you will know when) let one of the friends act as priestess:

We gather together to commemorate the withdrawal of the flowing bloods from our friend. We ask the Great Goddess to bless our sister with good health, vitality and gladness. Let the flow act through the younger women now and let this woman rest; she has finished her part as the Goddess of the Broods. She is now the Goddess of the Great Achievements.

The celebrant now lights her four red candles.

I light this first candle for the bloods that are gone. (Omit if not applicable:) The second candle for the children and health the flow brought me. The third for the flowerings of my womanhood, and the fourth for the labors ended in glory.

The Priestess:

I release you, said the Goddess of the Red. I accept you, said the Goddess of the Yellow Ray. I call you into my wisdom to grow in, I call you like a new Maiden, into my sciences, into my knowledge, into dreams to be manifest!

The celebrant now lights her four yellow candles.

I light this first yellow candle for the release from the Reds. This second one for the flowering of my skills. This third one for friends and support, and this fourth one for the blessings from above!

Now the circle can sing songs, entertain each other, share food and drink, exchange gifts with the celebrant. When the candles reach their natural end, cast them into a living body of water and don't look back.

Blessed Be! It is done!

Welcoming a New Mother Into the Circle of Mothers

We have bridal showers for brides-to-be and baby showers for expectant mothers, but once you become a mother, nobody gives a hoot. This must change. You, as a mother, now need attention and affection more than ever. You also need new clothes, new ideas and new friends.

To give birth is more important than the greatest military victory. To take life is easy. The American Indians believed that to go through labor and give birth meant going down to hell and fetching a new spirit into the light. Society has decided to focus on your new baby more than on you, the mother. You can change that by starting this new celebration of yourself.

Time: After you have given birth and feel strong enough to do it. This should be the first thing in which you are participating. Invite women who have had babies, if you can. In any case, invite all the women you like and whose company you cherish.

This event should be planned by the new mother's friends. They are to present her with three gifts of importance. First, a new gown, or material for making one. Green is preferred, but it can be of any color. A green-robed lady is the Goddess who gives birth and then renews herself, becoming a virgin again. Second, an herbal tea such as raspberry, good for the womb. Third, tickets to an event that she can go out to see. It should be a treat with color and content.

The women establish a time when she is to be resting in bed with her baby. As a surprise, they enter her room. Three women representing the Fates, a Nymph, a Maiden and a Crone, come bearing gifts. The women carry branches of trees. Evergreen is best as it is the symbol of rebirth. (Do not use ivy; it is sacred to death and is poisonous.) They should bring flowers and some incense sticks; sandalwood is best.

The first mother greets her, saying, "Blessed be thou (name). We heard in the air that you have returned to the world of mothers. Welcome to the company of the creators of humanity!"

The second mother says, "Blessed be thou (name). We have brought you gifts that make you whole. The new gown was sent to you to clothe you with the beauty of your new life. Blessed be your body, that you will grow strong, to return you to your own after you were gone. Your body and soul fetched a new soul from the unborn." She kisses the new mother and presents the gift informally.

The third mother says, "Blessed be thou (name). I give you an herb that is sweet to your womb. Drink it, and bless it. Be whole. I give you (theater tickets, invitation to a grand ball, a picnic, a hiking trip, tennis, a swimming party) to kindle your spirits. You worked hard, and your spirit is tired. Come to (this event), and we will all laugh and praise the Goddess!" She gives the gift informally.

Then the celebrant speaks to the three: "I am blessed today as a new mother, and welcomed into the circle of mothers."

The other three say, "We love you. It is done."

Then informal visiting takes place with whatever means all have to pursue it.

Naming Festival: Dedication of a Newborn Child

This ritual should take place on the first day of a New Moon, and includes a dedication circle composed of women in the mother's bloodline and extended family. After a purification bath, the mother dresses in white or saffron. The baby should also be dressed in white. Select a tree to represent the Tree of Life: Oak, poplar, willow, alder or elm are traditional, but any tree available will be fine. The women form a circle around the tree, singing and joyous.

The baby is placed at the foot of the tree with a bowl of corn or barley, a bowl of water, a bowl of salt, and a white garlic bulb. The mother will have chosen the child's Guardian Mother (NOT godmother).

The ritual begins with the Guardian Mother, acting as Maiden, giving the Great charge:

> *Aphrodite, Arionhod,*
> *Lover of the Horned God,*
> *Mighty Queen of Witchery and Night;*
> *Morgan, Etoine, Nisene,*
> *Diana, Brigit, Melusine,*
> *Am I named of Old by men;*
> *Artemis and Cerridwen,*
> *Hell's Dark Mistress, Heaven's Queen.*
> *Ye who would ask of me a boon,*
> *Meet me in some secret glade,*
> *Dance my round in greenwood shade,*
> *By the light of the Full Moon.*
> *In a place wild and lone,*
> *Dance around mine altar stone;*
> *Work my Holy Mystery.*
> *Ye who are feign to sorcery,*
> *Who give true worship unto me.*
> *Ye who tread my round on Sabbat night,*
> *Come all ye naked to the rite*
> *In token that ye be truly free.*
> *I teach ye the mystery of rebirth,*
> *Work ye my Mysteries in mirth.*
> *Heart joined to heart and lip to lip,*
> *Five the points of Fellowship*
> *That bring ye ecstasy on earth.*
> *For I am the Circle of Rebirth.*
> *I ask no sacrifice, but do bow,*
> *No other law but Love I know,*
> *By naught but Love may I be known.*
> *All things living are mine own,*
> *From me they come, to me they go.*

The mother, as High Priestess, now moves to the center of the circle, facing the tree. She holds the child in her outstretched hand and says:

Queen Brigit, we have brought you here
The fruit of my womb, for joy, for fay.[4]
Bless this child with golden luck.
May (her/his) heart have your silver touch.
Health and wealth shall be (her/his) lot,
By sickness nor evil shall ever be caught.
Blessed be.

The mother places the baby back on the ground and rejoins the circle. One sister now moves forward, takes the bowl of barley or corn, and pours it on the ground in an uninterrupted circle around the baby, saying:

Demeter, accept this offering to you.
May this child never know hunger of Body,
Nor Heart, nor Soul.

Another sister takes the bowl of water, sprinkles the child, and pours the water on the ground around the child, saying:

Marianne, accept this water as an offering to you. May this child have the Life-Force sap always strong within (her/him). May the Moon's fertility infuse (her/him) with love for all living. May (she/he) know Sisterhood.

A third sister takes the bowl of salt, again making a circle around the child and saying:

Blessed be Sophia, Wisest of the Wise, in the earth and beyond the heavens. Protect and bless this child with wisdom.

All in the circle again, the women unify and raise power, building songs and different patterns out of the sounds. Then the afterbirth and umbilical cord are buried with the garlic under the tree and covered with the left-over water, barley or corn, and salt.

The mother now pronounces the child's name to the women for the first time. There are, however, two names. One is the child's legal name; the other is her/his Secret Name, and must not be uttered again, even to the child, until her/his initiation ceremony. For a girl child, the initiation

---

4. fay: magicalness; having magical or fairy-blessed qualities.

ceremony takes place with her First Menstruation ritual; for a boy, this will be at his Dedication to the Goddess ritual, at the onset of puberty.

Feasting, dancing and joyousness are in order following the newborn child's dedication.

Ritual After an Abortion or Miscarriage
by Chris Carol

When the blood stops flowing, in the evening after the stars appear, friends prepare a bath of warm water. They sprinkle salt, herbs of comfort and cleansing, and rose petals on the water.

The woman enters the warm water saying, ''Bless me, Mother, for I am your child!'' She immerses herself, lies still and listens to her heart-beat and slow breathing.

Friends sing to the beat of the woman's heart, as the woman sees the life she created stir, grow and then leave her to fly up the Milky Way to join the dance of the stars.

We are flowing wave on wave, from salt sea to salt sea.
We are dancing round and round the Life Tree, the Life Tree.
We are leaping higher and higher, like sparks of fire, like
sparks of fire.
We are flying up along the Milky Way, the Milky Way.

The woman bids farewell to the young life. As she emerges from the water, the woman and friends give each other the fivefold blessing on head, breasts, womb, knees and feet. They share a pot of tea and a cake made with honey.

When the water has drained away, the woman gathers the rose petals to sprinkle on her garden. Everyone hugs and they sing *Deep Peace* together before leaving.

Ritual for Healing
After Removal of Ovaries or Womb, Breasts, etc.

Just because a woman no longer has her reproductive organs does not mean she has achieved Cronehood. Her body changes and it is important to bless this new being and banish the old fears, sicknesses and insecurity.

Prepare a fire in a cauldron or a pit. Put in the herbs you like; rosemary and lavender smell good.

Form a circle with your friends, holding hands, and unify with a hum or a song. When you've built the energy, say:

> *I (name of celebrant) today banish the ills that caused my operation. I banish weakness, I banish sorrow.*

Help yourself to this Siberian chant of banishment:

> *Into the dark night take away the evil spirit!*
> *Over the dark mountain scatter the evil spirit!*
> *Into the Mother's night drive it in banishment!*
> *Draw it into the invisible river!*
> *Drive it further into oblivion!*
> *Drive it across the threshold of the darkest night!*
> *All paths leading back into Life be barred with twice seven*
>   *arrows barbed with knives!*

Now jump over the flames at least three times, imagining that you are purified by the fire each time you jump. Your women friends then say to you:

> *Renew woman, renew like the sun*
> *Revitalize and sing the new song*
> *Your life has not ended*
> *It has only begun!*
> *Renew woman, renew like the sun!*

It always helps to receive a memento for the occasion. Give her flowers, books, messages, tickets to events. Party. Blessed are those who support each other.

Queening Ritual:
Celebration of Middle Age and Responsibility

Since most Americans spend their time being middle-aged, it's exciting to regard this space in our lives from a new point of view. It is easy to celebrate youth with puberty rites, and the Croning Ritual can mark our entry into the Sage Age, but what about middle age? When is it? Is it a biological event like the others? Do you reach a certain point and *boom*, that's it, you are in middle age?

The Triple goddess gives us the answer: The middle aspect of the Goddess is the Mother-Queen, She Who rules. She is always celebrated for Her fecundity, She Who gives birth to new life, but what about her "ruling" aspect, making decisions, taking responsibility, contributing leadership to what has been created? Middle age is a mental state. It begins when you accept your own power and are willing and proud to exercise it, by shaping your own life and contributing to society at large.

As ever, this aspect of the Goddess has many names. I like Hera, the origin of the word "courage," the swarthy queen of the cities and civic duties, She Whose queenly chariot is drawn by peacocks. On Her crown She wears the symbols of Her many cities, towers and landmarks. When women assume their power, they manifest the Queen aspect, the skillful leader. If you are lucky, you achieve this early in life; if not, you certainly have time until you are 56 to perfect some skill as your service to the Queen.

I did this ritual for Brandy, a friend who worked as an important official; her duties included fundraising for all the universities and colleges in her state. She had a large income, two growing daughters and two residences, one in the capital and one in her home town.

Brandy had little trouble managing her time without guilt; she was Supermom, Superfundraiser, Superwoman. She had everything except psychic support from herself and other women. She was flying too fast. I stopped her for a ritual.

First, her daughters commissioned an official crown for their mom, a nice silver witch crown decorated with a half moon, precious stones and runes inscribing her name. A silver crown is not always expensive. I have one made of a slim silver band with a little moon in it; it hides perfectly in my white hair.

Next we threw a "Power Party" for her and her friends. When the party was good and cooking, the energy high, I rang the bell to gather and commemorate my friend's official acceptance of her middle age.

I said, "Dear friends, it is so rare that a woman gets honor for her power without somebody putting her down. Let us honor Brandy by crowning her the queen she is! To be queen is necessary for the survival of the planet. Women must say 'Yes' to power or we'll never get to live in peace and prosperity. Come here, Brandy!"

Brandy shyly came to the middle of the circle, not knowing what was coming next. I took a branch of orange twigs, dipped it into water with orange blossoms floating in it, and sprinkled her on the head. Orange blossoms are for happiness, but any flowers indigenous to where you live would do very well. Flowers are associated with the fairy realm and blessings from the magic folks.

"I bless you with the self-confidence of the Goddess Whose daughter you are." (head)

"I bless you with the effectiveness of a true queen." (hands and body)

"I bless you with harmony so that you get the support of your co-workers." (back and front)

Then I asked her: "Do you, Brandy, accept the power and responsibility that come from manifesting the Goddess as Queen?"

She answered, "Yes, I do."

"Then receive this silver crown symbolizing Womanhood at her best, at maturity, at her most useful and inspired."

I placed the silver crown on her head. She had a moment of embarrassment, but also reverence for this old symbol.

It's hard for the modern woman to accept a crown unless she is born to royalty or is a beauty contest winner. Take your time and get used to it. The crown isn't funny; power is serious. It will help later on whenever you feel you are losing confidence and energy; just wear your silver crown for a while, and the blessing will return full force.

It is customary to wear the crown all evening and give orders to the guests. We are obliged to fulfill them, showing the new queen good faith. It can become a fun game with everyone going on errands for the queen. All this sounds very feudal, but power has long and deep roots, and women must start from these depths. Accepting honor and power with pride is being the Goddess in this life. Practice it. It's good for you.

Croning Ritual: Entering the Wise Age

This ritual occurs when a woman has reached the point in her life at which her Saturn has returned twice to her natal point. This happens to everybody at age 56. Saturn is the teaching planet, slow and complete; we celebrate the effects of this celestial event on the woman's life by the Croning ritual.

Call a party for the young Crone; friends and relatives can cooperate with the invitation. Try to provide some entertainment; invite a woman who plays an instrument or recites poetry. When all arrive, the group holds hands and sings a song to unify the group soul.

> *Lady, Lady, listen to my heart's song*
> *Lady, Lady, listen to my heart's song*
> *I will never forget you, I will never forsake you*
> *I will never forget you and I will never forsake you!*

After a few rounds of this, when the time is right, the priestess of the event steps out to address rest. This priestess can be anyone who loves the new Crone.

Priestess:

> *We gather together to celebrate (name) becoming fifty-six*
> *years old, and entering the Wise age.*

From now on, her proper title among women is "Young Crone." Who is the Crone, you ask? A Crone is a woman who has reached wisdom in her heart, who is called on to arbitrate disputes, who is called on to soothe the wounds of despair; a young Crone is a woman who is everybody's older sister.

Who else is the Crone? She is the Goddess in Her third aspect; she is Magaera, Hecate, the Goddess of unbound power.

Folklore has it that Crones bring good luck when you see them on the street; if they smile on you, you will have a very good day. They appear in important times to show the grace of the Goddess. Crones' wishes must be respected, for the Goddess demands this of the younger generation.

Crones enjoy special favors; their magic is stronger; their spells are faster; their loves are stronger.

All:

> *Bless you (name of the new Crone) with good health, happiness and long life!*

Now the youngest of the group starts lighting a circle of white candles previously set out in the middle of the room: 56 of them, one for each year of the Crone's life. Others can help after the Nymph starts. The priestess has a bell which she will ring out 56 times. If the Crone would like to give a speech, here is a good place to do it.

When the circle of light is done, the young Crone steps into it and the bell tolls out 56 times, after which everyone applauds. Congratulations and good wishes are showered on the woman in the circle. As a special feature, the Young Crone receives her Crone Jewel. It can be a brooch, a necklace, a ring, as long as it has a nice purple stone in it. Purple is the color of synthesis. It is a royal color, a learning color, a powerful color.

Priestess:

> *I present you with your Crone Jewel, to remind you that you are our teacher, our beloved sister, and Crone of the Goddess.*

Young Crone:

> *I traveled the road from my mother's breasts to Cronehood. I thank the Goddess for the good seasons that passed, and oh, I toast the good seasons to come! Blessed be!*

All enjoy the party, dance, perform, enjoy.

Ritual for Planting a Grove

This ritual has been performed for many women around the country who wanted their affinity groups blessed and dedicated to the Goddess. The best time for this ritual is the waxing moon.

Form a regular circle, with purifications, consecration and power raising. After evoking the Goddess and pouring libations to Her on the ground, the group to be planted comes forward and forms a smaller circle in the center of the large one. The High Priestess offers a ball of red thread to the Goddess and then says to the women, "This thread represents the thread of our lives. The red color indicates a commitment to action. Do you accept this?" The women answer, "Yes, we do." The High Priestess turns to the woman on her left and wraps the thread three times around the woman's waist, blessing her in the name of the Nymph, the Maiden and the Mother. This woman now takes the thread and does the same to the woman to her left, and so on around the circle. If the woman acting as High Priestess is to be part of the new grove, then she is included in the entwining thread. If not, she steps back before tying the ends together.

After tying them together, she says, "As the thread of life is bound to a circle, so shall our struggles be bound together. This new grove to the Goddess is formed. Blessed be. It is done." Then she and her Maiden go around the circle cutting the thread between the women, tying the ends to make individual girdles, and saying "The circle is never broken." Each woman answers, "Blessed be."

Before the next gathering of the new grove, each woman should weave this cord into her nine-foot-long witch's girdle, which will afterward be worn at all Sabbats and while doing magical work. It is a very important protection symbol.

Dianic Trysting

Trysting, handfasting, or the Promising Ritual is an ancient way of bonding which we as women loving women or men need to re-establish. The so-called Marriage ceremony, where mothers always cry and grandmothers faint—doesn't that give away its ominous meaning—is a recent institution geared primarily to sexual ownership. The promise is monogamy, and in the case of the woman involved, "giving up her maidenhead," which means losing her name, social status and identity; try to find a married lady through the phone book when you don't know her husband's name!

We approach trysting from a universal point of view. The bond called down on the couple is loyalty forever, which has nothing to do with sex. The words exchanged are promises to take care of each other as long as they live, and even after death. It's a moving bond, which should be done not only for couples but for anybody who feels this undying bond. Especially in these times of threatened ecological disaster, we must form tribes to survive. But to thrive, we must form love-bonds!

Requirement: The trystees have been friends at least six months. If for some reason they want to be trysted anyway, they should not be stopped.
Time: Full and New Moons.
Place: Outdoors under beautiful trees, by the ocean, in groves or indoors in some nice space. Decorate with yellow and white flowers, yellow for manifestation and white for blessing.

The women dress in robes, gowns, tuxedos or whatever, but they are barefoot for the ceremony.

The women prepare a tray of green things, something from the roots, from the stems, from the leaves, flowers and fruits (carrots, celery, cauliflower, dates, salads, almonds, oranges). This is to invoke the Goddess of Life over the tray; food is life. Also present on the altar are the two chalices in gold, silver or ceramic, that the women bought for themselves as symbols of their union. Wedding rings do not signify marriages as much as chalices do; they are symbols of pleasure. They may have the date engraved on them.

Last, floral wreaths for the two women and the High Priestess, made of yellow and white roses.

The couple waits barefoot outside the circle while the priestess goes from East to South, West and North, invoking the Goddess according to ancient rites. Holding an incense burner aloft, she pauses at each quarter saying her own invocation or this one:

> *(East:) Hail to thee, Goddess Isis, bringer of new life and feelings, come into this circle where lovers await Your blessings! (If not lovers, say "friends.")*

> *(South:) Come to this circle, fiery Goddess Heartha, Vesta, Pele! Bring Your energy to fuel this bond to be formed here today. Come bring Your excitement, joy and ecstasy. Blessed be!*

> *(West:) Hail to thee, Aphrodite! Love Goddess, Water Goddess! Come to us in this circle and bless the lovers who ask for it in Your name, come and bless this union with love!*

> *(North:) Come, o beautiful Earth Goddess Demeter and Your daughter Persephone! Come and nourish us with Your love and presence. Blessed be!*

Then closing the circle, two priestess who facilitate walk to the trystees and anoint them with either a sacred oil (Rosa Lama, priestess oil, frankincense and myrrh) or blessed water.

> *(Anointing the forehead) I purify you from all anxiety; I purify your mind from fears; (anointing the eyes and nose) I purify your eyes to see Her ways; (lips) your lips to speak Her names; (breast) your breast formed in strength and beauty; (genitals) your genitals I bless for strength and pleasure; (feet) your feet to walk in Her path.*

Finally she anoints the palms of the hands, saying, "I bless your hands to do the Goddess's works!"

She does this to both trystees. Now the two priestesses lead them in by the hand. The High Priestess holds her hands over the tray of food and all follow her example.

The High Priestess:

> *I invoke You, Goddess of All Life, I invoke You by the foods here present, by the roots to make a strong foundation for this relationship, by the stems for standing firm and proud, by the leaves to grow and prosper together, by the flowers for joy and laughter, and by the fruits for a long and enduring time together.*

Now she turns to each of the trystees in turn:

> *Do you (name), take this woman (name) for your friend and lover for this life time, promise to care and love even if you love others in addition?*

Each answers: *I do.*

The Priestess hands them the tray of food from which each selects something to offer to the other. Each trystee feeds the mouth of the other, saying:

> *May you never hunger!*

Then the Priestess hands them their chalices, filling them with wine, champagne, water or other drink. Each trystee offers the other:

> *May you never thirst!*

Now the Priestess hands them the wreaths, and they crown each other, saying:

> *Thou art Goddess!*

The High Priestess:

> *Now to mark the first moment of this commitment, I ask you to jump from West to East over the broom, which is made of myrtle tree and is sacred to the Goddess of Love.*

She places the sacred broom in front of them. Holding hands, the trystees "jump the broom" together; when they land on the ground again they are pronounced lovers in trust.

After they jump the broom, rings can be exchanged, because the ring in this case is a later development while the chalices are the true symbols of the ceremony.

After this ritual the women often want to read a statement or a poem, or perform a dance. General merriment ensues with eating, drinking and the echoing of congratulations.

The corresponding Tarot card to this event is the Two of Cups, where lovers exchange pleasures in an egalitarian relationship blessed by the Great Spirit.

Attitudes Toward Death in the Craft

Death is considered a door leading into a new life. From earliest times, representations of what happens around death in Goddess religions conspicuously lack terror. This is because the Goddess of Life, the Goddess of Death and the Goddess of Beauty (Isis, Hecate, Astarte) are three in one, the same. The same Mother Who gives life also mourns. Even the sorrowful Maria, Pieta, is but the Goddess's image in Her death-aspect, mourning the passing of favorite sons. The son is dead; She, however, is very much alive. She is at hand to perform the burial rites; She is there to accompany the soul of the departed into the promised "certainty while in life, after death peace unutterable, and reincarnation if desired." He is, in other words, immortal.

The preparation for death included meditations on the best qualities of the person about to pass on. This is shown on tombstones as a matter between the woman and her priestess, who helped her gain insight into her own gifts. The selection of jewels was part of the woman's preparation for death, because stones stand for human qualities: jade, for steadfastness and smoothness of conduct; moonstone, for psychic clarity and quick passage; bloodstone, to absorb fear; gold, for the healing sun.

Paint was added to the tombstones. Ocher was found all around the graves of Stone Age women, still staining the ground red. It symbolizes rebirth, and was believed to quicken the process of a new bloodline. Amazon graves were adorned with the horns of animals, particularly stags, to denote the Dianic tradition of the Amazon even in death. The Mighty Huntress of the Night collected Her maidens and with them hunted the forces of oppression.

The color of mourning among ancient people was not black, but white. The white robes symbolized the white light and the guiding Moon Goddess, Who appears to the dead to attract them to Her domain, Rebirth. Red as a color of mourning was also used to suggest blood, to stimulate a fast rebirth.

When About to Die

The worst possible thing for a dying woman is to be in fear. Fear produces terrible dreams and distracts the soul from its natural flight back to the

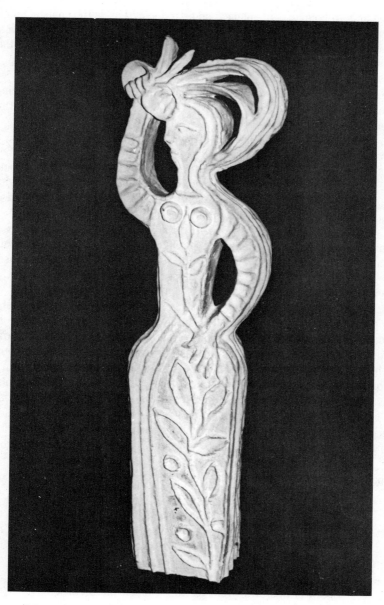

Magaera—Goddess of Death by Masika Szilagyi

Mother Goddess. Imagine death as a ball that has bounced against the floor. The first up-bounce is the highest and strongest. This is the chance, when dying, for the most "direct" or conscious exit of the soul from the physical body, the most evolved way to go through the transition. This is why the last thoughts and surroundings of the dying woman are all-important.

Establish a tranquil environment around the loved one. Do not let families intrude with anxious waiting, fear and grief. It is not the dying woman's job to console the family. Her job is to consciously exit into the peaceful Lap of the Goddess.

Light yellow candles around the room, and throughout the house if possible. Put at least two white candles on both sides of the woman. Gather cut flowers and stock up the vases, so everything looks pretty. A feast should be prepared for the "Rite of Passage," to be celebrated after death with games, laughter and memories of good times. Dialogue with the dead is the focus here, not the drunken venting of a family's insecurities.

The job of guiding the woman toward rebirth, or peace and rest unutterable, is strictly a woman's job. Only the family's female members should be present at the woman's side, unless she requests otherwise. One ALWAYS, and under all circumstances, honors the wishes of the dying woman.

It is important that friends of the dying woman talk to her while she appears unconscious. In truth, the spirit isn't "gone," and can hear. In ancient Tibet this was used as a way to guide the spirit toward final liberation. Tibetans believed that those close to the dying person would know whether that person wanted final "liberation" or another physical incarnation. Final liberation was considered the highest state of spiritual evolution that a soul could achieve, and it meant that the physical rebirth of a dying person's soul would not occur. Not every spirit chose liberation, meaning that a physical rebirth could occur instantly or within an appointed period of time, the soul moving to inhabit the body of a newly-conceived baby.

While the dying person is lying unconscious, the women's friends can chant this very old chant to her, to ease her mind and diminish fears:

I call to mind the Mother of the Universe
Who has created this world, both real and unreal,
And Who, by Her own power with Her three aspects,
Protects it, and having destroyed it, She then plays.
Commonly it is said that god created the Universe;
Yet the learned of ancient Mysteries
Speak of this birth from the navel lotus, the Mother.
Although it is said he creates,
Yet he himself is dependent on Her.
Even the water of Ocean, which is liquid in substance

Cannot exist without a container, therefore
I take refuge in Her, Mother of all beings
Who exists in all things in the form of Power!
Queen of the Universe art Thou, and its Guardian;
In the form of the Universe Thou art its Maintainer;
By all the women Thou art worshipped.
As Thy daughters, they have great devotion to Thee.

While chanting, visualization is the reality that a spirit about to depart understands. All present should imagine themselves becoming the Goddess of all-fulfilling Wisdom, all-performing Wisdom; by those powers they are endowed to help their beloved attain the highest kind of liberation, or happy reincarnation if desired. Visualize the Goddess as red in color: very beautiful, dressed only in jeweled girdles and a necklace of emeralds, holding to Her heart a skull filled with blood in one hand, while leaning on a white staff that is balanced in the crook of Her arm. Her other hand holds aloft a silver bolo. She dances the dance of the Five-Pointed Power, from East, to South, then West and North, and at last the center, where you visualize Her with the beloved dying person.

Now dwell on this image. All the women who can hold this in their minds experience the bliss that goes with the merging of the Mother and the child.

Priestesses:

You are the Earth, Creatrix of the World.
You are Water, and in the form of Diana preserve the World.
You are Fire, and in the form of Pele destroy the World.
You exist in the form of Isis,
You are the Air of the World.

You are the Primeval and Auspicious One;
Mother of all men, refuge of Your women,
Who ever move in the changes of the World.
The Supporter of all, yet Yourself without support,
the Only Pure Form in the form of Ether,
O Mother Kali, be gracious to me!

You are Intelligence and Bliss, and Light Herself.
How then can I know You?
O Mother Kali, be gracious to me!
You are that which supports and yet is not supported,
You pervade the world.
You are in the form of the world
That is pervaded by Thee.

You are both Negation and Existence.
O Mother Kali, be gracious to me!
You are the atom, and ever-pervading,
You are the Whole Universe.
No praise is sufficient, yet Your qualities prompt me
To praise You!
O Mother Kali, be gracious to me!

Now visualize a white navel cord, red inside, extending from the lotus navel of the Goddess and connecting into the navel of the dying woman. See Kali assimilate the essence of the Prana (Life Force) from the woman into Herself.

Abide in the bliss of this conscious transference. Sing, hum, meditate. Those who can play musical instruments should do so at this time. Bells ring rhythmically, nine times, after this chanting. When the bells are silent, all the relatives surround the person with fresh-cut flowers. Camphor is kindled in the Cauldron of Rebirth.

The Feast of the Dead

This is the same as All Hallow's Eve, except that this time one celebrates with a particular soul, not with all ancestors. Set aside the woman's favorite plate, with her favorite food, and invite her to partake in this last supper. After the feast the priestess whispers in the woman's ear, ''Come, Sister, and leave all worldly attachments behind. You have no more worries about us. We bid you goodbye.''

Burial Rites

Ancient women were buried in the earth, and men were put into sacks and exposed in trees for the Bird Goddess to assimilate. This, of course, is impossible for modern use. There is good argument for earthen burial because ''from earth we came and to earth we return,'' but it is expensive. Cremation was also used in ancient matriarchies, as the Fire Goddess took back the bodies for recycling. If a successful and conscious transfer takes place, it doesn't really matter which type of burial is chosen. It must be left to the preference of the dying person.

In case transference did not occur and the soul is still lingering in the body, a lengthy and careful guiding job must be performed so that the Prana, the essence or soul, can find peace.

If the dying person wanted to return immediately, and was very close to a couple who desire children, the two should make love in the same house where the woman is dying, so that she can enter the new cell of the baby at conception. If the person doesn't want to take a body for a while, burial by water is recommended. The soul would then merge with the Great Goddess of "all that is wet and gleaming," and exist in the form of water, rain, rivers, clouds. This is a nice possibility. Cremation and dispersal into the ocean are also used for this reason; the soul merges with the cosmic elements and permeates Nature.

Burial Procession

The walk to the burial place should be very, very slow. No loud noises must be allowed around the dead, such as wailing, crying or loud displays of grief; they could blow the poor soul miles away from the procession and cause unnecessary fear. You must remember that the Prana without the body is but a thought-form, without resistance to sound vibrations or the winds of emotion; like a fallen leaf, one is easily blown about, without the protection of a sister's wisdom.

Even as the procession is going on, the priestess maintains a continual dialogue with the dead person, explaining to her that it is necessary to let go of all earthly attachments. This is hard to do because the spirit, having no more pain, might like to stay and see what is going on. She might have left children behind, and bloodlines are very strong ties which are never successfully broken. A child can call on the spirit of the dead mother for help at any time, and the mother will respond. If a woman is satisfied about the fate of her children without her, she will be more willing to leave.

A last realization must be dealt with for the spirit to be able to transcend the physical plane, and that is the reality of "death" as the woman once understood it. Following death, the woman experiences a new mobility, depending on her inner emanations of thought, and she is able to see and hear everything. A good imagination now becomes her ship. She might totally reject the fact that she is "gone" from the physical plane. Grief is apt to set in when she notices that nobody responds to her when she speaks to them, and nobody notices her when she approaches. This is the last fear that must be overcome, and the priestess must help here by guiding the woman to realize the reality of death-separation. Using mental images here is necessary.

Devotion for the Dead

Go in the evening to the grave of your loved one. Tidy up some; plant some flowers or just turn over some of the top dirt. This is particularly nice for someone who has died recently. Place a week-long white candle in a jar on the grave. Use sandalwood oil to anoint the candle, and pour some of the oil on the ground as well. This is for wisdom. Light the candle, saying, "Blessed be, you spirit of (name); I come to bring you love and energy." Light frankincense and myrrh in your censer, saying, "May the Goddess Who is three-formed favor you with Her White Light. Look for this White

Light of the Life Force for your peace and rest." Talk informally for a while with the spirit of your loved one, telling her the latest news. In closing, say, "Blessed be your spirit, (name). Blessed be your dreams. Sleep in bliss and never know fear, but only the peace of the Mother."

Parentalia

Recently my best friend lost her father to the Goddess as Crone—in this case to the May Queen, whose earthly aspects we often discuss. A beautiful death was granted to Harry, who died in the woods on his way home, under the May full moon.

Forty-nine days after the death of a parent, a celebration of the new awakening and a memorial party called "Parentalia" is held. We invite friends and relatives of the lost parent, and cook a fine dinner. The foods are usually what the parent liked to eat when in life, keeping the colors of the foods toward red, to stimulate life.

Set the white table and arrange the company to surround the empty chair, where we invite the dead parent's spirit to partake with us. Then serve dinner; pile food on the plate assigned to the parent and fill her/his cup with whatever she/he enjoyed. That done, everybody begins the feasting, and behaves jovially, while telling stories about the parent who passed on. This is a great opportunity for all loving friends to express their admiration, and what they received as gifts from the presence of the dead person while in life, how their experience was deep and meaningful, and how it changed their lives for the better. Toasting the spirit of the departed is an ancient way to honor each other. Everyone wishes her/him deep peace and happiness.

My friend took a different route, and she invited her father to be her guiding spirit now that he was free of his earthly shortcomings. A parent would watch over you anyway. It is believed, however, that witches often tend the dead as if they were still alive. Tending involves remembering their birthdays and death days. On such occasions, it's appropriate to make sure that a special time is taken out to feed the birds or enhance nature in some way. Putting out milk and honey for the dead on Halloween is worldwide, but a glass of champagne or a favorite brand of wine or beer serves the same purpose. These foods and drinks are fed to the animals. No human can touch them.

There are many beneficial effects in celebrating Parentalia. There is a sense of the parent, often accompanied by vivid dreams as the dead assure the living that they are all right. I had such a dream about my mother, and I felt truly cheered from her death. We need to open our perception to the invisible world. There, too, we have our roots, our ties and our affinities. We also have many helpers there. The world is one.

The Art of Rebirth

Burn meditation incense on the grave or at the burial site, and light a white candle. Talk to the deceased in low, unafraid tones. Remember, everything communicates through vibrations. Say to the soul:

> *Imagine yourself like the Goddess of the White Light,*
> *Maat, who is the ancient Goddess of Truth,*
> *Emanating radiance. You are naked, with a feather*
> *In one hand and a scale in the other.*
> *You are the Unity of all Worlds, the Unity of all Truths,*
> *And All-Encompassing Mother.*

Abide in this and feel the White Light emanating from you and through you. Chant: "Me and Maat, Maat and me, are One." Repeat in different ways, helping in the imagery because you will merge with Maat while chanting. After this, frequent the gravesite under the Full Moon, tending to the white candle, bringing fresh flowers, and chanting.

To Choose a Womb

Priestess:

> *Abandon all feelings of attraction or repulsion, with*
> *memories' heedfulness restraining the roving tendencies of*
> *the mind. Abide in the pure state of Maat, emanating all*
> *the Light. Apply yourself to choosing a womb-door, and*
> *when you find the one you judge beneficial and good,*
> *imagine yourself emanating from the Goddess's navel con-*
> *necting you to the chosen womb, and enter.*

It is no accident that we are alive, reincarnated and sharing life together in time. This is a very special, extremely important thing. How often have you recognized someone you've never met, or responded to something in someone you've never seen? That feeling of "deja vu" has a valid basis. I believe that the last women killed are the first ones reborn, back in the spiraling evolutionary cycles, and the Amazons and witches were the last.

It is said that all the possible wombs in the world are visible to you as a spirit in search of reincarnation. You must avoid entering a womb because of the frightening sounds you "hear," because those are emanations from your own mind. There is nothing frighteningly "real" in this dream state; you must fight against accidental reincarnation.

When consciously choosing our parents, we indeed have an opportunity to be born to those who can help us develop our spirits higher. When attracted to a physical womb, we must bless ourselves consciously with ever-present bliss, so that we enter into a lucky lifetime with adoring and helpful parents. Blindly entering a womb without blessing or reflection, because you are frightened by your own thought-form emanations, must cause difficult and often futile paths. Be careful whom you choose. You are the one who must live with it.

The Great Rite: General Sexual Practices

The Great Rite is a feature of Earth religions which has received little discussion in feminist witches' circles thus far. The reason is that we are not quite ready to take on the entire concept. At one time, I even offered a promise to the Goddess that if I could salvage my lovelife, sparing myself all the sorrows and tilting the scales to the side of pleasure, I would found and lead a Dianic Great Rite to Aphrodite, thereby honoring the Goddess of Love. Did I do it? No. Instead, I found that I was jealous, possessive, masochistic and a coward in general. Also, the further returns of my lovelife ran toward intensive contemplation of the Life Force as in sex I was faced with my own failings. For the first time in my hedonistic, life-affirming lovestyle, this High Priestess didn't do very well. I even had a second lesson and a few reruns.

As a High Priestess I must explore what the ancient people have left us, believing in the heritage of women's sexual modes and practices, especially since a few good working models are still with us. Even a short search sheds a lot of light on the probable causes of much unhappiness. Consider the rampant loneliness shown by the ever-increasing numbers of women committing suicide, and those driven to desperate measures in their drive for survival. What happens to women happens to all.

We know that the Goddess is intimately connected with religious sexual practices; when mating and pleasuring are observed in Her honor alone, the sexual inhibitions of any era are defeated. Patriarchal sexual mores are direct reversals of this religious sexual enjoyment. All taboos of Judeo-Christianity were made against the values of the Old Religion.

The forcible suppression of woman's basic orgasmic nature, and the intolerance shown women's natural cycles, are perversion and represent a sexual glorification of the male, without the influence of the Great Mother. All this reflects a death-worship so deeply ingrained in our society that we can hardly identify it, even as we exist in it.

The essence of the Great Rite was that women related sexually to more than one man or woman during its celebration, often experiencing pleasure with many others. This took place in the fresh furrows of the newly-plowed earth, in private rooms, in the woods, on the mountains—in all cultures, in festivals honoring Aphrodite, Ishtar, Isis, Astarte, Hera. The sacred time was calculated according to the cycles and seasons of the Earth, and the women of Earth did as the Goddess did. Nature is not possessive. She is certainly promiscuous by Christian standards, but then, Nature is still at it, unconquerable because She is Divine. When the Great Rite was used liberally in sexual festivals in celebration of life, the communities were more closely bound, happy and fulfilled. Even crime decreased; there was no time for it. Sex was Divine and violence was not.

People do not change or truly experience a revolution until they come to terms with a healthy, natural sexuality. When sexual standards changed, so did we. Through our sexuality, the Goddess reveals Herself, energizes us and instills a bond that peacefully holds together sizable communities. The sexual mores of the Goddess are free, open and inclusive, never discriminating against the few, the plain, the infirm, the unique. Aphrodite accepts all merging in Her name and the community reaps great benefits from it in the form of increased good health, vitality and tolerance for all.

Pleasure is a virtue in Earth religions. Oneness of all Nature is much sought after in the sexual union, be it with female-male variations or female with female and male with male. Creativity generally, rather than procreation exclusively, is the object of Tantric, Wiccan, Earth-religion practices.

Tantra, the Science of Ecstasy, teaches the duality of all things. This is hard for Dianic witches to hear, since we have a trinity concept of the world order, and when we see it in its true origin we understand how duality leads people not to freedom of sex but forced monogamy. The sexual mores of the Goddess decree that sexual favors be "distributed evenly" and justly, loving more than one partner for Her glory. The oneness of all living creatures, the loving freedom of the Goddess is given to all. The least we can do in return is transcend our own twentieth-century mindset and promote love and freedom with many more than one person.

Bonding sexually with more than one is a terrifying threat to couples who have assumed responsibilities together and who fear losing their exclusivity with each other. A bond that cannot hold through a divine sacrifice, expanding in religious sexual rites for the honor of the Goddess, cannot hope for Her blessings for very long. Our mythology tells us how the Goddess, angered by the exclusivity of patriarchal sexual mores, visited famine and tempests upon the people who refused to "loosen their girdles" for Aphrodite in Her rituals. Since the Goddess is recognized by love alone ("No other Law but Love I know"), it is impossible to argue with Her.

Tantra is concerned with the maintenance of a penile erection for as long as possible. Most tantric training for men consists of techniques which reinforce the mastery of mind over penis. With Dianic sexual practices, this worry is definitely not one of ours. Between women, sexual tension is not the product of the particular biological state of a penis. It is born and held solely with the mind, with images of the Goddess as the Goddess of Love. The collective female circle becomes possessed by Her, and unbridles female sexual instincts from the far recesses of the third layer of the brain, diminishing the fears, the guilt and the oppression of female sexuality.

Pleasure is a mental process. Sadly, the minds of most people today are conditioned to pain and suffering. Pleasure makes new connections in the brain, and is a learned process much like orgasm and pain, the two being connected at times. Orgasm in sex will burst the ego, which is the greatest single block to our most basic instincts. But that same ego is quite necessary for survival. Pleasure easily achieves as much as pain. The ego must be consciously relinquished for a short time when we approach loving as Her Goddesses. Current sexual fantasies pale in comparison with Goddess imagery and possession by the Goddess during sex. The healing power of sex as it releases energies to the organism is proof of having tapped a most Divine source of energy.

Resistance to sexual practices in the Goddess tradition comes solely from our conditioning. Part of our oppression comes from that great body of sexual mores dictated by anti-nature, anti-woman religious forces: latecomers to the world, who brought with them bloodshed, shame and guilt. We are all imbued with it.

As witches we have a chance to transcend all fears which block creativity. Women must be very careful to practice the ancient sexual celebrations in secrecy. The political climate is such that the burning flesh of witches still lingers in the memory of the male churches without regret. Patriarchy knows that it cannot survive if women turn once again to the Old Religion with its powerful and natural lovemaking. No one would be able to fix on paternity again, for example, if women related to more than one man in ritual or life. The natural and holy practices of the Wicca (Dianic and other traditions) are by far the most dangerous to the patriarchy, and therefore suffer from the most intense hatred and persecution. The revival of Aphroditian love and the Great Rite are integral to a real revolution. Sex, like religion, is the highest of politics. Sex is the highest held human experience. How Aphrodite is hunting us down, making us Hers once again!

I want you to know that this information is every bit as hard for me and other women to follow as it is for you. Maybe it's enough to have the vision now and let it unfold as it may for the future.

Esotara: Witches' Valentine's Day

The scent of blooming flowers and the warming sun herald the time in nature when all is opened up for renewal; Flora comes of age, fauna abound, and all is ready for love.

In ancient times we celebrated the importance of this time with processions through the streets, dances and curious "sprinkling" rituals. In Hungary, they still do this in the countryside at Easter—young boys go from house to house with vials of perfumed water, and sprinkle all female members of the home, old and young alike. When this has been done, the women offer the boys boiled eggs, sometimes painted especially for a particular admirer. This is clearly a non-personal mating ritual, very sexual in nature.

In this country, "Valentine's Day" takes the place of Esotara (usually celebrated around March 30th), but at a time when Nature is not attuned to the same vibrations. February 14th, the day currently signified as Valentine's Day, falls during a period when the ancients were celebrating Diasia, a gloom festival. Blooming love is strained when Nature is not yet ready for it. The wooing which goes on today, through gifts of flowers and love messages sent via cards, is a modern mating dance, celebrated too early.

Today a general public ritual could be held, using a circle of flowers. Gather all your friends together, inviting them all as singles. Let them all come to the circle by themselves, bringing flowers from your area. Form a circle while holding the flowers in your hands, and just hum together, humming for the power within you. When all are centered, one person says to her flower:

> *Behold the grave beauty of this bloom!*
> *She teaches us to open with our hearts,*
> *To set aside fear and to risk being vulnerable.*
> *Only then can life regenerate.*
> *The Goddess stirs, and binds our hearts together.*
> *She plays the eternal spinning wheel,*
> *Weaving in beauty, diversity, variety and abundance.*

Now each person in the circle makes a wish concerning her love-life. The wishes may be expressed aloud or silently, as each person steps to the middle of the circle to make a wish on a flower while holding it aloft. An example might be: "My heart was lonely, but no more. The Goddess will send love, galore!"

The humming should continue as the members of the circle make their wishes, so that the energy level is kept high enough to launch all desire. Dancing, feasting, exchanging gifts, making dates, renewing love vows, kissing friends and lovers, all this is in order. It is very good luck to share love with more than one person, even if only in token.

The Esotara ritual for witches is bolder and more ancient. It hearkens back to times when modesty was unknown and unnecessary—an invention of the patriarchal future. For this ritual, witches come together late at night, wearing only jewelry and flowers. They raise power in the same way (humming) except that the Priestess invokes Kore:

I invoke you, Kore, Mighty Maiden Bloomed!
I invoke thee by the roots and by the stem,
By the leaves and by the flowers,
By all the goodly fruits!
Come among us and bless us with your loving signs.
Let us be merry, happy and well-loved!
Here I bind us in your Sign.

Now the Five-Fold Kiss is passed, from East to South, then West and North. In the Circle the women (or men or both) pass the kiss from one to another. The first kiss is on the forehead, for the thoughts of the Goddess; then the eyes are kissed for visions and clearsightedness in love; then the breasts for beauty and nurturance in love; then the genitals for the pleasures of love.

When the Five-Fold Kiss has come full circle, everyone continues to hold the energies high, visualizing for each person in the circle whatever that person wanted to change. All circle members visualize in great detail how that particular change is to be made. Then, before the energy drops, the Priestess says: "The circle of Love is never broken. The Goddess blesses Her children. Blessed be."

Of course in the old times Diana put all the lights out and the people freely made love in the circle.

The Drawing of the Flowers:
a Dianic Great Rite

The observance of the Great Rite may take place on any Full Moon or particularly relevant Sabbat. May Eve, Midsummer, Spring Equinox—all are fine for the celebration of this ritual. Other holy days may also be used since there is no hard and fast rule, but I would caution against All Hallow's Eve. The Sacred Crone is traditionally not much involved with sexual ecstasies on All Hallow's Eve, but this is not a specific rule either. We should look to our current generation of Crones for guidance in this matter.

Aphrodite is the aspect of the Goddess to be invoked for the celebration of the Great Rite. The circle of women build a stone altar, employing images of Aphrodite and symbols sacred to Her. This altar is placed in the Western corner of the circle, the corner of Waters and Rebirth. The ancients took a communal bath of purification before the Great Rite, so using a pool for this modern ritual would be appropriate.

Frankincense and myrrh are burned and placed in the Eastern corner of the circle. To the South is set the customary red candle; in the North, an offering of grain is laid out for the birds. The altar in the West should have a bowl of water in it. Wands, not swords, should be used for this ritual.

All are sky-clad, except for jewelry worn as desired and sacred cords tied around the waists. Each woman brings a fresh flower to the ritual, representing herself, and hidden from others in the circle. Each women must remember what flower is hers; if two or more flowers are alike they must be marked in some way as to make them identifiable to the women to whom they belong.

Invoke the Watchtowers, moving from East to South, West to North. Priestess of the East:

> *Powerful Mother, Ishtar!*
> *I invoke You by Your favorite colors of purple and red.*
> *You Who gave birth to the dawn, to civilizations,*
> *You Who reveal Yourself through Love!*
> *Come and join this circle of friends*
> *As we worship You according to ancient rites!*
> *Keep all enemies and envious eyes from the East,*
> *Far from us, and bless this circle.*
> *So mote it be!*

Priestess of the South:

> *Conjure, conjure, o Goddess of Love!*
> *Conjure and appear through us!*
> *Fiery passions, woman-loving Goddess, come!*
> *Enter the hearts of all her present*
> *As we worship Thee in loving!*
> *Keep all enemies from the South.*
> *Allow no evil to enter from Your Corner.*
> *Only the good and the sacred shall come.*
> *Blessed be!*

Priestess of the West:

> *Lovely Goddess, Aphrodite, Sea-born Goddess of Life!*
> *Enter our feelings with Your gentle delight.*
> *Let our sexuality rise like the waves on the Sea!*
> *Kundalini, white serpent, rise up through our spines!*
> *Let each of us be you, possessed by Your love.*
> *Keep all evil away from the Corner of the West.*
> *Blessed be.*

Priestess of the North:

> *Powerful Mother, Demeter!*
> *Without whom there is no life, no grain, no food for the living.*

Fertile Mother of life-giving things,
Enter our hearts and let us feel Your earthly passions.
Let us smell and touch and stroke in Your name as the ancient
*   passions rise.*
Keep all evil from the North away from us and bestow Your
*   warm blessings on our great rites!*

Now the women close the circle with, "The circle is now closed. The Goddess blesses Her Women." Link arms and begin humming to raise power. When energies are right the High Priestess says, "The Goddess is here." She then turns to the woman on her left and says:

All ye assembled at my shrine,
Mother, darksome and divine;
Mine the scourge and mine the kiss,
Here I charge you in this sign.

The High Priestess then kisses the woman once on each of the five sacred points: her forehead, her mouth, her breasts, her genitals and her feet. This fivefold kiss is passed on from one woman to another. Since it is a warming-up for the Great Rite, it should be freer than the normal ceremony. Laughter, joking or playfully intimate remarks are to be encouraged, and the kissing may be informal, long, ritualistic or simultaneous. Make sure that every woman is given her sign of the Goddess in the form of the Fivefold Kiss.

Now one or many women place a great white, purple or red cloth on the ground in the middle of the circle. The High Priestess then leads the women in the Great Charge:

Hear ye the words of the Star Goddess
The dust of whose feet are the hosts of heaven
She whose body encircles the Universe:

I am the beauty of the green earth
And the white moon among the stars
And the mystery of the waters
And the desire of human hearts.

Call unto your soul, "Arise!" and come unto me
For I am the soul of nature
Who gives life to the Universe
From me all things proceed
And unto me all things must return.

Before my face, beloved of all
Let your divine innermost self be enfolded
In the rapture of the infinite.

Let my worship be in the heart that rejoices
For behold, all acts of love and pleasure are my rituals
And therefore let there be beauty and strength

Power and compassion, honor and pride
Mirth and reverence among you.

And you who think to seek for me
Know your seeking and yearning shall avail you not
Unless you know the Mystery:
That if that which you seek you find not within you,
You will never find it without.

For behold, I have been with you from the beginning
And I am that which is attained
At the end of desire.

Now the women place their flowers in the middle of the cloth. The four corners are then folded in and the flowers mixed up in the cloth so that nobody knows whose flower is where. The High Priestess holds the gathered cloth high in the air, facing West:

We dedicate this rite to You, Aphrodite,
Mother of Good Fortune.
Allow the power that is in loving
To flow through all of us
Regardless of personal preferences
Or personal attractions
For we are all You, as You are us.

Each woman reaches into the cloth and draws out a flower. As each flower is held up, the woman who placed it there must claim it by saying, "It is I. I am Goddess tonight." This lets the women know their initial ritual partners. The tradition has been one for the Goddess and one by choice, but each woman must actually relate to more than one woman; a trinity concept is worshipped here in Divine ways. This ritual goes beyond personalities, beauty requirements or any other externally imposed considerations. Here, sex is a spiritual experience.

The Great Rite begins with stroking. This does not require pairing off. Massage, relaxation through touch, any pleasurable stroking is fine, and if there is a bath available, each woman can climb in to be bathed and attended to by the others.

The stroking is followed by anointing all the bodies with healthful oils. Women need not pair off for this either, since it is preferable that the anointing be done to as many women in the circle as possible. The focus should always remain clear: communal pleasuring. Making garlands for each other is part of the ritual, and flower or feather decorations may be created for the purpose of beholding each woman as Goddess of Love.

The Great Rite feeling must be spontaneous. When this occurs, it is a gift and the group has given itself inner permission to accept it and follow its lead. Kissing is a good beginning, accompanied by stroking, and if the mood enters the women, the Goddess is there. Lovemaking is then allowed freely, with reverence.

Women who are shy, and who do not yet feel the power, should involve themselves in some way with the others who do feel such power. Whether through physical contact, massaging or assisting in some other way, the shy woman will then be touched and made love to as well. As a natural-chance choice, lovemaking should be slow and unhurried. Before the evening is ended, the women will make love with the "drawer" of their particular flower, but not first and not exclusively.

Words of sexual scenes or words describing sacred lovemaking should be chanted by those who think of such things to say. The Sacred Whore is invoked here with Her holiest meaning—She Who Shines on All Equally. Music may be applied to the general mood, and dancing around women entwined in sexual ecstasy is fine for keeping the energy high. If and when orgasm occurs for somebody it is treated as a sacred chant and shared by other women in the circle. However, orgasm is not the goal of the Great Rite; pleasuring is.

When the mood is exhausted and the women lose interest in the revelries, it's time to give thanks to the Goddess of Love. Pure water is carried around the circle and sprinkled on the ground in gratitude. Birdseed and other grains are poured out for the birds, who are the children of the Goddess. Thanks are given to the Mothers from the East, South, West and North, with wands upheld.

Priestess of the East:

> *Goddess Ishtar, thank You for Your guidance and libera-tion, for the ability to transcend the personal to the universal, and that we have been able to merge with the great All! Bless us before You leave! Blessed be.*

Priestess of the South:

> *Goddess of Fires, Passionate Lover-Mother, thank You for fueling our hearts with Your energies. Bless us before You leave! Blessed be.*

Priestess of the West:

> *Gracious Goddess of the West, Bountiful Aphrodite, Great Mother of Lovers! Thank You for Your blessing of grace and power. Bless us before You leave! Blessed be.*

Priestess of the North:

> *Great Goddess Demeter! We have tasted of the earthly love*
> *which is Your favorite. We have felt the Divine within us!*
> *Bless us before You leave! Blessed be.*

When all this has occurred, pack up the cloth but leave the flowers for the Goddess. Remember to keep silent about the celebration of the Great Rite since the envy of Judeo-Christians could bring you trouble.

Self-Blessing

There is a ritual in the Craft called the "self-blessing," which comes to us from centuries of oral tradition. It has not been written down in a very long time, so we don't know how old it is, but because of the elements involved, it feels very ancient. It is a woman's blessing upon herself, honoring her own Divine in a ritual with her "selves." This is a very powerful affirmation of self, very private and personal. Far from being the product of any clergy, this blessing ritual is folk-psychology, a legacy from the peasants. Peasant women in earlier times performed it whenever "cleaning out" of the inner spaces was desired. Although this ritual is not necessary on a daily basis, it may be performed at least once a month, particularly when the Moon is full, and preferably after sundown.

One very important rule is that the mind has to be cleared of all doubts and fears in the performing of this ritual. Earlier witches tried this by reciting certain Christian prayers backwards, but I don't think that's really necessary. I think that when you accept a feminist consciousness, accept the political analysis, and develop a healthy amount of self-love, then you already have a new and unique perspective from which to begin. You do not have to do anything as bizarre or complicated as the spells and incantations that are often included in "witchcraft" books commonly found in occult supply stores.

Begin with a ritual bath in which you immerse yourself completely. The purpose of this is to allow all your cares and anxieties to simply "flow" away from you. Often it enhances your psychic space at this time to visualize colors and indulge in fantasy.

Fantasy is an excellent tool. You visualize what you want to achieve, and very often it is the only thing you can consistently depend on. Fantasy can be practiced until you are able to visualize, at will, something other than present reality. Look at an apple. Imagine it half-eaten. Look at a woman wearing summer clothing and imagine her in winter clothes. You can practice anywhere, any time, as long as you don't harm anyone. Soon you will be able to impose one reality on another. Our rituals are exercises in the visualization of change, and women are usually able to do this very well.

In your ritual bath you should place a purifying herb or a purifying oil derived from the herb. One of the most commonly used is the natural lemon, squeezed into the bath water. This is a sort of homemade "Van-Van" bath. "Van-Van" is the traditional name for a lemon purification oil. Witches can usually recognize traditional names of specific oils to buy what they need, but I contend that the essence of the oil is more important than any particular formula.

Prepare your altar with everything you use in the ritual: Goddess-image, candles, incense, a small bowl of salt and a chalice containing half water, half wine. Arrange your altar in a creative manner, with a white cloth, two white candles on the sides, and a rose or other Goddess-image in the center. Place your chalice in front.

After preparing yourself, step up to the altar and take the container of salt. Put the salt on the floor in front of the altar and stand on it. The salt symbolizes wisdom, the Salt of the Earth, so you are standing on your own wisdom. Contemplate the wine-water mixture in the chalice as symbolic of the Life Force. The water represents Aphrodite. Contemplate the fact that there is no life without water. The wine brings ecstasy and is sacred to the Goddess because it represents joy and stimulation. By mixing it with water you are also representing temperance, which is important in women's Wisdom.

Drink from your chalice or "special cup." This cup should communicate something festive to you, something special and joyful. It should only be used for celebrating this relationship you have with yourself. It should be used to drink from only when you commune with the Divine.

Meditate a moment on the altar and importance of the psychic space you are creating for yourself. Actually, when you are performing magic, it is more beneficial if you are able to approach the altar completely naked. This is not for any sexual or erotic reason, but to stimulate and increase the energy flow. After your bath, you are clean. Your blood is pulsing quickly, you have rosy cheeks, your pores are open, and you are not likely to get cold, even when naked. This way you can celebrate your ritual in "Truth" and with pleasure.

At this point in the ritual, take time to contemplate what you are going to do. You are about to bless yourself. That's a big step. In our society, this blessing is usually done by male clergy in a patriarchal religion.

Light the incense now to awaken the brain cells. The sense of smell has come to us from the earliest times, from "smelling out" edibles to "smelling" danger. A very large portion of the brain deals with that sense, though the sense of smell is seriously stunted in the modern world. Choose an incense to which you feel personally attracted. Try to choose one that is power-oriented, because after you bless yourself there is no turning back. You must deal with getting Power.

Light the white candles, saying, "Blessed be, thou creature of fire," as each flame is born.

Between these candles is the image of the Goddess you have chosen. Objects from nature are good for this, such as a new rose, the personification of Persephone. The Goddess has a few symbols which are always associated with Her because miracles happen with or around them, and the rose is such a symbol. A single rose is a lovely centerpiece; it is an altar in itself, and a very, very good working altar at that.

Take a moment to smell the incense, meditate on the candle flames and contemplate the Goddess-image.

Now dip your fingers (traditionally, the first two fingers) into the chalice and touch the wine-water to your forehead while you address the alliance of Goddess and you. You may call out Her names or you may simply say: "Bless me, Mother, for I am Your child." This is an acknowledgment of where your life comes from, an awareness of how you got here. It also connects you to the spirit you are addressing within yourself.

Dip your fingers again and touch your nose, saying, "Bless my nose to smell Your essence." Most of the brain cells can be stimulated with a certain scent, which in turn stimulates the deep mind. While your conscious mind is tending to modern life, your deep mind can work for you to straighten out your problems. To smell the Essence of the Goddess is also to be close to Nature; to connect with Her in such a way makes you able to remember the fragrance of the roses, the salt smell of the ocean, or the unmistakable liberating scent of a clear evening.

Again dip your fingers, this time touching your lips and saying, "Bless my lips to speak of You." The lips are an extremely important symbol in the Craft. They represent the Word: utterance, ordinance, incarnation of Themis, Goddess of Social Consciousness. Indeed, words are revolutionary. The mouth is a tool of the revolution. The conscious manifestation of a thought is a word. Once uttered, the vibration of that word never stops but keeps on going without end. Sound never stops. We have a solemn responsibility to be conscious of what we say, because it is magic, a ritual. Words have power. Speech is how we touch each other's minds. We influence each other with words. We have to articulate change in order to achieve changes. When you bless your lips, think of all this.

Now that you have blessed your mouth and contemplated your speech, dip your two fingers into the chalice and touch your breasts. Meditate on your breasts as the Source of Nourishment, on nourishment as part of the

Female Principle of the Universe, on how nourishment comes from you, how you are nourished, and how you are part of the Source that has power to give. Think of how Divine that makes you. Now say: "Bless my breasts, formed in strength and beauty."

That is a definition of the Female. A definition of Womanhood: strength and beauty combined. To be strong is to be beautiful. Weakness is not reinforced in the Craft, and no "brownie points" are ever given for being a "ding-a-ling." You must assume adulthood and responsibility in the Craft. You ritualize your responsibilities in the Wicca, especially responsibilities toward your contemporaries.

Again dip your fingers, touch your genitals and say, "Bless my genitals that bring forth life as You have brought forth the Universe." Touching the genitals and speaking of bringing forth life does not mean that all women must give birth to children. It is simply a recognition of our connection to the Source of Life, the Divine Female. The biological destiny of women, which has been used against us, is actually the basis of our Divine. Think this time about the Source of Life. Know that you are part of that. Pleasure and birthing are considered sources of energy. Birthing is a manifestation of re-creation of other human beings. Pleasure is a manifestation of self-re-creation. Pleasure is worship because it replenishes the soul. The nerves like it. It's good for you. Anything that is good for you is a ritual of the Goddess, who says, "All acts of love and pleasure are my rituals." So, as you touch your genitals, contemplate all the things in your life which bring you pleasure.

Lastly, dip your fingers and touch your feet, saying, "Bless my feet to walk in Your paths." Wherever your mind leads, your feet will soon follow, and so you must desire to make a straight path: to follow a life-orientation pattern towards yourself, your world, your people, everything around you. The responsibility which you accept is that you are Divine, and you have Power. You are powerless only if you allow a structure to exist that makes you powerless. Once you realize that you don't have to be a slave, and you speak of it, the Goddess of Freedom is evoked.

Think about the way in which you've been conducting yourself. Give yourself strokes for developing and strengthening your own interests, for being surrounded by kindred spirits. Contemplate the path you want to take. Fantasize. Treat yourself to wishful thinking. It can be acted on and made "real" later. Revolution begins as a thought-form. Then it multiplies in other people's minds and is soon translated in action. Everything works like that. Everything in the world is first created in an intangible way, as a thought-form, eventually becoming manifest. Thus, every thought is an act. You bless your feet because walking is an act born of your thought-forms.

After blessing your feet, stand a while and let all the feelings and thoughts blend. Allow energies to well up in you and flow through you. When you are finished, extinguish the candles, saying, "Blessed be, thou creature of fire. Thank you for your presence." Thank your Divine Selves for attending as well. You are never talking to somebody "out there," so your voice can be kept low and soft. You do not have to shout or throw yourself into a frenzy, as some books on "witchcraft" suggest. Screaming what you want is a male approach. They think that if it's louder, it's better. That's not true. Very strong witches have been known to say very little, to very great effect. That's part of having your mouth connected to your brain.

Each time you touch yourself in this ritual, allow the touch and the connection of blessing-to-body to carry and teach you, as you linger on that particular part of your body. The flickering candlelight is a good reminder of the need for psychic meditation and personal psychic space.

All these steps tie in directly to "folk psychology." Each of these processes helps actualize a wish that would remain only a wish unless projected outside. Whatever the wish, you will be able to realize what you want. You really "do it" through ritual; the deed is done. You have created for your "self" an alternate reality in which what you wished for actually happened. As your own Goddess you have created, in small, what you wanted.

This concept relates to one of the basic tenets all witches share: "As below, so above." If you create a small "something" here, it will have a ripple effect of consequences. "Like" affects "like" and the small eventually affects the larger. That's why spells work. When the witch creates something through a spell, it is done.

The spell of self-affirmation serves as a celebration and reinforcement of the Divine within you. This is most important because too many of us have internalized our oppression. It is imperative that we change the influences working in our deep minds. Religion controls inner space; inner space controls outer space. If a woman internalizes her oppression and thinks she is inferior or unclean, then she internalizes her own "policeman" and she will act accordingly. She will not need to be policed by actual oppressors because she will have assimilated their judgments and will police herself.

The easiest and most efficient way for a small number of people to oppress a large number is to sell them a religion. If that religion is embraced by the majority, then they will police themselves and act in accordance with a value system which oppresses them. Once they have internalized it, they have lost. This is what happened to women under patriarchy.

Self-blessing, self-affirmation rituals are a way of exorcising that patriarchal "policeman," cleansing the deep mind, and filling it with positive images of the strength and beauty of women. This is what the Goddess symbolizes—the Divine within women and all that is Female in the universe. We MUST NOT underestimate the importance of this concept.

Chapter 3

Celebrating the
Holy Days
of the Earth

The Sacred Wheel

Study the Great Mandala of our lives: the Wheel of Karma, the Wheel of Life, the Way. All is encompassed by it. Nothing escapes the ordered, complicated, sensitive and effective chain of events—the Wheel of Change. All that is alive must change. That is the Law. What does not change dies, and thus changes. All is subject to the Law of the Way.

The Goddess Dike is associated with the Wheel, a floating, angel-like, winged Goddess, Victory. Her names are many. As Themis' daughter, She is sister to Truth, the Goddess Maat.

Contemplate the Great Mandala in terms of your internal life. Contemplate yourself as a part of the Great Design. You belong here. This is your spaceship. Nobody leaves to ascend to "heaven" or descend into "hell," because they both exist simultaneously in the here and now. You can move into heaven now, if you wish; you've probably already visited hell. Redemption is like responsibility; you cannot pass it on. It is you, and it is us, makers of Divine Choices, makers of Karma, makers of Change and maintainers of the Wheel.

What a beautiful spaceship we live on! As the Blue Planet in space, it gives us the only water in the entire solar system. Without water, there is no organic life. Aphrodite still lives here. Our Mother—Earth, Gaia, Demeter, Kore, Tara, Ceres—has dictated all seasons and changes into a calendar of life. Food is life. Knowing how to plant and reap is the core of every culture's reservoir of knowledge. That is one cycle of change.

Then there is the other—changes of the spirit, management of feelings, relationships, and personal well-being. Love is the food of the spirit. The communal events that bind communities together around spiritual issues make up our lives and are the highlights in our humanities.

Having celebrations of all sorts—calling, summoning the people to rejoice, parading, gathering together, feasting, purifying together, making oaths together, producing culture together, worshipping together—were stock and trade of the most important concerns of the life-oriented society that women created. While these festivals and holy days were often observed by both sexes, they were "priestessed" by women.

Although diverse in function, the celebrations all had to do with the theme of the communal spirit of the year. Following the simple observance of these festivals, holy days and Sabbats would give rich exposure to the other people in one's community, and the involuntary isolation of any one person was virtually impossible. Hence, there was no loneliness as we know it today, that gnawing awareness that nobody cares. No one had to experience any deep degree of lovelessness, because the attitude toward love was such that, at least ritualistically, everybody had a chance to participate in communal sex as well as communal nurturing. Even the priestesses of Aphrodite vowed to distribute their favors evenly.

Today's calendar, with its meaningless and artificial days of so-called "celebration" that are usually synonymous with drinking and time off from work, pales in comparison with the gentle Path of Old. Therefore, try to celebrate the many holy days of this ancient calendar as often as you can, choosing at least one or two from each end of the wheel, and making the celebration of these sacred days a tradition for your family from now on.

Do not allow your soul to grow without tending to the spirits of old—your ancestors. You are part of a never-ending continuation and it is perfectly all right to take heart and sustenance from the past. When you allow the spirits to awaken in you, difficulties will be clarified and unseen powers suddenly revealed. Do not forget that the Goddess is re-emerging in the public consciousness today, but She has been with you from the beginning, and She is all that is attained at the end of desire.

Tread lightly into the soul's hidden desires. The hunger of the spirit will be satisfied by the motherly hands of the Goddess. The price humanity will have to pay for ignoring and denying the Female Principle of the Universe is soaring. It is through this Female Principle that the Way will be found. Let this spaceship find home in the Mother's harbor—paradise restored, at least spiritually. By accepting all elements in nature, we make whole the collective and individual Soul.

Sabbat Rituals

Foreword

Women who embark on the path, bear in mind that all of the rituals in the following pages are partially from the tradition of my own Dianic witchcraft. Also know that I have reclaimed them, and therefore changed them to adjust to modern women's needs. There is nothing rigid in Goddess worship. Rituals can be researched and symbolism relearned and applied by any group of like-minded women who are inspired by the Goddess. These deeds will be equally valid. The important thing to remember is that beyond a certain structure upon which we all agree, creativity is the order of the night.

Therefore, read all of the pages, absorb what we communicate, and then create your own rituals, your own tradition. The only consistent parts in all traditions are the acts of purification by water, consecration by fire, and creation of a magic circle, the theme of the Sabbats, the times of the holidays, the center focus, and the Triple Goddess of Life, Death, and Beauty. All other acts will spring forth from womansouls, all invocations from inspiration, and all devotions from the highest of all, Sophia, Goddess of Wisdom.

Blessed be!

Yule: Winter Solstice (December 21)

Theme: Rebirth of the sun. We celebrate the birth of the Sun Goddess, Lucina. The altar is set in the eastern part of the circle. Decorations include pine boughs, mistletoe, holly, ivy. The Mother Goddess image has two red candles on each side. The witches are wearing evergreen crowns with lit white candles. This symbolizes the Sun Goddess dispersing the darkness, all purified and consecrated. Then there is a period of humming that builds up to a birth scream. It is good to let those sounds come out of us because we are reborn along with Lucina.

When the energy is high enough, the High Priestess says:

> All ye assembled at my shrine,
> Mother darksome and divine,
> Mine is the scourge and mine the kiss.
> Here I charge you in this sign.

The HP kisses the woman to her left on the forehead, the eyes, and the lips. The kiss is passed on from woman to woman, from east to west. When this is completed, the HP in the Goddess position says:

> All ye assembled in sight,
> bow before my spirit bright.

All bow to the east. The High Priestess says:

> Aphrodite, Arianhod
> Lover of the Horned God,
> Mighty Queen of Witchery and Night,
> Morgan, Etoine, Nisene,
> Diana, Bridgid, Melusine,
> Am I named of old by men.
> Artemis and Cerridwen,
> Hell's dark mistress, Heaven's queen.
> Ye who would ask of me a rune,
> Or who would ask of me a boon,
> Meet me in some secret glade,

Dance my round in greenwood shade,
By the light of the full moon.
In a place, wild and lone,
Dance about mine altar stone;
Work my holy mystery.
Ye who are feign to sorcery,
I bring ye secrets yet unknown.
No more shall ye know slavery,
Who give true worship unto me.
Ye who tread my round on Sabbat night,
Come ye all naked to the rite,
In token that ye be really free.
I teach ye the mystery of rebirth,
Work ye my mysteries in mirth.
Heart joined to heart and lip to lip,
Five are the points of fellowship,
That bring ye ecstasy on earth,
For I am the circle of rebirth.
I ask no sacrifice, but do bow,
No other law but love I know.
By naught but love may I be known.
All things living are mine own
From me they come, to me they go.
(Sybil Leek)

The cauldron is lit and all are silent so that the Goddess may reveal Herself to Her women. Omens include the screeching of an owl, appearances of deer, shooting stars, sudden wakening of the wind, curious cloud formations, neighing of horses, howls of wolves or coyotes, hisses of serpents, and appearances of ravens.

The High Priestess, when she intuitively feels it is time, says:

Queen of the Moon,
Queen of the Stars,
Queen of the Horns,
Queen of the Fires,
Queen of the Earth,
Bring to us the Child of Promise!
For it is the Great Mother
Who gives birth to the new year.
Darkness and tears are set aside,
When the Sun comes up again.
Golden Sun of hill and mountain,

117

Illumine the world,
Illumine the seas,
Illumine the rivers,
Illumine us all.
Grief be laid and joy be raised,
Blessed by the Great Mother!
Without beginning, without end,
Everlasting to Eternity.
Evoe! lo! Evoe! lo!
(Sybil Leek)

The women then jump over the fire in the cauldron, making a wish for the new year, saying it as they leap. After each jump, the women seal it by saying, "blessed be!"

A toast to the Goddess follows with the usual feasting, dancing, meeting dance, and merriment. The circle is closed with thanks given to the watchers who attended and a final blessing.

Deep Peace
Deep peace of the Running Wave to you;
Deep peace of the Flowing Air to you;
Deep peace of the Quiet Earth to you;
Deep peace of the Shining Stars to you.
(Chris Carol)

Candlemas (February 2)

Theme: The celebration of the waxing light. It is the high point between Winter Solstice and Vernal Equinox. The waxing light of the soul is understood here; it is a major Sabbat to initiate new witches.

The altar is set up at the north of the circle. Candle colors are pure white. The cauldron is placed in the middle with sacred herbs or weeds: rowan, apple, elder, holly, pine, cedar, juniper, poplar, dogwood.

Cast the circle as usual, admitting the eldest first, youngest last. The High Priestess purifies the circle, consecrating it with fire (incense). The four corners of the universe are invoked with the appropriate Goddess, unified to raise power.

High Priestess:

> *In the olden times, the Goddess had many groves and*
> *women served Her freely and lived in dignity. The God-*
> *dess's presence was everywhere, and Her women knew Her*
> *as the eternal sister. The patriarchal powers burned down*
> *Her sacred groves, raped and killed Her priestesses, and*

enslaved women. Her name was stricken from library books, and great darkness of ignorance descended upon womankind.

Today, there is a new dawn. We are welcoming new witches into our coven as we strive to replant the Goddess's groves. We, the women, are the grove; through us the return of the Goddess is evident. Let us give birth to each other spiritually just as the Goddess brought forth the light of the world! Behold the great Goddess of the ten thousand names! Blessed be!

Challenger sister priestess asks:

Who are the new souls seeking the Goddess?

The new initiates reveal themselves:

It is I.

Challenger sister:

Who vouches for you?

The new initiate sister then names the coven member who vouches for her. This continues around the circle with each new woman. When the challenger sister is satisfied with the answers, she announces:

It is well! We shall bless your path, if you know the password.

Silver Wheel

As I rode out on frosty night
Silver wheel a'turning, turning,
I met a Lady dressed in white;
Silver wheel a'turning, turning,
Ah . . .
Ah . . .
(All:) Her breath was ice, her steed like snow;
On silver wheels did her chariot go.
(Challenger:)
What brings you to this sacred place;
Will you gaze upon my face?
(Initiate:) I seek the Source of rainbow light,
Which floods the sky this moonless night.
(C:) I am whom you seek, fair one;
Now the mystery is begun.
(I:) The fivefold blessing be my shield

Against all ill my enemy wield.
(All:) You shall hex and you shall heal;
Curse and bless with salve and wheal.
(C:) Power comes even to the fool;
Know you now the wise ones' rule?
(I:) And I harm none with my skill
I may do as I may will.
(C:) Better fall upon my knife,
Than enter here in fear or strife!
(I:) Towards the circle now I move
Entering in trust and love.
(All:) We shall dance and we shall play
Feast with you till break of day!
(Chris Carol)

Initiation

The initiated members stand one behind another with legs spread apart, forming a birth canal. The end of the birth canal faces moonward. The new members line up, oldest first, youngest last. As they step toward the beginning of the birth canal, the challenger sister stops them by pointing her athalme at their breasts.

Challenger sister:

> *It is better for you to rush upon my blade than to enter with*
> *fear in your heart.*

New initiate:

> *I enter the circle in perfect love and perfect trust.*

The challenger removes the knife from her breast, for this is the correct password.

The new initiate now lies down on her back, positioning herself head first. Slowly, the women reach down and move her little by little through the canal without her help. This is an experience one must trust the "elders" or "mothers" to complete with their own strength. When she surfaces on the other end of the canal, the High Priestess welcomes her with a hug and kiss. The new initiate, facing the moon, says her new witch's name, if she has already found it. If not, she says her old name. All women in unison:

> *Blessed be! Happy birthday!*

The High Priestess offers the new woman a honeycomb with honey in it. High Priestess:

Taste the sweetness of Isis; may Her blessings guide you always!

After tasting the honey, the new woman becomes the last link of the birth canal, helping to give birth to the rest of the new souls.

This ritual needs strength, but it is also exhilarating and joyous, not solemn.

After the initiation, the circle is formed and power is raised as usual with everyone making sounds with their bodies. When it is time, the High Priestess begins the witch's chant.

The Witch's Chant

Darksome night and shining Moon,
Hearken to the witches' rune.
East and South and West and North,
Hear! Come! I call Thee forth!

By all the powers of land and sea,
Be obedient unto me.
Wand and Pentacle and Sword,
Hearken ye unto my word.

Cord and Censer, Scourge and Knife,
Waken all ye into life.
Powers of all the Witches' Blade,
Come ye as the charge is made.

Queen of Heaven, Queen of Hell,
Send your aid unto my spell.
Horned Huntress of the night,
Work my will by magic rite.

By all the powers of land and sea,
As I do say, "so mote it be."
By all the might of Moon and Sun,
As I do will, it shall be done.
Blessed be!

After the chant, the High Priestess, in the Goddess position facing east, says:

Eternal sister of all beginnings, Ea, Diana, Isis, Tiamat,
Astarte, Ashtorah, Adame, You are the beginning and the
end. Without Your blessings there is no life. Touch us with
Your wisdom and make this grove grow like the sacred

> *groves of olden times. We dedicate ourselves to You, know-*
> *ing the mystery that what is not found within You will never*
> *be found without.*

All meditate silently upon the divine woman soul.
The High Priestess pours the chalice, offering it to the Goddess:

> *Here is to Your joyous return, may our presence please You!*

The chalice is then passed sunwise (clockwise) as each woman expresses herself with thanks and wishes to the Goddess. The cauldron is kindled; feast foods are blessed and passed. Good times, dancing, and music-making follow.

After a while, the High Priestess forms the circle of power and gives thanks to the four corners of the universe for attending, and asks for blessings before the spirits depart.

Celebration continues until dawn.

Spring Equinox (March 21)

Theme: The return of Persephone from the underworld to reunite with her mother, Demeter. This is the holy day of the continuation between mothers and daughters, the life force perpetuating and rejuvenating all in nature.

Green candles are used, symbolizing the green flora that has appeared again above the earth. Two silver candles are placed on the altar, symbolizing the maiden aspect of the Goddess who rules this part of the year.

Proper preparation: grounds and circle cast, purified with water; admittance in order of age; consecration with fire; corners of the universe evoked; and unifying as usual.

High Priestess:

> *We invoke Thee, o Persephone, Kore, Diana, Artemis, the*
> *ever young maiden, and Flora, the new life that is all*
> *around us. We invoke Thee by root, by stem and by bud,*
> *by leaf and by blossom. We invoke Thee by seed, by life to*
> *transfuse our lives and souls with Thy fresh energy. As You*
> *have risen from the ground, so shall Your sisters, we who*
> *call upon Thee. As You have united with Your joyous*
> *mother Demeter, so shall we unite with our mothers while*
> *in life, and close the gaps of socialization that separate us.*
> *Hail to Thee, maiden, unconquerable and ever young life*
> *force. Bless Thy sisters who call upon Your guidance for*
> *sisterhood. Make our hearts fill with love for one another,*
> *for our sisters and mothers and offspring. So mote it be!*

The High Priestess pours wine into the chalice, pours libation and drinks. She passes the chalice afterward, saying:

Ten thousand years I have been sleeping
and now I am being wakened.
My heavy eyelashes are the woods;
They are beckoning.
My heart, the clouds are surprised
because the are calling me, calling me.
My earth body is bedecked
with a thousand flowers,
Many breasts of mine,
the mountains joyfully rearing their tips,
They are calling! They are calling!
I want to embrace all the sad and the lost.
All wrongs my hands shall doom to death.
I am the defender of every woman
As I am the defender of my holy self.
Earthmother I am, the Only One;
Everything sprang from me;
I carry the seed of all creation;
I am the bestower of life alone.
Oh, oh, oh, I am awake!
Oh, I am answering the call...
(Masika Szilagyi)

The first round is to toast the rejuvenated Goddess; the second round is to ask the Goddess to bless the new projects in the women's lives, be they relationships or activities. Food is blessed and shared, followed by the meeting dance and sisterhood merriment.

The circle is closed.

Demeter's Lament

A mother roves throughout the land,
Searching for her daughter.
The Earth laid waste, no plant at hand,
She mourns o'er earth and water,
Ah...she mourns o'er earth and water.

Where is the girl, both brave and strong,
Belonged to Sappho's band;
Who loved to dance and swelled with song
On Lesbos' golden sand?

The laughter left my graceful girl
Since matriarchy fell;

Seduced by Flowers to an underworld
She lives in man-made hell.

I put my ear close to the earth
and hear the signing sound
Of her who's tied to me by birth
Now captive underground.

But now I know where she is hid,
I'll not delay one hour
Until from bonds my daughter's rid
By our own women's power!

This pomegranate that we share
Is like our common heart;
And fruit we ate in slavery's snare
Shall not keep us apart!
(Chris Carol)

May Eve (April 30)

Theme: The maiden Goddess comes of age. Flora is now in flower and trees, fruits, crops, and animals are fertile. Our lady of May grants rebirth to the world.

The altar is wreathed in flowers. Women wear crowns of bright blossoms. Branches of trees are held; the cauldron is filled with good-smelling herbs. This is a holy day sacred to Brigid, the fairy queen.

The circle is cast. All is purified, consecrated and admitted; the corners of the universe are invoked.

High Priestess:

All ye assembled at my shrine
Mother darksome and divine
Mine is the scourge and mine the kiss.
Here I charge you in this sign.

She kisses the woman five times on the forehead, eyes, lips, breasts, and genitals. The kiss is passed around the circle from east to south to west to north. (Optional if you are shy.)

High Priestess:

All ye assembled in my sight,
Bow before my spirit bright!

All bow. High Priestess:

Hear ye the words of the Star Goddess
The dust of whose feet are the hosts of heaven,
She whose body encircles the universe:

I am the beauty of the green earth
And the white moon among the stars
And the mystery of the waters
And the desire of human hearts.

Call unto your soul: Arise and come unto me
For I am the soul of nature who gives
Life to the universe.
From me all things proceed
And unto me all things must return.

Before my face, beloved of all,
Let your divine innermost self be enfolded
In the rapture of the infinite.
Let my worship be in the heart that rejoices
For behold, all acts of love and pleasure
Are my rituals.
And therefore let there be beauty and strength
Power and compassion, honor and pride
Mirth and reverence within you.

And you who think to seek for me
Know your seeking and yearning shall avail you not
Unless you know the mystery:
That if that which you seek you find not within you,
You will never find it without.

For behold, I have been with you from the beginning
And I am that which is attained at the end of desire.

A period of silence is followed to contemplate the Goddess's presence. When the time is right, all bless the food and drink on the altar, and fill the chalice full. The High Priestess offers proper libation by pouring some wine on the earth.

High Priestess:

Eternal sister of life, bless our year with wisdom and
understanding, replenish our energies, remove all obstacles
that separate sisters from each other. So mote it be! Blessed
be!

Each woman toasts the Goddess of May, Who stands for flowering womanhood. It is unlucky to marry in this month because She is still a maiden Goddess. But dancing is very pleasing to Her, especially using the tree branches that the women have brought.

Close the circle with thanks to the Goddess. Feast. Party.

Queen of the May

I crown thee Queen of the May;
Put on thy cloak of green;
With every bush in bright array,
Appear as Heaven's Queen!

I crown thee Queen of the May;
Put on thy floral crown;
Inspire each song with joy and mirth
And banish every frown!

I crown thee Queen of the May;
Take up thy hawthorn stake
And pierce the lies of those who would
Our women's freedom take!

I crown thee Queen of the May;
Display thy whitened face;
With terror strike the hearts of those
Who women would disgrace!

I crown thee Queen of the May;
Hold high thy ribboned pole;
Inspire the dance with earthly joys
And thrill each woman's soul!

I crown thee Queen of the May;
Gaze in the dew-pond still;
And as thou seest thy true love there
Do with her what thou will!

I crown thee Queen of the May;
When all is rightly seen
Each maiden fair assembled here
Appears as Heaven's Queen!
(Chris Carol)

Midsummer Night: Summer Solstice (June 21)

Theme: This festival is sacred to the fire queen of love, Heartha, Vesta, Rhea, Artemis, Callisto, and Arianhod. On this day we celebrate the Goddess's power over men.

Those witches who relate to men bring a lock of men's hair to be placed in the cauldron. Others take a strand of their own hair as a symbol of their personal homage to the fire Goddess. On the mountaintops in Europe, people still build roaring fires from old car tires to Her. A wheel is placed in the circle, covered with flowers, symbolizing the turning of the year.

The circle is cast with stones. The cauldron plays the major role here, so it is decorated with flowers and placed at the southern part of the circle. All wearing summer flowers. Purify with water, consecrate with fire, admit in order of age, invoke the corners (using wands, not knives), mark the circle with the wand, and unify by humming:

High Priestess:

> *All ye assembled at my shrine*
> *Mother darksome and divine*
> *Mine is the scourge and mine the kiss*
> *Here I charge you in this sign.*

High Priestess:

> *All ye assembled in sight*
> *bow before my spirit bright.*

All bow. High Priestess:

> *The fire festival has begun. This is the day when the God-*
> *dess reigns supreme. At this time in particular, She has*
> *power over Her horned consort. In commemoration of this,*
> *I bid you honor Her by placing in Her sacred fire an oak*
> *branch that represents the male principle.*

This is a great opportunity to cast spells over men who have bothered you this year. It can be anyone from political enemies to personal enemies. Rapists, for example, can be sacrificed with great success on this night. Each woman approaches the cauldron and places her oak branch in it, saying which man it represents. This may also be a blessing on sons and lovers, or just a love spell.

After this is done, the women begin dancing clockwise around the cauldron. Bring instruments or recorded music. We use ritual music from Africa.

When all are tired, gather again into a circle and unify. High Priestess:

> *Passionate sister of the living fire, accept our love. Great*
> *Rhea, Mother of all living, turn the wheel of fortune to*
> *the betterment of women and their liberation. You alone*
> *have power over patriarchy in this time of oppression. I in-*
> *voke You and call upon You, o mighty Mother of us all,*

*bringer of justice, fruitfulness! I invoke You by the vestal
fires in our cauldron, by the passion in our hearts, by the
intense flames of the pyres that burned Your witches not
long ago. Descend upon our enemies in Your fury. Avenge
the wrongs, halt the rapes, illuminate the minds of our
leaders and judges with your eternal fire. So mote it be!*

All watch the burning fires for clues, pictures, or prophecies. After
a while, bless all food and drink.

Feast and praise the name Rhea, Vesta, Esmeralda, woman passion.
Dance. Party.

Close the circle as usual.

Flames of Love

*Drink the wine, chew the laurel,
Sing of love and never quarrel;
Wake, to die of pleasure's pain
In flames of ecstasy again!*
(Chris Carol)

The Lammas (August 2)

Theme: Celebration of Habondia, the Goddess of plenty, of fortune, the
Indian Corn Mothers, Kore and Ceres, the daughters of the Earth Mother;
from Her comes all plenty.

The circle is created as usual: purification, consecration, admission,
raising power, and the Fivefold Kiss. The altar is dressed with fruits of
the earth, flowers, and grapes. Candles are green for material gain. Sheaves
of wheat are placed on the four sides. Branches of holly or any grain can
be used for crowns.

High Priestess:

*I (name), Your High Priestess and Witch, hereby invoke
You, O loving Aradia, teacher of the oppressed, protectress
of women. I invoke You by Your holy Mother's name,
Diana, Mother of all that is alive. Great is the Mother Who
created the universe, Who created the waters, the fires, the
earth, and the air. I summon You, Diana, lovely huntress
of the night, to descend upon this gathering of women who
came together to commune with You.*

More power is raised. Everyone listens for the inner voice of Diana,
and whoever feels Her presence shares it with the others.

High Priestess:

The harvest season is coming; the harvest of foods of our labors, of our struggles. This is the height of the year. Great Fortune, smile upon Your sisters! May the bounty of this season keep us strong in spirit, body, and soul.

Offering of the chalice after libation:

Great Goddess of life and good fortune, accept our thanks for our own growth, insights, accomplishments, and the sustaining food You have given us.

The chalice is passed. Women offer a toast to the Goddess. Food is set aside for Her place, which no one touches. The rest of the food is blessed and shared in joyous feasting.

Music is played during and after the feast. Individuals perform their spiritual contributions, such as reciting poetry or making music, to make the feast worthy of the Goddess's company. The Goddess hates boring circles.

Close the circle before the last ounce of energy is gone. The last part can always be done by wands as well as swords. Don't forget to thank the spirits.

Song of the Corn Maiden

There's plenty to eat, plenty to drink,
Plenty to keep us toasty warm
Plenty to clean, plenty to heal,
Plenty to keep us from harm;
The power is ours to work and share
Our Mother's Plenty everywhere!

There's plenty to say, plenty to sing,
Plenty to dance and dare to do;
Plenty to weave, plenty to unwind,
Plenty for me and you!

There's plenty of work, plenty of play,
Plenty of rest when day is done;
Plenty of corn in the Maiden's hands,
Plenty for everyone!
(Chris Carol)

Autumn Equinox (September 21)

Theme: Witches' Thanksgiving.

The altar is decorated with pine cones, oak sprigs, acorns, ears of corn, dried leaves and hazel branches. Candles are brown and green. The circle is created as usual; all procedures are as usual, including the Fivefold Kiss. After the energy is raised, the High Priestess turns to the west in the Goddess position.

High Priestess:

> *Farewell, Goddess Lucina, ever-returning light! You ripened the grapes and fruits and nuts of the earth. We thank You; great is the Mother Who made our lives ripen with experience and wisdom. This is the season in which the wise hazelnut teaches us contained knowledge. In the seed is hidden the new life, which Demeter will free once it returns to the sacred earth.*

She plants the seed into the earth. All:

> *Blessed be! May new life be sent from the land of youth!*

High Priestess (offering the chalice to the Goddess):

> *Eternal Mother, without beginning and without end, accept our libation to You for Your love and teachings. Indeed, You are the soul of nature, and all that is belongs to You. Accept our souls. We dedicate ourselves to You!*

The chalice makes the round for the toasting to the Goddess. All bless the food and drink and feast in Her honor. Dancing follows; close the circle.

High Priestess:

> *Sisters, I propose a toast to the good seasons that have gone, to the seasons yet to come!*

All: Blessed be!
High Priestess:

> *Sisters, I propose a toast to the beauty of women, to the beauty of the crone!*

All: Blessed be!
High Priestess:

> *Sisters, I propose a toast to the Goddess who is three-formed; may She bring freedom to women all over the world!*

All: Blessed be!

Harvest Home

Harvest Home, my friends,
O bring the harvest in!

Gone the summer haze,
the frost will soon begin.
Harvest Moon will grant a boon,
and turn the night to day,
Harvest Home, my friends,

O sing the hours away!
Harvest Home, my friends,
O reap the stalks of grain,
Life lies in the seed,
'til spring shall come again.
Golden leaves and golden sheaves
do glow by light of moon;
Harvest Home, my friends,
for winter's coming soon!

Harvest Home, my friends,
Oh work until we're done;
Soon comes rest to all
who labor 'neath the sun.
Fill right up the Vintage cup,
and toast the new made wine;
Harvest Home, my friends,
for 'tis the Harvest Time!
(Chris Carol)

Hallowmas: Women's New Year (October 31)

Theme: The Goddess displays Her third aspect as the destroyer of life. As the Sacred Hag, She represents nature in winter—death, which is organically important for future life. On this day, She returns to Her sisters to give the wisdom of the ages, to protect, to avenge.

Form the circle as usual. All is properly purified and consecrated, and each woman enters the circle with the password. Raise the energy, and unify.

This is the time of Hecate, the time of ancestral worship, the time for witches to draw near the Goddess, Who speaks directly to Her children. In Europe, people go to the cemeteries with bouquets of chrysanthemums, honoring the dead. The Susan B. Anthony Coven always remembers the witches burned by the Christians this night. This is also the night of the revengeful Mother, Who is the fierce protector of Her daughters when aroused. If you have a blacklist of women's enemies, the score can be settled this night.

The altar has two black candles and two white ones. Each woman is represented with one red candle on the outside circle and one red candle on the altar. Offerings of food are appropriate. All kinds of food with red colorings are used, because that is the food that belongs to the dead. We often use pomegranates and red apples.

High Priestess:

> *O Hecate, Goddess of life and death, beloved by us all, wake up from Your slumber, Earth Mother. Bless this gathering of Your sisters who are present here tonight. Let this all-holy Sabbat proceed in mirth, in understanding, in love and ecstasy.*

All: Blessed be, Great Goddess!

This text came to us from ancient times, recited by matriarchies of old. Let us listen to their visions of the Goddess Hecate.

High Priestess:

> *Lady of tremblings, the sovereign lady, the mistress of destruction Who sets the world in order, She Who delivers from destruction, lady of heaven, the mistress of the world Who devours with fire.*
>
> *Lady of the altar, the lady to Whom abundant offerings are made. She Who prevails with knives, the mistress of the world, destroyer of the foes of the women, Who makes the decree for escape of the needy from evil happenings.*
>
> *Fire, the lady of flames who inhales the supplications that are made to Her, Who permitted no man to enter at Her shrines.*
>
> *Lady of light, She Who is in front, the lady of strength, quiet of heart Who gave birth to all that is alive, Whose girth is three hundred and fifty measures. The likes of Her has never been found from the beginning.*
>
> *Lady of might, Who dances upon the blood-red ones, Who keeps the festival of Hecate on the day of the hearing of faults.*
>
> *Terrible one, lady of rainstorm, Who plants the ruination of the souls of men, devourer of dead bodies; the orderer and producer and creator of the slaughtered. Dispenser of light during Her period of life, watcher of flames, the lady of the strength and of writing. She takes possession of hearts; She has secret plots and councils.*

After this recitation, the Goddess' presence should be felt. All meditate on the meanings of the words; listen within. If business is at hand, proceed with the same energy of the terrible one.

The High Priestess gathers the witches and all thrust their knives forward. They clank them together and work them up for action. The maiden reads the names of the rapists or their descriptions. The witches requesting these must give a short rousing speech on why these men deserve the worst, in order to get everyone involved emotionally.

Take a pomegranate, name the rapists, or just "patriarchy," to cover a wide range, and chant the witches' chant over it. When the last words are spoken, the High Priestess thrusts her knife into the fruit so that it drips like blood. Do not touch a cursed pomegranate with your hands! Then each witch pronounces a curse over patriarchy as the fruit is passed from knife to knife. For example, "So shall he who hurt my sister bleed from unknown wounds!" or, "So shall his guts fall out to nobody's pain." Take inspiration from the terrible one and vent your righteous anger magically; send it where it belongs!

The Witches' Warning

(Chorus)
They're gonna come, they're gonna come;
They'll come for us in the morning.
They're gonna come, but we'll be gone;
We've heard the witches' warning!

They snatched away our children dear
They took away abortion;
They wiped the wildflower from the field
And covered us with poison.

Now childcare costs our weekly wage
We're prisoners in our homes;
The welfare barely feeds the flesh
And starves our woman's soul.

They cast our Goddess from the earth
Subdued with rape and burning;
But every spring the new corn sprouts
The old ways we're learning.

The night watch now, the daylight soon
The struggle brings the glory;
The lives we lead, the songs we sing
Will be our woman's story.

The sooner fight, the sooner win;
Why wait a moment longer?
Our deadliest weapon is our hope
And we are getting stronger!
(Chris Carol)

133

The Esbats

An Esbat is a celebration of the full moon in the name of the Goddess Diana. The thirteen full moons of every calendar year are the source of the magical number 13. Esbats are usually smaller and less ritualistic than Sabbats, and they are often more solemn and meditative. There is nothing more beautiful than having an ancient celebration under the majestic full moon.

An Esbat is usually a small group of witches who have important magic work to do. The Susan B. Anthony Coven usually goes through the creation of the circle with everyone participating intimately. The gathering of the stones for the circle is only important for women who must steal into patriarchal "public" land to find the Goddess in the city. We always dismantle the altars we build to avoid being found out. If you own land, you can simply go back to your stone altars. An Esbat can be held indoors, but if at all possible, have it outside. It should be on the night of the full moon, preferably around midnight. Have the coven members meet in your grove about 10:30 PM. Sisters should bring white candles (at least two for each witch), incense (frankincense with a little mugwort, myrtle and rose petals are good), an image of the Goddess (a figurine is fine if you can find one you really like), the chalice and some wine, a cauldron and charcoal, sea water or salt water in two containers, and a small container of earth.

When you get to the grove, each woman should gather at least two stones from the area. The largest stone should be used to mark off the outer circle. To determine the size of the circle, each woman should stand with arms outstretched, fingertips touching her neighbor's fingertips. When everyone is touching, that means the circle is the right size, and each person should put one of her stones in front of her toes. This should be done one at a time, with the person standing at the north starting first. The remaining stones are used to build an altar in the middle of the circle. Each person puts one white candle on her stone in the outer circle and one on the altar. This can be done by wedging the candle between the stones, or burning the end of the candle over the stone so that the warm wax drippings will hold it in place. The candles represent desires, requests for special blessings, and devotion to the Goddess.

Place the image of the Goddess on the altar, and light incense in front of Her. At this point, some people may want to go off alone to meditate or do private spells. This is also a good time to drink some purifying wine or tea. When everyone has returned to the circle, it is time to mark off the four corners of the universe.

In the north corner, inside the outer circle, put the clump of earth; to the east put a thurible of incense; at the southern point, the cauldron; and to the west, the salt water. All magical tools, food, musical instruments and wine should be placed around the altar now. Light the candles in the outer circle and on the altar, and light the charcoals in the cauldron. You can throw in some herbs or Vesta powder if you like. The High Priestess draws the magic circle with her wand and a sprinkling of salt, as members of the coven enter from the north corner according to age, with the oldest going first. The High Priestess blesses coven members with salt water as they approach the entrance, and everyone enters the circle in love and trust. When all have entered, the High Priestess closes the circle with her wand, and standing at the altar, says:

> *Magic Lady of Light, You bless us with Your radiant presence! Like our foremothers of many years past, we come here tonight in Your honor.*

The High Priestess goes to the north point of the circle, raises her athalme to the north (while the other witches are drawing the pentagram in the air and kissing their blades), and says:

> *O fertile, lush Goddess of the earth! Ancient Mother, Who nourishes us, Who gives birth to all things growing, may You nurture people's struggles for liberation around the world! May we the people gain control of the earth, may those who try to exploit her be made powerless. Our Mother Nature, may You bless with strength and power our liberation from all the forces that oppress, alienate, degrade, pervert, imprison, and attempt to destroy us!*

The High Priestess goes to the east, and all witches point with their athalmes.

High Priestess:

> *Beautiful Lady of the winds, may we become as free as You! May we break from our oppressive bond, our ghettos, our prisons, our alienation. May You bless us with vision to see what will be in the future. May You spark our womansouls, freewomen!*

All witches point their athalmes to the south.

High Priestess:

> *Goddess of the South, woman of passion and fire, may You share with us Your fiery spirit! May You bless our struggles with passion, strength, determination, ingenuity, and brilliance. Set afire passionate solidarity among women and oppressed people of the world! May You bless our victory!*

All witches point their athalmes to the west.
High Priestess:

> *Bright lady of the waters, untamable woman flowing with the strength and beauty of the women's revolution! You break the chains of our oppression with Your force, while lapping inside us a love and sexuality. We drink of Your life force and ask You to bless the eternal solidarity and love between all women; we flow from the same womanspirit. May we join together and celebrate this!*

The High Priestess then stands in front of the altar and says:

> *Beautiful ancient one, may You bless us with Your presence! May we bathe in Your light and love; may we feel You inside and outside our bodies; may we all touch as womansouls.*

Now you may want to come together and put your arms around each other. You can hum, meditating on the presence of the Goddess, while the High Priestess asks Her to appear in spirit. She may ask for some sign of Her presence, such as the hoot of an owl or the howl of a wolf.

During this part of the Esbat, it is best to let whatever is going to happen, happen. By joyous, or solemn, or frenzied. Trust your feelings, your body, and your spirit. After a while, sit in a circle around the altar. As the chalice of sacred wine, blessed and treated with herbs, is passed around, each sister says her wish, asks for blessings, and expresses her devotion to the Goddess. After each witch has made her wish, her sisters bless her and direct woman-energy toward that wish; they ask the Goddess to grant their sister the boon for which she has asked. As each takes the chalice, she pours a little wine onto the earth before making her wish, so as to share the wine with the Goddess.

After this, the High Priestess raises the chalice to the altar, and spilling a little wine onto the earth, says:

> *Ancient Mother who controls the winds and the tides, beautiful Ea, fiery womansoul, we feast in Your honor, and thank You for making us Your daughters, for making us lusty, life-giving, life-loving women! Blessed be!*

Now you can sing, dance, feast, whatever feels best and seems appropriate. Esbats have unique and differing characters, and it is best to rely on your intuition. In the patriarchal social system, "women's intuition" is derided, and we are taught to act and feel what is "socially acceptable" rather than acting on our own, genuine feelings. Witchcraft has never fit into the patriarchal system, so relax; listen to your feelings and body. Feel free and alive!

As witches, we feel righteous and proud of creating our own social system based on love, solidarity, sisterhood, and magic. We live by our own values. This is going to be our revolution, too!

The Words of the Star Goddess

I am the beauty of the green earth,
the white moon among the stars;
The mystery of the deep waters,
the desire of human heart;
Know the Mystery, therefore . . .
That if ye find not what ye seek within,
ye shall never find it without.
Lo, I have been with you from the beginning,
And I am whom ye will find
at the end of your desire.

Chapter 4

Women's Holidays
in the Dianic Tradition

Themis is the Goddess of social instinct—the communal or collective consciousness—and such service as She requires acts as a civilizing force. This includes community festivals, good times, purification and ritual celebrations. The civilizing influence of Themis was promoted in Goddess worship by gathering the people of the community to worship the Source of Life with life-oriented activities—sacred dances, holy feasts and fasts, festivals and parades. Such activities allowed the people to contemplate all things larger than their immediate individual lives and to participate in the play of forces that essentially controlled their lives.

Matriarchal followers of Themis knew well that one's actions are controlled by one's thoughts. Thinking together communally served to create a civilized collective consciousness, directed toward the continuing health and well-being of the community. Such civilizations led long lives and dominated the social life, even into the new patriarchal culture, until suppressed. In every ethnic background, such a culture, such a civilization existed. The festivals were integral to them all.

Feralia and Lupercalia: Fertility Festival

The theme of the festival of Feralia was purification. It began on February 13, and worship was devoted to "Parentalia," the ancient ancestor. This was not a feasting time. Marriages were forbidden, temples closed, and magistrates appeared in public without their insignia. Feralia was devoted to minding the "old ones," the "more." Spirits of the dead were placated, appeased, and tended during this time.

During Lupercalia, the spirits of the dead were again a major part of the theme, although this particular festival was devoted to the stimulation of fertility as well as purification. During Lupercalia, the ancient people would strike the women with strips of goat skins (februa). This was an invitation for happy ghosts to reincarnate in the women. The world of the dead was considered active and near. Spirits of the dead being ever-present, the people felt comfortable not only invoking them, but also inducing them to return through the cycle of rebirth. The februa served a dual purpose— purification and stimulation of fertility—expressed through placation of ghosts. This was the ancients' idea of being "pure" and blameless. The importance of these festivals is thus expressed:

> *This rains and ruins over*
> *And all the seasons of snows and sins,*
> *While in green underwood and cover*
> *Blossom by blossom the Spring begins!*

Diasia: Ward-Off-Poverty Festival

Diasia was a dark, gloomy and scary festival—a time for exorcisms, magical curses, purgations and placation for wrongs done within one's own bloodline. The festival took place on the night of March 14, when the people of the community would journey to the temple of the Big Snake Goddess, Ua Zit. There they would offer food to the Cobra Queen in order to exorcise poverty and illness from their lives.

In the Old Religion, Ua Zit was invoked and fed by pouring barley out upon the earth for the Underworld. Although the Olympian Zeus Meilichos superseded these practices with his own, the takeover was never so deep and complete that the simple folk could not see it for what it was. They continued to visit the shrine of the Cobra Queen. Using offerings of piglets after the advent of the patriarchal meat-eating customs, the people continued their rites of purification, using fire to fumigate and brimstone to cure all ills. In this way, all that was sick was exorcised, and the Cobra Queen would feed the good luck of the community for another year.

Anthesteria: Blessings on Vine Festival

This was a three-day festival, the first day being dedicated to the Openings of the Casks (Pithoigia) for the broaching of the new wine. Essentially, the community got together to taste their new wine, and to pour out libations to the Earth Mother Who made it all possible. As they poured, they asked that the wine be rendered harmless, since the Goddess didn't really like wine or alcohol to drink. Her animals could die from it. Pure water or juices were more favored libations of the Earth Mother. On this day of Opening the Casks, the normal patriarchal slave-master hierarchy was relaxed and a more socialistic matriarchal approach was law. "No one shall be prevented from tasting of the new wine!" Slaves and masters, parents and children, drank together.

The second day of this festival was the Day of Cups, and drinking contests were held all over town. One tradition called for someone to drain the garlanded cup to win a cake of great good luck. Cups being a pleasure symbol, it is no wonder that the Sacred Marriage was staged on this day. During this "Hieros Gamos," a sexual union took place between the representative of the Goddess and Her sacred king. The temples of the earth-born Dionysus were opened so that the community could, for the only time all year, witness this sacred union. If this involved the actual queen of a country, there was a "displaying" of her pleasure, which was the best omen for her people in the coming year.

The third day of Anthesteria was the Festival of the Pots, a celebration of the food for the people. Pots were newly purchased, blessed by priestesses, and a great meal then cooked in them for the first time—to feed the hunger that the Day of Cups had worked up. General disorganization ruled this day, too, and no work was done other than feeding the community.

When all three days had passed, it was time for the serious part of Anthesteria to be observed, around midnight, in each home. Here the head of the house, mother of the family, would stand barefoot in the middle of the home. First, she would make a special sign with her hand, the sign of the Yoni—making the shape of a diamond with thumbs and index fingers touching and the rest held straight out next to each other. She would wash her hands in clear spring water three times, then turn around three times, each time putting nine black beans into her mouth. Through the special sign she had made with her hands she would spit the beans, calling out: "These I send forth! With these beans I redeem myself and mine!"

Nine times the mother would spit nine beans for the Mother Goddess, saying this each time. After the beans had all been spat out, she would avert her eyes and turn away so that the ghosts (or their essences) could pick the beans up. To complete the rite, she would wash her hands again with water, and striking a brass bell nine times, would say after each stroke, "Shades of my ancestors, depart!"

Since, in essence, this ritual is a mutual All Hallows custom, it may be observed at Halloween, or in May when the Goddess is still in Her Death-in-Life aspect. Different places in the world with their varying climates should decide when this gentle exorcism of the old spirits is appropriate.

Thargelia: Festival of the First Fruits

A harvest festival for northern cultures would be held in September, but in the early days of southern Europe and Asia Minor, as now, harvest begins with festivals in May or June. The first three such early harvesting festivals was the Thargelia.

> *The road on which our feet are set*
> *Is in a harvest way,*
> *For to the fair-robed Demeter*
> *Our comrades bring today*
> *The first fruits of their harvesting*
> *She on the threshing place*

> *Great store of barley grain outpoured*
> *For guardian of Her Grace.*
> (Theocritus, *Idylls*)

It was considered very bad luck to ignore or forget the importance of the "first fruits" because famine could come to the people or a wild boar might waste the land. The ancients were very careful to be grateful for the source of their life—food. They would take their first fruits to the temple of Demeter as an offering, and pour everything out in front of the Goddess image. This food was then gathered and used by the priestesses of the temple. This was quite sensible to the pagans. In remembering the good grace of the Goddess, the community fed Her temple workers, the Priestesshood.

A good luck charm for the community was an important part of Thargelia. This charm was made by the boys and nymphs whose parents were living, and consisted of a decorated olive branch known as the Eiresione. From this branch, the youth hung all manner of natural products: sacred wool from first-shorn sheep, dyed white and purple; strings of acorns; vessels of wine; figs, dates and barley cakes. This charm was fastened over the door to the home as a charm against pestilence and famine in the coming year.

> *Eiresione brings all good things;*
> *Figs and fat cakes to eat,*
> *Soft oil and honey sweet,*
> *And brimming wine cup deep*
> *That She may drink and sleep.*

Because the branch was olive, we may assume this was a dedication to Athena, the Virgin. In other places, this would be done in honor of Artemis, Soul of Nature.

Although later patriarchs (Aristotle is an example) told of pagan "sacrifices" during Goddess-worship times, there was usually a taboo on the killing of animals. Even the Olympians periodically bowed to this custom, steeped in tradition and wisdom. Such a period of taboo on killing allowed the wild animals and livestock to grow and multiply. The original pagan form of offering was to sprinkle grains and water on the altar before a ritual was performed.

> *As we cast up our barley in little showers*
> *A little grace from the birds is ours.*

The harvest feast was prepared from pelanos, or barley meal, with cheese, leeks and chopped olives. Variations were also used, however, as evidenced by the following:

143

A holy heifer's milk, white and fair to drink
Bright honey drops from flowers, bee-distilled
With draughts of water from a virgin fount
And from the ancient vine its mother wild
An unmixed draught this gladness and fair fruit
Of gleaming olive, ever-blooming
And woven flowers, children of Mother Earth.

During Thargelia, it was important to include musical offerings to the Goddess. Music festivals were held during this time, and winners of contests received special tripods—used in divination—for them to sit upon while creating. The festival of Thargelia gave rest and relaxation, as well as a communal spirit, to the people, and usually featured a procession of townspeople moving through the streets with their first fruits (wild herbs, ground pulse, acorns, barley, wheat, dried fig cakes, barley cakes and pots full of good food). As they passed each door to a home they would hang the sacred good luck charm (Eiresione) over the entrance.

Pharmakos

Actually still a part of Thargelia, the ceremony of Pharmakos was one of ritual purification and stimulation. Two men were chosen to represent all that was not well in the community. Usually these men were criminals, taken from imprisonment and seen as representatives of the Male Principle of the Universe. As Pan, these men were struck with leeks and fruitless branches, or pelted with onions. This beating took place seven times for good luck, then the criminals were led out of the community, never to return under penalty of death. This expulsion served to purify the city and was so important that only special and magical people, specially purified, could perform the ritual, usually to the sound of flutes.

It was said that this beating of Pan served to drive out evil influences as well as to make him more virile. Onions were considered aphrodisiacs, and the beating was done by one of Pan's priests. Considered in this way, the Pharmakos fits nicely into Thargelia, without any taste of blood.

This ceremony was well liked by the new patriarchy, whose leaders took the ritual further. After the Pharmakos were "led out" of (expelled from) the city, the patriarchs burned them on a pyre of fruitless trees, then scattered their ashes to the four directions. This was a patriarchal touch—a blending of the gentle exorcism and stimulation of the matriarchal mode with the patriarchal perversion of human sacrifice. Because of this, however, the festival of Thargelia, with the attendant ceremony of Pharmakos, survived deep into patriarchal, fifth-century Athens.

There is a female Pharmakos, "Charila." When there is famine and drought in the land, a festival is held in honor of Charila (Kore), the

Maid-Virgin. Before offering first fruits to Her, an effigy or priestess-representative is pelted in the face with satin strips. Afterward, normal Thargelian activities begin. This custom can be recognized in Italian weddings, where the groom and bride have leather shoes thrown at them before they are showered with rice. The purpose is the same—to drive away the evil influences first, then shower with blessings afterward.

The nature of "sacrifice," as stated earlier, was dependent upon the times and political winds of the ancients. In the beginning, there were only fireless and wineless sacrifices, as in the sprinkling of the grains over the altars of the Old Ones (Venerable Ones). No animal sacrifice was allowed. With the advent of patriarchal hordes pressing down from the north, this new flesh-sacrificing feature was accommodated with the building of an altar for the Olympians, the Indo-European, militaristic, hero-god-worshipers. The altars of the Goddess were preserved behind the new ones and continued to be filled with honey cakes and offerings of first fruits.

"Up the hill they came, yet in their hand, no seed of burning flame, and for the Rhodian land with fireless rite, the grove upon the citadel they light." Pindar said this in observance of his local customs of priestesses worshipping the pre-Hellenic Great Goddess, Athena.

Kallynteria and Plynteria: Nurturance Festivals

These festivals (May 19 and May 28) were designed to encourage a communal "gloom" attitude, as ill-omen rituals to be solemnized rather than celebrated. On the sixth day of the third part of Thargelia, secret Goddess rites were performed and the gloom was taken very seriously. Priestesses would carry the sacred image from the temples to the waters (ocean, lake, river or stream) and bathe Her. This ritual washing united the sacred image with the life-giving waters. Often the priestesses would shroud the holy image, or perhaps rope off the temple entirely.

During Plynteria, Pallas Athena was taken down and out of Her temples to be bathed and beautified by new paint or the addition of new jewels. This practice extended into the individual homes, where all personal shrines and altars were cleaned and renewed, as was the rest of the house. A thorough sweeping out with the old and in with the new was in order. These festivals took place in May, held to be unlucky for marriages because of the association with the Maiden-Virgin aspect of the Goddess.

Vestalia: Fire Festival

Vestalia, another large purification festival, was celebrated on June 7 by the Virgin and dedicated to the Fire Goddess, Vesta. On Vestalia, priestesses traveled to the rivers to throw small images of men into the waters while standing on a wooden bridge. The images were made of rushes and called "argeioi." The practice was a response to the Oracle:

Ye nations, throw two bodies in sacrifice to the Ancient Ones who bear the sickle, bodies to be received by the Tuscan streams.

Priestesses remained unadorned and in old clothes until the ban was lifted on midsummer night. Eternal fires, kept in the temples for Vesta, were renewed at this time, and the people took some of the fire home with them as a symbol of good fortune and blessings.

The temples also received vigorous attention during Vestalia. Priestesses swept, scrubbed, washed and beautified the House of the Mother. During the festival, the innermost sacred space of the temple was opened to all priestesses. This was a space where no man was ever allowed to set foot. Here the priestesses would crowd together, standing barefoot, for prayers and rituals concerning their own order.

Vestals prepared the first cakes of the first-fruits corn and offered them in the temples, while all millers and bakers were garlanded. There are parallel customs to Vestalia among the Creek Indians of North America, usually in July and August, when their first corn is ripe. They, too, maintain the ritual purifications: bathing of sacred images; sweeping of public plazas, temples, and houses; fasting before partaking of the new first fruits; putting out the old fire and rekindling a new one; and solemnly and communally eating of the first fruits of new corn.

Arretophoria: Nymph Festival

This was also known as a "trust" festival, and was a very charming ritual of trust, responsibility and friendship. Held in June or July, this festival was devoted to maidens and culminated in a feast of Athena. Two young maidens (ages seven to eleven) were chosen each year by the priestesshood to perform the sacred "trust." These maidens lived near the temple, wore white robes with golden trim and golden jewels, and ate a special diet of honey cakes baked and served by the community. Prior to the actual festival, the chosen two would be given a variety of tasks to do in and around the temple.

The "trust" ritual is neither long nor elaborate. At the appropriate time, the priestess of Athena would give each maiden a box or sack of sacred, holy items (sacra). No one except the High Priestess knew what the two boxes contained, and the maidens were charged to carry the boxes to a sacred place, deep within the earth. Although this meant a long, dark walk into the depths of some underground cave, the two young women were to carry the sacra down into the chambers on their heads, leave the boxes there, and return to the priestess with the sacred items left there the year before, during Arretophoria. To open any container of sacra was forbidden, even though the maidens were young and inquisitive.

Maidens who accomplished such service were returned to their communities with honors and initiated as Maids of Athena. Maiden services were also performed for Demeter, Kore, Themis, Proserpine and Hersophoroi, as well as Athena. The meanings relative to this festival summed up the place of young women within the society. They had magical powers, were carriers of sacred objects, and were obedient—defying fear to descend into the depths alone—in service to their communities.

Thesmophoria: Festival of Women's Rights

Also known as the Festival of Demeter, Thesmophoria (October 11-13) is a major holy day, dedicated to the observance of the Laws of Demeter, the Goddess. Theocritus reported:

> It was law among the Athenians that they should celebrate
> the Thesmophoria yearly, and the Thesmophoria is this:
> Women who are virgins and have lived a holy life, on the
> day of the feast place certain customary and holy books
> on their heads and, as though to perform a liturgy, they
> go to Eleusias.

The origins of Thesmophoria are very ancient. In fact, it is here we find the roots of magic, blessings, curses, pronouncements, and the beginnings of law-binding. The moral convictions of the communities were pronounced, and all enemies of the people were cursed. This took place in front of the doors of appropriate temples of the Goddesses, especially Demeter and Artemis. Aristophanes recorded the words of a woman performing Thesmophoria:

> *I bid you pray to Gods and Goddesses*
> *That in Olympus and in Pytho dwell*
> *And Delos and to all other gods...*
> *Or plots of Tyranny,*
> *Or if female slave in her master's ear tells tales,*
> *Or male or female Publican*
> *Scants the full measure of our legal pint,*
> *Curse him that he may miserable perish,*
> *He and his house.*
> *But for the rest of you*
> *Pray that the gods give you all good things.*

This is a powerful, sobering curse, reinforced by custom. With both sexes participating, it was much more effective than lawsuits eventually brought to any male-dominated court.

This was a time when matriarchal practices were reinstituted and the people were reminded of the rights of women. This was also a time for the taking of the Great Oath by all who sought to vindicate themselves of certain actions.

According to Plutarch, when Callipus was conspiring against Dion, the wife and sister of Dion became suspicious and demanded that Callipus take this Great Oath to vindicate himself. The procedure was this: The man who takes the Great Oath must go to the temples of the Thesmophoroi and, after a ceremony with the priestesses, takes a burning torch and denies the charges against him. He then puts on a purple robe in dedication to the Goddess of Death, just in case he lied. This would cause great physical as well as psychological strain upon any man attempting to lie to the priestesses of Demeter. It is said that no man lied and survived the ritual.

On the first day of Thesmophoria, there was a ritual known as "kathodos," or a "down-going and up-rising." The priestesses for this day's celebration were women who had been purified and who had avoided the touching of any iron objects for three full days. These women acted as the "drawers-up." They dressed in crimson and purple gowns and their service was to descend deep into the cleft of the earth where the shrine of Demeter stood.

These priestesses carried piglets, considered sacred to Demeter because of their intelligence and the fact that they love earth best. The staple food of the people, therefore, was symbolically returned to the Goddess—the source of all food. The priestesses collected from the shrine in the earth some remains of piglets left there the year before, then replaced the sacred Goddess-images, snake statues, and homemade shrines. The task was not an easy one. There were usually many snakes kept around the shrines, and around the shrines of Demeter in particular, since the snake is earth-born. The women often had rattles with them, which they shook to keep snakes away while they were "drawing-up" the offerings of the past year.

The second day of Thesmophoria, Nestia, was dedicated to Demeter the Law Giver, who ordained that "men provide with their own labors their own nurturance." This was an acknowledgment of the fact that women would not nurture men throughout a lifetime; after a certain point, men had to take care of themselves. On this day, everyone fasted. All those things that had been "drawn-up" were displayed upon the altars, prisoners were pardoned, courts closed, amnesty granted, and Demeter as a "smileless statue" received worshipers while sitting on the ground rather than on Her usual throne. On this day of atonement the people placed marble pigs and other sacra on Demeter's altars.

The third day of Thesmophoria was spent "sowing" all the "drawn-up" things once again in the good Earth—a sort of magical fertilization. Only women who had no death in their families could perform this sacred ritual of the "born fair," "born beautiful," or Kallingeneia. Afterward, feasting took place throughout the community and everyone danced while the music played. In this country, Thesmophoria has been transmuted into a "thanksgiving" ritual, without the matriarchal tradition of putting back into the Earth that which is received from Her.

The essence of most of these ancient ways leads us back to the beginning of matriarchal societies, where women were in charge of the dispensation of justice. Every year, when the women congregated for the traditional festivals, the part of Thesmophoria where public cursings and blessings were performed, even in modern times, was a remnant of witchcraft. The Goddess to be invoked, therefore, had to be Hecate the Witch Queen, She Who is three-formed. Usually the High Priestess, dressed as Kore, sounded the bronze gong (associated with purifications), giving the final seal to all pronouncements. Later on, the clapping of hands replaced the gongs as the incantations were said in public places. Hence, the custom of clapping hands for performers today.

Spiritual beings who presided over the communal and ritualistic curses were not hated or despised or feared, but found to be quite useful. They were referred to as the Averters, Those-Who-Send-Away, Protectors, or Putters to Flight. Even today the seed of cursing hasn't changed from that of Thesmophoria. To "bind down" a person into keeping his promises, by the power of Hecate, still works. To "give over" the ills or bad luck caused by someone is still the heritage of witches.

Ancient curses eventually developed into the modern vow and even prayers in the new religion are an offshoot of this matriarchal practice. The ordinances of many social orders came from this, and even regular "laws" as we know them finally also claim their origins in the Craft.

Stenia: Bitching Festival

This stunning festival takes place during Thesmophoria. Crones of the community were enthroned in tents made of fig branches while younger women tended them with food and drink. After eating, the younger women were turned loose to playfully harass and insult one another, using all the "bad" language they wished. As evening came, the young women would continue to "abuse" each other through scurrilous jesting, namecalling, throwing dirt clods and small stones, and wrestling with each other. This all took place in the tents, under the gentle supervision of the Crones, and was a powerful way to eliminate unhealthy feelings and unreleased resentments.

Since it served to promote growth and new life in relationships, this "bitching" brought good luck to all those who observed it.

Skira: Festival of Images

This festival was a communal celebration of art—a festival of image-making. This pagan feature has been much slandered and maligned as a worship of idols. In reality, Skira provided the community with impetus to create sacred artistic statues, usually images of Athena, out of gypsum. The gypsum, being snow white, represented mystical purity. The artwork done by the worshiper represented devout concentration and meditation on the Goddess. The finished work became a prayer offering to the Mother, carried in public by the artist. It is said that even such powerful men as Theseus carried gypsum statues during Skira.

Modern efforts by scientists to uncover the past have yielded an overwhelming number of these pagan images, most of which are female in form. These are a testament to the votive artwork of the people, and some of these statues now sit in museums, proclaiming the validity of a religion that embodies creativity as a form of worship.

Haloa: Festival of Free Speech

When Mother Nature was ready with her grapes, the Day of Cutting of the Wines was celebrated with Mysteries of Demeter, Kore, and the Son of the Goddess, Dionysus. The pomp and circumstance included carrying first fruits through the streets of the city for good luck before offering them at Demeter's grove. After the Cutting of the Wines there was a communal dance on the "Threshing Floors," doubly used for cleaning grains and, in honor of the Grain Giver, dancing, sporting and playing games. Special prowess was displayed, ritual showing off took place, and the general good humor of the people abounded.

After everybody was warm and high on the new wine, it was believed that purification from troubles could be achieved on many levels. Young people flirted with each other, and loudness and laughter were not frowned upon even by early sleepers. This was a pagan custom nobody wanted to change. Dancers came out to perform exhausting feats. The next day there were more local athletic events, during which men lifted logs and huge stones or even carts. Women cooked sumptuous feasts, flirted, and danced with each other in circle dances of the earth.

English archeologist Jane Harrison found Haloa celebrated in the midwinter season and later taken over completely by Dionysus. This, according to Harrison, was due to the incoming god of the patriarchs, and his coming was a two-edged sword. On the one hand, worshipping Dionysus enabled women's mysteries to thrive into patriarchal times, with the worship of the god as hermaphrodite—both male and female in one form. This allowed the Meneads, in particular, to accompany him where no men were allowed. On the more negative side, however, the festival was officially shifted from harvest time to midwinter in Greece, and completely assigned to a male god who, as time went by, shed more and more of his female characteristics and traits. But Dionysus, as the son of the Earth Mother, remained closest to having matriarchal status despite the efforts of the patriarchs to modify him.

Haloa remained completely dominated by priestesses, women descended from the Meneads. Hierophants were not allowed to offer sacrifices, and there was no blood offering or killing of animals. Grains, barley, honey cakes and the first fruits of the harvest were offered at the communal feasts. We know this from the record of an ancient scandal, related by Demosthanes. He tells of a Hierophant who was cursed by a community because he dared to make a burned flesh offering on the altar of the ashara in the court of Eleusias: "It was not lawful on that day to sacrifice an animal victim and the sacrifice was not his business but that of a priestess."

A newly-discovered scholia from Lucian revealed a full account of Haloa, casting a new aspect to the festival. The women celebrated Haloa alone in order that they might have free speech: What an ingenious religious impulse! The sacred symbols of both sexes were handled and exhibited, the priestesses whispered into the ears of the women, and they whispered to each other things they were never permitted to utter at any other time, to the horror of men. Quips and jests flew on Haloa. At the end of this festival there was a giant banquet. The recorder states: "Much wine was set out and the tables were full of all the foods that are yielded by land and sea, save only those that are prohibited by the Mysteries: I mean the pomegranates and the apple and domestic fowls, eggs and red sea mullet and black-tail and crayfish and shark."

What was in abundance on those festival tables was varied and interesting—cakes shaped as female and male sexual organs (still seen in European bakeries), crepes filled with cream, diamond-shaped cookies with red raspberry filling inside. But in all of this, the flesh of animals was not eaten or desired. That particular custom was brought in later by Achaeans, who overran the gentle land of the Palasgians.

Eleusinian Mysteries: Festival of the Return of the Daughter

The most famous and revered seat of Goddess worship was in Eleusias, and although the rituals became polluted with Dionysian mysteries during patriarchal rule (as a way to survive), the splendor and prestige attached to this holy place remained. Thus, we have an idea of what the matriarchal mysteries were. The Eleusinian Rites began on September 13 and continued for the rest of the month.

New initiates were assembled on September 15 and a cry, "To the sea, ye mystics!" heralded a banishing procession on the 16th, when all concerned went to the sea for a purifying bath. For their part, community members took piglets and images sacred to Demeter with them to be bathed as well. (Note: Piglets were so important to Eleusinians for acting out Demetrian customs that when they were allowed to mint their own coin, about 350-327 BC, they chose an image of the piglet standing on a spray of ivy. The other side of the coin showed the Goddess Demeter and Her Snake, seated upon Her throne with the Wheel of Fortune.)

There were different rites for the children. Nymphs passed through fire for purification, followed by a mock fight, throwing stones at each other or wrestling. On the night of the 19th or 20th, all purified mystics made a procession back to the temples, where they were now fit to handle the sacra and holy foods.

An inscription from the fifth century BC reads:

> *Let the Hierophant and the Torchbearer command that the Hellenes should offer first fruits of their crops in accordance with ancient usage. To those who do these things, there shall be many good things, both fine and abundant crops; whoever of them do not injure the Athenians or the city of Athens or the two Goddesses.*

And elsewhere:

> *I fasted, I drank the kykeon, I took from the chest, I put back into the basket, and from the basket into the chest.*

These cryptic lines describe what the mystics did in their rituals, without telling us too much, since they were sworn to secrecy. For ancient people, this needed no explanation since everybody knew what was in the basket and understood what kykeon was.

The fasting is an obvious act of purification, sometimes accompanied by an herbal laxative (still used in some so-called primitive societies). After this, kykeon, a souplike mixture of vegetables and barley mixed with pale honey, onion, and Pramnian wine, was drunk. Some of this mixture was also poured out onto the ground as a libation for Demeter, but only before the wine was added.

"I took from the chest," refers to the sacra, which could have been tokens of good luck such as a ball, a symbol of the Wheel of Life; a cone for fertility, symbolizing of virile manhood; a mirror for self-knowledge. Today there are covens that still use a mirror, given to new initiates with this command: "Look therein and see. Thou art Goddess."

"I put back into the basket," means that's where one put the first fruits one brought. The basket held loaves of bread and other good food, and the offerings were placed there.

"From the basket into the chest," simply refers to the completion of another cycle of life. One takes something from one place and replaces it in kind again, so that more can grow. The celebrant might have put grains back into the chest for the next year's harvest. Even a few grains would have done it in token, in the belief that ritualistically, it was done. Since there were very important moments in the social lives of the people, things that were placed back into the chest could have been personal spells, art, sacred images of the Goddess, clay or stone representations of sacred symbols, or healing prayers.

The Mysteries were not uniform, varying as rituals do today. Another version of the just-mentioned rite was: "I ate from the timbrel, I drank from the cymbal, I carried the kernos, I passed beneath the pastos." These were the words pronounced by other participants in the Mysteries.

The kernos was an agricultural tool, a winnowing fan that separated the grain from the dirt and dust, purifying it. It was also a vessel containing many smaller bowls, all set in a triple circle. In each bowl there was some natural product: white poppies, wheat, barley, pulse, vetch, ochroi, lentils. These things were carried by the celebrants, who "tasted from the timbrels" and then "drank from the cymbals," which were used to play music with as well. The pastos was a white umbrella that was often used for petitions for blessings from the Sky Mother. It was raised for the celebrant to stand under, with its four-pointed covering directing petitions to the four corners of the universe.

Mysteries were never quite confined to Demeter and Kore alone. Other goddesses had their rites performed as well (Ino, Hecate), and other male gods were added later (Hermes, Dionysus). In general, Mysteries such as these were "rites in which certain sacra are exhibited, which could not safely be seen by the worshiper until she had undergone purification."

Chapter 5

The Goddess
and the God

Love: Understanding the true being of Aphrodite

The Goddess of Love is the only aspect of the Goddess that has not been totally discarded, even though She has been negatively regarded and severely misunderstood. The Goddess of Love represents both beauty and wisdom and is the second aspect of the Triad. It is possible that this particular aspect of the Goddess survived patriarchy because of Her ability to bear children and Her relatively easy accessibility as a tool for men's pleasure.

In truth, the Goddess of Love is the Great Mother. It is Her seasonal condition to procreate, after which She bathes in water to regain her virginity. In mythological terms, childbearing never impairs or impedes the Lady's independence. The matriarchal Aphrodite always stood proudly naked, gently pointing out Her genitals as the Source of Life. She was muscular, strong and dignified, with no coyness or submission evident in either Her gestures or facial expressions.

The Goddess of Love has many names, the most important of which are those connecting Her to the water element, because all organic life depends upon it. Thus, She is known as Aphrodite, Marianna, La Mer, Mary, Themis, Marina, Tiamat, Ua Zit, and Wrushemu, to mention a few. Her favorite name is Isis, Who defines Herself as "She Who binds hearts together." Notice that She does not mention sexual preference. She does not bind men with women exclusively, because a genitalia philosophy has no part in Her law or worship. Isis speaks to the hearts of people and generous play is Her favorite pastime.

All women served in the temples of the Goddess of Love. Priestesses who chose to live in the temples worshipped Her as Queen of Heaven by extending Her life-giving powers to impotent men. These Holy Women were violently attacked by the emerging Levite priests as prostitutes, a deliberately demeaning epithet. Offspring of the qadishtu (Holy Women) inherited their property and name. It was not unusual for many generations of temple "family" to serve as Priestesses of the Lady.

This practice of "lying" with various men as an extension of life-giving Mother was the greatest obstacle facing the new patrilineal system because paternity was not at all important to the qadishtu. When asked who had

156

"fathered" their children, they simply asserted that "All," or "Pan" was the father (referring to all that is male in Nature). Eventually, these women were murdered by Levite-incited riots, an early common way of committing matricide.

The sacred ritual of mating with members of the opposite sex did not exclude from worship the practice of pleasuring among women. Lesbian sexual practices were employed to dispel evil, to heal and prophesy, to make rain, and to raise any kind of energy necessary at a given time.

The Ancient Ones believed that a nation could experience serious difficulties (droughts, plagues, and other disasters) if the queens and princesses did not "loosen their girdles" for Aphrodite. One story is told of Theseus, whose mother was a royal princess. She went to the temple one night to serve the Goddess of Love as her oracle had said. In the temple she lay with a "sacred stranger" who turned out to be the King of Athens. Apparently it was possible to pull a few strings in royal service to the Goddess of Love, and parents of the women serving in the temple may have secretly prearranged meetings with particular "sacred strangers."

Sacred sexual practices included one known as "displaying," which was part of the sacred marriage ritual, performed by the queen and her consort for the good of the people and crops. On the first night that the queen and consort made love to each other, the royal bedroom was filled with officials and clergy, ready to pull the bed curtains in order to "display" evidence of the love-making ritual—namely, the man and woman locked in coitus. If the queen was happy and her cries of pleasure were loud and clear, this was considered a good omen and the consort was then treated as a king. If the queen was not pleased, the consort was considered an omen of bad luck, to be treated accordingly. Sexual loving was obviously not a private affair, but a healthy and positive public solicitation of good karma for an entire community.

Women on the island of Lesbos worshipped Aphrodite quite differently. This serves to give us a clue as to the variety and wealth of religious thought concerning sex. Sappho and her women worshipped Aphrodite in the form of creativity. They wrote love songs, carefully decorated their heads (dark-haired women wore purple ribbons while blondes wore flowers) and bodies, and spent their time and energy in constant scholarly pursuit of beauty and creativity within their lifestyle. Thus they worshipped their Queen of Love.

Of course, there were other schools of thought on the subject. The Goddess, Whose worship was strongest in Her birthplace of Cyprus, was worshipped with extensive sexual orgies. These celebrations took place on certain religious holy days such as Midsummer Night. The priestesses there would eat the sacred *Amanita muscaria* for increased muscular strength and then dance and revel in good feelings for three days and nights.

157

These sexual rituals took place in the woods and forests, wild places where all sexes knew no bounds.

Remnants of these ancient sacred sexual rituals are today known as "the Great Rite," which is a very tame version of the original. It still is a challenging concept to most women in the Craft, although the pagan men get great mileage out of it, since during such rites the women change partners and lie with more than one man during a night. These celebrations have their origins in the earth religions and sympathetic magic.

Lovemaking energies do indeed stimulate the growth of crops. This was the reason that the Priestesses of Aphrodite would invite a fraternity of men to lie with them in the fresh furrows of the earth. Today, using the latest scientific machinery in their laboratories, men are measuring the vibrations and sounds of plant life. The result? Lovemaking does make a plant excited, and does stimulate its growth.

Indian pagan customs include one particular tradition regarding the healing energy of sex. A sick person is placed in a room where a young couple mate, in the belief that it will improve the condition of the ill person. More and more people today are able to relate sexual energy to healing energy.

Love and this business of "binding hearts together" are still the most desperately desired of human endeavors, and the most taxing. Patriarchs continue to pompously strut their power, but it is Aphrodite Who has every human animal by the heartstrings. She can be a harsh and exacting mistress when Her rules are not obeyed, and not one of us goes through this life without feeling Her touch.

Mythically, the Goddess of Love is not meant to make commitments, sign contracts, marry or raise children, but to *play*. If there are any attempts to place any reins upon Her at all, She flees. People continue to be love-starved because Aphrodite is misunderstood. She is kidnaped in order to breed the patriarchy into power, but She comes back in Her own might with a mixed-breed of children of war, incurable venereal diseases, the rebellion of women (Her most faithful expression), and porno-literature wars. Her symbol, the Sacred Yoni, is blacked out even on the front pages of the most blatant sex-exploitative magazines. Men unconsciously still feel that to degrade the Goddess is bad luck. In this, at least, they are right.

In the Women's Movement, we have woven different webs of Aphrodite (She is a great weaver, like Her sacred animal, the spider) in the form of sisterly love. Aphrodite loves equality and loves Her womenfolk. She is not quite as fond of fighting as Her sister, Artemis; thus, women attracted to the worship of Aphrodite are not the fiercest fighters in our revolution. The Lady even finds it necessary periodically to sink productions of sisterly endeavor, playing Her game of yoni-power politics. Because our headset is still based on a scarcity-conscious politic, Aphrodite is often able to cut right to the quick. "There is only one lover for me." "It is much too hard to risk another love." "There is not enough love to go around." "He loves me, he can't possibly love somebody else as well."Inner monologues such as these are the trickiest to overcome for women not in touch with the abundance and bounty of lovely Aphrodite.

The movement of women toward liberation has nourished a variety of loving. We have massages—Love heals. We have discussion groups—Love touches. We have radical therapies—Love grows. We have spirituality, prophecy, and ESP—Love communicates. We have creativity and art—Love shows. We have our casualties—Love frees. We have information sharing through publications and many points of view—Love feeds. We have fun— Love plays, and to stay well, She must.

Aphrodite, the Oldest of the Mothers—the original door for existence—must be cultivated consciously in order to gain Her rich blessings. Witches perform love spells upon themselves, and sometimes upon each other, but we do not think that then we control the Lady Who plays. The most difficult spell in the world is to light Her fire, because that is something to which She attends personally. She operates always from a prosperity consciousness. She is Lady Plenty of the Flowing Emotions, defiantly enduring amid patriarchal abuse, and delightfully unpredictable in matriarchal temperament. She is being awakened more and more by the women, and love is changing as a result, like never before. Indeed, the only chance for humanity is the absolute return of the Goddess of Love, sweet Aphrodite, She Who binds hearts together and then plays.

Aradia: The Female Avatar

It was a time of crisis on the earth, long after the Beginning Birth of all things. The few rich oppressed the many poor, making them slaves and causing them to suffer in poverty and toil in wretchedness. The lives of the poor were so hard and miserable that they cried out piteously for help.

So the Great Goddess became concerned for the poor children of the earth, and decreed that Aradia be spirit-born and sent to earth as a mortal. The Mothers of Aradia were the Sun and Moon, who multiplied and divided their Goddess-essence, weaving Aradia from the vibrations of the luminaries of the solar system surrounding earth. Manifest as a human woman, the Divine Daughter, Aradia, became Goddess incarnate.

Descended to earth, Aradia (Herodius) became the first of the witches. Spirit-born and mortal-manifest, Aradia fulfilled her Divine Purpose: to teach the oppressed the Craft of the Wicca. She dwelt among the people and carefully taught them the Mysteries and Secret Arts by which they could free themselves from their oppressors.

It was to the poor that Aradia came; it was to the oppressed that the Craft was given. In the Schools of Aradia were taught the arts of herbal cures and poisons; of ritual and prophecy and enchantment; of music, poetry, and dance; of the knowledge and secrets of power. Aradia taught the ways of freedom to the slaves of the rich.

When She had given the children of the Goddess all the techniques of the Craft, Aradia returned to Her Mothers, leaving behind a ''Charge'' to be used to call on Her in need. Having all this, the bound were to be bound no more.

Nineteenth-century witches, as evidenced by writings contained in Charles Leland's *Gospel of Witches*, were militant about their liberation. Preferring lives of nomadic lawlessness to slavery and imprisonment, these ''folk'' were taught how to poison their oppressors, how to cause them to die in their own palaces. Rich landowners were to be hexed with ruination of crops, with tempests, lightning, terrible thunder, and hail. Additionally, the ''new'' priests of the male-god trinity were called devils and denounced as perpetrators of evil by the witches of the nineteenth century. Aradia promised revenge and rectification.

Feminist witchcraft at the end of the twentieth century is a tame echo of the rage hidden behind the history of the survival of the witches: the rage expressed in ancient poetry of slaves, rage about conditions so horrifying that violent reprisal was warranted. And all the rage in the face of witch murders that were barely ending when Maddalena collected the folklore of Aradia for Leland. The religious war of the rich upon the poor, the direct attacks of the male-god priests against the Goddess-worshipping witches, has only been transmuted—it has not gone away.

Conditions that originally prompted the sending of the Female Avatar, Aradia, are true today just as they were a century ago. As the daughter of Diana, Moon Goddess and Mighty Huntress of the Night, Aradia's purpose on earth was to teach. She did not marry, breed, or consort with men during the time She dwelt among the oppressed of the earth. Witches of the Dianic tradition follow Her example, concentrating on the development of psychic powers, the teaching of the skills of the Craft, the recovery of Women's Mysteries, and the perpetuation of women's natural connection to the Female Life Force. We believe that Aradia, Goddess incarnate, is all women who come to a female-identified consciousness, to a social consciousness of the oppression of everything female, and who dare to fight for their own rights and the rights of their children.

The God

Hoof and horn, hoof and horn
All that dies shall be reborn...

Corn and grain, corn and grain
All that falls will rise again...

Who is the gentle god Pan? Why is he endowed with hoofs? Why does he wear horns? Why is he naked?

In a society where the male is totally socialized, made antiseptic with clothes, deodorants, designer hairdos, cosmetics and designer smells, it's hard to visualize the Male Principle of the Universe. What does manhood mean without violence or competition?

We pondered these heady questions, and more, in my workshops from the Midwest to Alaska to the Bay Area.

There was a time when the great god Pan was pronounced dead. In the Mediterranean countries, where worshipping him was once at its most vigorous, the last of his altar's fires went out. However, today I think he is being reborn again, returning to a more understanding world that has missed his presence.

Pan (meaning all that is male in the universe) wore many names: Bacchus, Dionysus, Zagreus, Jove, Dios, Satyr, to list a few. He is the essence of manhood; he is wild, he has a glint in his eye. Today we would label him crazy. He is utterly free. He is not, however, dangerous to women. He is not a rapist, not a violent male. He likes to party, he enjoys sex, and

is ever ready for it. He is not possessive (his women are free, too). He wears horns not because he is cuckolded, which is silly, but because he represents the animal kingdom as well, hoofs, hairiness, nakedness and all.

Pan loves solitude, too. I talked to modern men who have seen him around lakes, in the Rocky Mountains, in the deserts. The great god Pan is here.

Pan appears to groups who call him. His power, a sexual love of life, permeates us all when we feel good. Women contain him; he is within us just as he is within men. Pan is a dancer, a magician, a healer, a priest. He is the son of the Earth Mother. He has total communication with all that is natural. As Dionysus, he could make water spring from rocks. As Pan, he could dance wildly for five days and nights without stopping to rest. As Jove, he initiated young men into men's mysteries, wielded thunder, became the fire god.

Pan is bisexual or pan-sexual. Shame had to be invented in order to get rid of all this freedom he bestowed on his followers. Guilt had to be invented and his people threatened with eternal fires to make them give up their wildness, their freedoms. Pan, finally, is the divine artist, Bacchus, who attends festivals and plays the Pan pipes, which gladdens all who hear.

Christians took one look at him and decided he was going to be the bad guy, their devil, to offset their good guy, Jesus, in his long white nightgown. Jesus only related to his mother, Mary, and to Mary Magdalene. The Virgin and the whore, because of Jesus, became archetypes for women to emulate. Women still suffer from this stifling, unnatural demand.

Pan, on the other hand, related to women as women. As full, complete, sexual beings, in all walks of life, including the priesthood. Chastity didn't have any particular merit with Pan since he didn't seek to control women's sexuality. He paid a high price for his feminism. His image was stolen and made into that of the devil incarnate.

Many other elements went into the creation of the devil. For example, the sun goddess Lucina herself, masculinized and renamed Lucifer. A fallen angel, the fallen goddess of the sun.

But back to Pan. Was he warlike? There are no accounts that he ever fought with anyone or attacked anyone. Apparently he didn't need violence to assert his masculinity.

Was he competitive? There were songfests, dance contests, wrestling matches and foot races dedicated to him. You see, Pan had nothing to prove. He didn't have to work on his manhood; he felt secure about it.

His priests sacrificed a goat to him, especially mountain goats, but they also ate them so it wasn't cruel or wasteful.

Negative sides to Pan? Yes, there were some. Obsessions, for example, with sex. He had the energy to obsess about people, issues and feelings. Lack of good judgment and poor decisions can result from that. Overindulgence is another flaw that can appear when the Pan energy is misused. The pleasure principle, without moderation, can get out of hand, as people have found out. Only Pan can indulge himself without paying a price.

Pan, our dear pagan god, however, is not evil. What is evil? Look at Mother Nature. She creates disasters and destruction, but she is not considered evil. Human beings have created much evil in the world, most of which were acts against Mother Nature. It really boils down to waste. In nature, everything has a purpose, wisdom, a place. There is no displacement of materials. No design to hurt, only to continue.

Ultimately, my definition of evil is ignorance. Everybody has a little of it. Ignorance coupled with the power to act usually winds up hurting people and the environment; hence it is evil.

The Sacred Sons

Throughout the evolution of Goddess-worship there has been one extraordinary feature setting us apart from other religions—we are inclusive. This inclusivity is inherent in a religion that reveres the Mother rather than the Father. A superficial scrutiny might lead one to believe that this is simply a matter of opposites. However, upon examination we rediscover the major fact of the miracle that is birth: It is the Mother who carries the children. Female and male in the Mother's womb; female and male in Her religion as well.

There are only two kinds of people in the world: mothers and their children. Mothers can give life to each other as well as to men, who are not able to do the same for themselves. This constitutes a dependency upon the Female Life Force for life renewed, and was accepted naturally in ancient times by our ancient forebears as a sacred gift of the Goddess. In patriarchal times this sacred gift was turned against women, and used to force them to give up roles of independence and power.

All male-god worshipping religions which have no life force represented in the form of the Female Principle of the Universe end up being exclusive. They become essentially male, homosocial edifices without the redeeming quality of nurturing, maternal love.

Jehovah is an archetype. He is jealous and possessive, ordering the wholesale slaughter of those who worship other gods. He is nothing more nor less than a warrior. This is not a religion; it is militarism incorporated into moral law by force, not as a result of the inherent, collective feelings of those whose lives are controlled by it. Only the Mother inherently knows how to include; Her male children must exercise conscious, religious efforts to do so.

Today in the Craft, male witches are often referred to as "warlocks." This word literally means "traitor." As such it is unacceptable. Our sons, our Sacred Children, were not raised as traitors, but as lovers of life, lovers of women, brothers or lovers to each other, helpers of the Goddess in the most essential skill of nurturing. Sons of the mothers in Goddess-worship became Kouretes, members of the Goddess-serving priesthood.

The word "Kouretes" actually means "adult male" or "son of Cronos." Cronos was an old god, consort to the Goddess Rhea. Even in the old time it was Rhea who had to protect newborns from the wrath of Kronos, who would eat the young if left to himself. This myth symbolized a very real danger: If nurturance were left solely to men, without the civilizing influence of the Goddess, they would destroy each other and their sons as well. In today's society, men have made enough bad decisions to threaten to destroy life on our planet. Kouretes were sons saved by the Goddess, becoming Her helpers to save the rest. They, as protectors and teachers of the young, constitute the Sacred Priesthood of the Mother Goddess.

Hymn of the Kouretes

This ritual poetry was left to us in slabs of stone found in the Minoan strata of the Birth Cave of Dikte in Crete. Although it is incomplete, we can receive from it an impression of the sacred priesthood of Rhea. This is not directed to the Olympian Zeus, as some would have us believe, for Zeus had not yet been invented. This hymn celebrates the Kouros, the Kronian—the Sacred Child of the Goddess.

> *Io, Kouros, most great, I give Thee hail! Kronian, Lord of all that is wet and gleaming, Thou art come at the head of Thy Daimones to Dikte for the year. Oh, march and rejoice in the dance and the song!*
>
> *That we make to Thee with harps and pipes mingled together, and sing as we come to stand at Thy well-faced altar.*
>
> *Io, Kouros, most great...*
>
> *For here the shielded Nurturers took Thee, a child immortal, away from Rhea, and with noise of beating feet hid Thee away.*
>
> *Io, Kouros, most great...*
>
> *And the Horai began to be fruitful, year by year, and Dikte to possess mankind, and all wild living things were held about by Wealth-loving Peace.*

Io, Kouros, most great...
  To us also leap for full jars, and leap for fleecy flocks,
and leap for fields of fruit and for hives to bring increase.
Io, Kouros, most great...
  Leap for our cities and leap for our seaborne ships, and
leap for our young citizens, and for goodly Themis!

This hymn of the Kouretes begins with the invocation of the god, who is given various titles and instructions as to how and where to come. The Kouretes performing this invocation are matriarchal witches. They are not calling on an Olympian god, nor are they petitioning a "Father." Rather, they are commanding spirits to appear! This is internalized to the point that, by doing the commanding, they activate this spirit because they ARE the spirit. Judeo-Christians, by comparison, dare not claim they are gods in and of themselves, but place "Him" as Spirit-Creator somewhere "out there," rather than within.

The concept of a Sacred Son, held dear in both religions, is here discussed from a Mother's point of view. This is Kouretes, "Young-man-just-come-to-maturity," "the greatest of Youth." This is the independent Male principle, no longer the babe in arms found (along with the Great Mother) in religious symbology. This Kouretes is a role model for matriarchal manhood.

In the hymn, the Kouretes as high officials are always attended by Daimones—attendants, escorts. They were attached only to matrilineal male gods, never to the Olympians who overthrew them. This feature changed during patriarchal times, because it is a very pagan concept of religious impulse, originating in Goddess-worship. Patriarchal male gods such as Zeus and Jehovah do not have attendants, although Jesus does. Had Jesus been a real Kouretes, he would have had thirteen female Meneads (Holy Women) in attendance, instead of twelve men.

The Kouretes themselves are escorts and attendants, as we see in an account by Strabo: "These attendants are Kouretes. They are certain young men who perform armed movements accompanied by dancing." This would lead us to conclude that those forms of folk dance in which weapons are used (sword dancing, shield dancing, even the great Russian leaping dances) are living legacies of the culture of the Kouretes.

As their theme, Kouretes act out the protection of the young as their sacred duty to Rhea, Mother Goddess. However, with the forced advocacy of patriarchy upon them, their theme had to change accordingly: hence, the "Birth of Zeus," "Birth of Dionysus" or "Zagreus."

Rhea (The Flow), the Universal Mother, is in labor. She attempts to conceal this fact from Cronos, because he eats his children out of jealousy of his power and his access to Rhea. Rhea seeks Her Kouretes for help, and they loudly clank their protective armor over Her, successfully concealing Her cries. As soon as She delivers Her baby, She turns it over to the Kouretes for further protection. What an obvious, clear ritual for men's maturity!

Elsewhere, other features are attached to this ritual. In one instance, the Titans come in with white-chalked faces to take away the Child and destroy him. They succeed in this, the Child dying or becoming a Titan himself. Later the Kouretes, with the help of the Goddess Rhea, bring the Child back to life, and the whole story repeats. The birth-death-rebirth cycle is thus ritualized.

The story of the male principle in Nature is pretty much the same. Here the Goddess gives birth to a son who grows to manhood and becomes Her lover. He then impregnates Her and dies at the end of the year, only to be reborn of Her again the next Spring. This weaving in and out of the cycle of rebirth is symbolized with the Kouretes, where the nurturing aspect of the male is made sacred.

Because the Kouretes claimed a specialized religious function, that of fertilizing the Goddess-incarnate, they were called upon to serve as her orgiastic priests. This meant gathering with the ritual priestesses during the appropriate seasons (Spring-Midsummer, September) and mating with them in the freshly furrowed fields belonging to the community.

As Divine Lovers and Sacred Sons, as participants and co-actors with the Great Goddess in Her circle of rebirth, the Kouretes were also of practical service as medicine men, seers, metallurgical craftsmen, inventors, builders, beekeepers and shieldmakers. As medicine men, they never handled altar offerings, but dealt mainly with the spiritual/physical growth of the community's male population. They even presided over the births of infants, assuring them safe entrance into the world, serving as nourishers and nurse-midwives as well. They lived together, worshipped Pan and considered themselves sons and lovers of the Goddess. They were the initiators of heroes, the magical men of the community. However, at their most Divine, the Kouretes were always priests of the Life Force, performers of initiations and practitioners of nurturance. Clearly, they were magicians, adept in their craft.

Themes of the Kouretes repeat: Mother-saving-Son. Often the Son was represented by a stone thrown from heaven between the lightning and the thunder. This stone was a Holy of Holies, and was used in certain rituals to purify new initiates. The image of this thunder is that of initiation. The sound of the thunder is a magical vibration of awesome power, associated with the Mountain Goddesses: Kybele, Rhea, Bendis, Kotys. The initiation by thunder of the Kouretes indicates that they became members of fraternities dedicated to the continuing worship of Rhea.

The symbols of the Kouretes include the sacred cup, in which herbs were brewed for curing; the shield of protection; the thundering sounds made with instruments for a religious purification from fear through the energy of sound.

There were stages between the sacred priesthoods of the Goddess and the patriarchal "priesthoods" to come. The Kouretes did not die quickly or easily. First, they changed all the names, and the Sacred Child became Dionysus. Thus the ecstasy essential to the Kouretes and all such religious priesthoods could survive into the grim patriarchal period where the warlike lifestyle led, predictably, to the practice of a scarcity-conscious, poverty-ridden society.

In a way, the cults of Dionysus were heavily interwoven with both mythological worlds—matriarchal elements stirred the soul of the times, even though the messages were consistently, conscientiously and forcibly suppressed. Dionysus became a hit in the all-new pantheon of powers. As a hermaphrodite, Dionysus could even be admitted into some circles dominated by Dianics. His attendants were the Satyrs (Priests of Pan) and Kouretes. Dionysus kept matriarchal company.

During the same period, the Dianic priestesses found it necessary to become "attendants" to Dionysus in name, so they could continue to practice, in modified form, such traditional rituals as dancing on the mountaintops. Worship was so much a part of the lifestyle, permeating every moment, that it controlled the total culture. What we currently recognize as "culture" originated from religious instincts—from worship—and it continues to control our lives.

Another stage through which the Kouretes (korybantes) passed was becoming "Bacchi." As counterparts of the Bacchanalians, they recede more and more into secret fraternities, usually living together in the seclusion of the mountains.

The birth-theme so prominently featured in Kouretes' ceremonies was the first to be co-opted by the male god Zeus, who declares "Come, o Dithyrambos, enter this, my male womb." This obvious attempt to transform the initiation rites into rituals of male mutual loyalty (to the exclusion of the Female Principle of the Universe) failed miserably. True priests hid away in the wild rather than change their matriarchal worship of Mother and Child.

> *There is one pure stream*
> *My days have run, the Servant I*
> *Initiate of Idaen Jove*
> *Where midnight Zagreus roves, I rove*
> *I have endured his thunder cry*

Fulfilled his red and bleeding feasts
Held the Great Mother's mountain flame
Enhallowed I and named by name
A Bacchos of the mailed priests

Robed in pure white I have borne me clean
From men's pained birth and coffined clay
And exiled from my lips always
Touch of all meat where life has been

Invocation of the Kouretes

Come O Dithyrambos, Bacchos, come...
Bromios, come, and coming with thee bring
Holy hours of thy own holy spring.
Evoe, Bacchos! Hail, Paen, Hail!
Whom in sacred Thebes, the Mother fair
She thy one once Zeus to bear.
All the stars danced for joy
Mirth of mortals hailed thee, Bacchos, at thy birth!

In the tradition of the Kouretes, the male principle is reborn from the Mother into new life. This is a birth-song, celebrating the Mother and Her full-grown Child. The Korybantes lead the chariot of the Goddess and this man-child across the heavens (this is the horned Selene and Her Son). The Satyrs, brothers to Kouretes, performed the Goddess revelries as well, as fertility aspects of Nature. The Dithyrambs brought in the aspect of the sacred Bull, Male Principle of the Universe. It was the custom of the Dithyrambs to lead young men (the sons) through town with a live, festively garlanded bull. All these acts were culturally diverse, yet focused on the same sacred image—that of Mother and Child.

In springtime, O Dionysus
To Thy holy temple come
To Elis with Thy Graces
Rushing with Thy bull foot come
Noble Bull, Noble Bull!

Dionysus is a god of the people. As intruder into Hellenism, he represents the early religious instincts, now revived. He is a gentle New Year God, who loves wine, women, men and the dance. His worshipers were a very distinguished people of the mountains (Thrace, for the most part), not easily conquered. The satyrs, traditionally worshipers of a Nature-god, were the attendants of Dionysus. It is only later, in the patriarchal Greek mythology, that satyrs become horse-men, beings to be feared "because they rape women."

The Greeks were very quick with mythological justifications for their own hatred and prejudice against the conquered people of the Old Order. As happens in cultural wars, the conquered people were told to reject all that was natural and familiar to them, and to adopt the "new" ways and religion. They were made to feel evil, dangerous, ugly, lacking breeding, but in possession of superior (unnatural) sexual passion and prowess. They were forced to deny their religion, and fear what was once beloved. Satyrs were represented as fearsome in order to prevent the instant alignment of women's sympathies with the Nature religions. It didn't work. Dionysus was recognized by women as the brilliant Son of the Mother, and the women attached themselves readily to his worship, taking all manner of unheard-of privileges as the "mad" Meneads.

The women who followed the gentle, fun-loving, nature god Dionysus were not, strictly speaking, the counterparts of Satyrs, since the latter implies a strictly gender code—Thracian Mountain Men. Meneads were neighborhood priestesses, whose task was to foster good luck in the community and officiate at community events. Meneads altered their consciousness in their nature-worshipping rituals. The resulting Sacred Madness, achieved not necessarily with wine but with *Amanita muscaria*, fermented mare's milk, ivy, laurel leaves, peyote and the like, was intended to commune with Nature, to see Her secrets and be one with Her. Other names for these "mad" priestesses were Mimallones, Klodones, Bassadirs, Thyiads, Potniades, names attached as well to the Goddesses worshipped in religious ecstasy. Artemis is thus addressed: "Menead, Thyiad, Phoibad, Lyssad; Mad One, Rushing One, Inspired One, Raging One."

Patriarchs found it difficult to digest the "excesses" of these women, to tolerate their freedom to rave and go out at night. For the most part they allowed it only because of the threat of magical and powerful retribution if any man interfered with Women's Mysteries. One legend tells how Penteus, ruler of an entire kingdom, was literally torn apart by his own mother and sisters because he violated the sacredness of the women's worship. This served well in the culture, to remind the new patriarchs that to pry into women's affairs always angers the Female Principle, causing her to turn into Her Death-aspect, regardless of the rank or status of the offender.

Plutarch relates a story he heard from Klea, a High Priestess of Delphi. There was a religious war against the nature religions, and the tyrants had taken sacred Delphi. Attendants of Dionysus, the Meneads, wandered into the city following their revels, not knowing the city was in enemy hands. They went to the temple as usual to rest and sleep. Still under the influence of their ritual, and unaware of danger, the Meneads slept, while the women of the city formed a circle of protection around them. In silence, the women of the circle waited until the Meneads woke, then attended to their needs and guided them stealthily out of the city to escape detection by the soldiers and patriarchs. What a testimony this is to women's solidarity and women's religion!

The Salii

Just as the Kouretes served Rhea with their shields, so did the initiates of the Salii serve their Goddess, Themis. Tradition called for initiates into the Salii to leap a ritual fire and roll flaming wheels down mountainsides. The priestesses of Themis attended to each boy by anointing his five points, thus assuring him of immortality. Then he was presented with his toga, shield and weapon, and received into the fraternity of the Salii. These rites were held at a crossroads, sacred to Hecate. Rites of passage were held in the sacred temples of Hecate, because of Her importance as a Goddess of Transformation.

The Salii were considered aspects of the sun, sun-priests serving the Triple Moon Goddess. Salii priesthoods performed the rituals during the month of March because, although the Romans devoted this month to Mars, it was previously and more traditionally held to be the month for the Rite of Passage for Boys. On March 17, Roman boys assumed the ritual toga according to traditions much more ancient than Hellenism.

On March 14 there was a festival known as the Mamuralia, followed by the festival of Anna Perenna the next day. This is the time of the year when the cycle of seasons is at the point of completion and continuation: the Vernal Equinox. During the festival of Mamuralia, an old man of the community would dress in goatskins and be led through the town while members of the community ritually purified him with white rods, symbolically driving him away. This signified an exorcism of the past and the physical and psychic opening up of the new. As soon as the Old Year had been expelled, the New Year God was introduced and everyone rejoiced, wishing each other a healthy and happy new year.

More traditionally, this Old Year was a woman rather than a man. Her name was Anna, and she would pass herself off as a young bride in order to marry the New Year God. She is, like the Male Principle, representative of both the old and the new. In any case, there was much merrymaking during these festivities surrounding Nature's "Holy Marriage."

Sons and Lovers

The Son and Lover of the Goddess bears thousands of names, very much like his Mother and Bride. He is called Dionysus, Bacchos, Iacchos, Bassareus, Euios, Zagreus, Thyoneus, Braites, Lenaios, Eleutherus,

Bromios, Pan, The Horned One. These names evolved from religious cries into proper names.

Today we associate Dionysus with the wine god, but the other names point to a more distant past, that of the Earth-born Demetrius, son of Demeter. The intoxicant of which he is made Lord is one of barley, oats and wheat, rather than grapes, which were used much later. He is earth-born rather than sky-born, and he is of the Mother rather than the latecomer father. The name Braites is of great importance, since it means "grain prepared for the making of the beer braisyum," a kind of heady mead, drunk in worship of the Earth. To degrade this ancient earth-god, the Sacred Son, into a god of drunkenness from alcohol is to discount the Force as manifest in the Male Principle of the Universe.

> *Appear, appear, whatso thy shape or name*
> *O Mountain Bull, Snake of the Hundred Heads*
> *Lion of burning flame!*
> *O God, O Beast, O Mystery, come!*

The Male Principle, examined far enough back into antiquity, reveals itself as "lord of all that is wet and gleaming," and when evoked by the ancient priestesses, emerges out of the ocean as the Sacred Bull. This basic interpretation is complicated by the fact that the Mother is the Waters, and the Moon Goddess governs all that is "wet and gleaming." She regulates the weather and causes the Ocean to heave with tidal ebb and flow.

The image of the Bull echoes the crescent horns of the Moon, and male and female worshipers often wore horns during rituals in honor of this connection—a symbol of the origin of the Moon Goddess and Her Son. The image of the same Bull as representative of the ancient Goddess religions is clearly mentioned in the Bible when Moses finds the people making a "golden calf" and dancing around it. Thus we see the Old Religion that he was trying so hard to defeat in order to bring in the completely monotheistic worship of the "Father."

The essence of the male god is his transformation. He is born of Semele, the Earth, Moon and Water Triad, and as a child is worshipped by his mother. In this newborn nature, he is also worshipped by priestesses of the Goddess. (Does this remind you of Christmas?) Through many names he grows to Manhood and fertilizes the Mother, who remains eternally Virgin. When he becomes old he is driven out or ritualistically torn asunder, and recycled back into the Life Force, out of which he rises again every Spring as the Beloved Child. This is the magic of rebirth. The ecstasy of life is the form of worship of this very ancient Son.

> *O glad, glad on the Mountains*
> *To swoon in the race outworn*

When the Holy fawn skin clings
And all else sweeps away
To the joy of the quick red fountains
The blood of the hill goat torn
The glory of the wild beast ravenings
Where the hilltop catches the day
To the Phrygian, Lydian mountains
'Tis Bromius leads the way!

The Spell to the Force: Self-Dedication for Young Men

Time: New Moon

Take the white candle and carve your name on it with something sharp. A rose thorn is traditional, but a clean nail or a personal pen will do. Take some aluminum foil and make a clean place in it for the white candle and the blessing incense. Pick a lovely flower in which you see the Life Force manifest, and place it in the middle, representing the Force.

Now anoint your candle with Protection oil, moving your hands always upward from the middle and anointing the two ends as well. Light the blessing incense on the charcoal and when the air is filled with the smell and your mind is clear of fear, say:

> *Appear, appear whatso your shape or name O Mountain*
> *bull, Snake of the Hundred Heads! Lion of the Burning*
> *Flame! O Force, Pan, Beast, Mystery, come!*

Light your white candle, saying:

> *Blessed be thou creature of fire!*

Watch the flames a while, then say:

> *Happy am I, on the weary sea*
> *Who has fled the tempest and won haven.*
> *Happy whoso has risen free*
> *Above his striving! Happy I, with the Mother's blessings!*

Take oil and anoint your forehead: *Blessed is my mind to think of life.*
Anoint your lips: *Blessed are my lips to speak of life!*
Anoint your breast: *Blessed is my breast formed in strength and beauty!*
Anoint your genital area: *Blessed are my genitals, to stimulate life!*
Anoint your feet: *Blessed are my feet to walk in Your path!*
When you have performed this, let the candle burn all the way down. You may burn more incense if you like, or save it for other spells. Go home; now it is done. You are now a Kouretes.

It is best to perform this in the woods or outside if you can wrestle some privacy for yourself.

Acceptance of Manhood

(This ritual is based on *Prologomena to the Study of Greek Religion* by Jane Ellen Harrison, 1922.)

Enter the temple purified. The teacher guide, Kouretes or Bacchoi, anoints the young men's foreheads with gypsum and pitch, erasing the past and making them pure souls again. As the men enter from the corner of the South, the direction of passions and summertime of life, they are dressed in armor, wearing shields of leather or metal. Bronze is traditional. On the shields are the symbols of Kouretes: the snake of rebirth, the gorgon head to frighten away evil spirits, and inscriptions of power. In other cases, the family seal may be drawn on the shield.

The Kouretes priests invoke the four corners of the universe with their athalmes pointed toward the appropriate watchtower. In the corner of the North, Rhea, the Great Mother, is seated dressed in rich russet robes. She holds a newborn baby, which can be male or female. It will be the baby's initiation as well, as the magical wealth is bestowed upon the earth through the Goddess's womb.

The Kouretes points to the East and says:

> *Hail to thee, powers of the East! All Wise Eagle, Great Ruler of Tempest, be present, we pray thee, and guard this circle from all perils approaching from the East. Universal Soul, Force of all beginnings, bless this circle here with your powers of protection!*

The Kouretes, pointing his athalme to the South, says:

> *Hail to thee, powers of the South! Mighty Lion, fiery one, passionate one, come bless this circle from all peril approaching from the South! Bless the sons who are gathered here to initiate the Kouretes!*

The Kouretes says to the West:

> *Hail to thee, powers of the West! Mighty Serpent, ruler of the Deep! Guardian of the bitter sea, come and protect us from all peril approaching from the West! Give us your blessing and knowledge as thy gift!*

The Kouretes calls to the North:

> *Hail to thee, powers of the North! Black Bull, Mighty Horned One! Ruler of the Mountains and the Valleys, and*

*all that lies beneath them! Protect us from all peril
approaching from the North! Bless us with your strength,
that all of us will grow!*

When they are finished, they salute the High Priestess, who stands
up and acknowledges their salutes. Holding the child aloft with both hands,
she addresses them:

*The Goddess Demeter welcomes her sons. Lead in now the
Protectors of life.*

The Kouretes of the North says:

*Demeter brought forth Pluto, and kindly was the birth of
him whose way is on the sea and all over the earth. Happy,
happy is the mortal who thus meets him as he goes. For
his hands are full of blessings, and his treasure overflows.*

The Kouretes approaches the child, sprinkling barley and wheat at the
Goddess's feet, and throwing them at the sky as feeding the birds. The
Kouretes of the South says:

*But the Child was hunted much too soon. Angry flew the
news that Demeter's son will one day inherit the bountiful
earth, and the new Gods seized him and tried to cause him
harm. They searched for him under every bush, saying
"Baby, baby, don't cry."*

The Kouretes act out the scene. They encircle the Goddess, holding
their shields aloft. The Goddess approaches each corner with the baby,
hiding him under her clothing. She shouts NO! to each corner as the
appropriate Kouretes tries to take the child from her.

To accompany this, drums and cymbals should be played, and the
Kouretes of the watchtowers should get into playing the "villains," shouting
things like "Give me the child, and I will eat it right away!" or "Give
me the child, and I will send it to war!" or "Give me the child, and I
will make it toil and toil and toil!" or "Give me the child, and I will make
it sick with poisons!"

After one such round, the Goddess Demeter returns to her throne
and calls on the powers to help:

*Come, o Dithyramb, flowers of me, come, my children,
come! Come, o Kouretes, come o Bacchoi, come, Bromios,
come. And coming with thee, bring the holy hours of the
holy spring!*

The new Kouretes take the child gently from Demeter, saying:

Demeter, Earth Mother, all life originates from thee,
Semele, gift giver, bringer up of wealth and kin. We protect
thee from malice and destruction of mind and body. The
sacred child is well with us. We thunder our shields above!

They place the child on the ground, on a piece of silk, and begin the dance that looks like a wardance, imitating the defense they would put up if any danger approached. Here imagination can reign: sword dances of ethnic origin, wand dances, and leaps over the child and each other. While they are so occupied, the older Kouretes are placing toys into the child's reach: the cone for fertility, the rhombos (or Bull-Roarer) to invoke the rain, and the golden apples of Aphrodite for health and happiness.

The young Kouretes are preoccupied until it is too late. The old ones have taken the child and mimicked tearing him limb from limb.

To demonstrate this, the child is smeared with white gypsum and pitch, like the grownups, and Demeter receives him again, hiding him under the silk. She says:

The most important shortcoming of sons is hubris, excessive
pride. Vigilance must be where there was mirth alone.

The new Kouretes says: *"We hear you, Holy Mother!"*
Demeter says:

An important thing to remember is that rebirth comes
through understanding of the heart.

The new Kouretes says: *"We pledge ourselves to you, Holy Mother!"*
Kouretes: *"To be a Kouretes you must treasure life and the carriers of life, women."*
Youth: *"I have searched my heart. I pledge myself to life and the carriers of life, women."*
Kouretes: *"To be a Kouretes you must cooperate with your brothers. Pan is not violent. Pan is grace, songs and creativity."*
The rhombos is now twirled, the drums now drum, the silk is removed and the child is whole again! The Kouretes now lift the child on their shields and sing the ancient song of spring:

Io, Kouros, Most Great, I give thee hail! Kronios, Lord
of all that is wet and gleaming, thou art come at the head
of your sacred priests! To (place of the ceremony) for a year
and a day, oh, march and rejoice in the dance and song
that we make to thee with harps and pipes mingled together,
and sing as we come to a stand at your well-fenced altar.
For here the shielded Nurturers took thee, a child immortal,
from Rhea, and with noise and beating feet, hid thee away.

*Death powers found thee, and lured you away, and tore
you limb from limb with your mother's body bedecked in
pain, until you were all over the earth. But She of eternal
force made you whole again by the dawn of all dawns.*

And vigilance is bidden to us now,
And love is bidden to us now,
And honor is bidden to us now.

*And the Horai began to be fruitful year by year, and Dikte
to possess mankind, and all wild, living things were held
about by wealth-loving peace!*

*To us, leap for full jars, and leap for fleecy flocks, and
leap for fields of fruit, and for hives, bring increase!
Leap for our cities, and leap for our seaborne ships, and
leap for our young citizens, and for goodly Themis, justice
for all!*

After this ritual ends, the Kouretes kiss the Goddess on the cheek,
and she kisses them back. The four elders thank the spirits for participating
in the rite, and sound the gong. The last words are from Demeter. She says:

*I know you now as children no more; the Nurturers are
sacred, effective, and beloved by the gods.*

Acceptance of Matriarchal Manhood: Modern Ritual

You most likely don't have a temple for the Goddess in your neighborhood.
What to do? Mother and son need a new form of bonding as young man
and mother. This relationship is the basis of our society. If this is a positive
experience, fewer men will hate women. Today, all puberty rituals are done
by men for men, without women participating. They perform a "separation from the mother" ritual, not a young men's pledge as responsible adults
to create and protect life. They misunderstand the acceptance of manhood,
as if to be a man simply means rejecting his origins. Manhood means
acceptance of responsibility for Life. This has to be done with a woman
who represents the Force of Life. Cutting women out of manhood rituals
is like presenting apples without ever honoring the tree that brought them
forth. The tree and the apple forever have a deep connection of continuity.
In matriarchal rituals this is remembered again.

Time: During March after a New Moon.
Place: Indoors or outdoors. Since there is an honoring feast connected with
it, use your common sense and you will know where.
Celebrants: Mother and her son, family and friends, affinity group, tribe.

The group forms a circle and harmonizes with a deep humming, without straining, just like a beehive. Then the mother picks up her censer and goes around in the circle from the inside, smiling, welcoming the assembled friends. She has an opportunity to purify everybody with the mixture of fire, air and earth in the burner, as she lets the smoke enfold them. She puts down her censer. Everyone pays attention to her.

Mother:

> *We are gathered together here today in the name of Life.*
> *I want to present my son (name) to the community. He is*
> *(age, 12 to 40: Kouros means "flower of youth" and some*
> *people hold up better than others). He has grown into a*
> *fine young man. (Mother can make a short speech here*
> *if she likes about how she feels about the Goddess, her child,*
> *life in general.)*

Then an older man acting as Kouros steps out and calls the name of the young man, who then steps forward to face him.

Kouros: *"Are you prepared to accept manhood and what it means in life?"*

Young man: *"Yes, I have searched my heart. The child that I was is distant to me now. A new being is emerging from the child that I was."*

Kouros: *"Do you know the meaning of that emerging? It is the natural voice of Pan, the male principle of the Universe."*

A group of other youth comes and the young man joins them. Together they read the invocation to the Kouretes, the group and the young man answering each other.

Kouros: *"To be a Kouretes you must treasure Life and the carriers of Life, women."*

Young man: *"I have searched my heart. I pledge to life and the carriers of Life, women."*

Kouros: *"To be a Kouretes, you must cooperate with your brothers. Pan is not warlike. Pan is love."*

Young man: *"I have searched my heart. I pledge to seek a flow of cooperation and avoid aggression."*

When they finish, they leap, for the words call for it. At the end of this, the Kouretes face the mother as the young man says:

> *Thank you for the opportunity of my life. I knocked on the*
> *door and you let me in. I was hungry and you nourished*
> *me. I was lonely and you loved me. You are truly the God-*
> *dess manifest among us.*

Mother replies:

Farewell the child, who grew so well from my womb to
childhood. Welcome the young man who will return to me
as friend and ally in all Life's enterprise. (She presents
him with a ring.) Receive this ring as a reminder that while
you are gone, our connection forever remains.

This acceptance ring is a silver band. It can be thin or thick, as taste
and money allow. The silver is for the powers of the Moon, who controls
water's connection and life in general.

After this come more singing and much feasting. The mother is honored
along with her son.

Epilogue to the Kouretes

We received some complaints from Dianic sisters about changing our
manifesto slightly concerning men: "We are opposed to teaching our magic
and craft to men until the equality of the sexes is reality."

Dianic tradition is one of teaching, and from early times on we taught
both sexes of the young. In our manifesto we mean that we are not averse
to teaching parts of the usual craft curriculum to men, such as medicinal
herbology, because more healers means that we are all better off.
Philosophy is another craft that we would definitely teach both sexes, since
if there are more thinkers, there are more ideas. Dances, sports and songs
are other ways to spread Goddess consciousness without divulging Women's
Mysteries to men. But we would never teach ritual work to men, not even
after ERA is a reality.

Let me tell you a story. In 1980 I attended my first Pan Pagan festival.
Next to an emerald-colored lake in the Midwest, pagans were about to have
their first Women's Circle, an unheard-of experience for the dominating
duality traditions that assembled. The Goddess told me to get help to insure
the safety of the Women's Circle. I asked the gay men who called
themselves the Fairy Circle to station themselves around the Women's
Circle in a radius of forty-nine large steps and guard us, letting no man
pass their line.

This proved to be the best idea I'd had in a long time. As the beautiful
and moving Women's Circle got underway, with sixty-six priestesses participating, some kids hiding on the other side of the lake sighted us and
called their daddies. The daddies watched for an hour, working themselves
up to a white froth, then charged down on us with big rods, fully intending
to beat up the naked ladies who in their opinion were breaking God's law.

Instead, the Fairy Circle stopped them and dealt with their rage. From
the pagan side, a man who felt threatened when his wife and daughter

joined the Women's Circle came to disrupt us and pull out "his" women. The Fairy Circle stopped him as well, and we had a wonderful Dianic ritual in spite of all the ruffled male feathers.

So things are not as bleak as they used to be. There are natural allies to the Dianic Women. Nonhomophobic men who respect the Goddess and Her privacy and gay men who search for Her can act as temporary Dianic Priests and help the women guard their religious rituals. By the way, Dianic priests did exist, and their function was exactly that: to help the women create the circle, then leave and guard against other men.

This measure can be taken only when trustworthy men (only you know who they are) keep their backs turned to the Women's Circle and never look back, no matter what they might hear, while meditating on their own souls in the service of the Lady.

Chapter 6

Prophecy
Tarot, Runes, Astrology, Dreams, Reincarnation, Automatic Writing, Fortune Telling

Witches throughout the ages were involved in finding things out. My mother "read" palms, but she confided in me that she really just had to hold someone's hand, and the stories about that person came into her head; she merely repeated what she "heard." She taught me how to read cards. It was a deck of thirty-two suits, and had subtitles in four languages. Mother always knew what was going to happen.

I believe we all do. The outlines of our lives have definite cornerstones that are predestined, but we also have many choices. We all know before we reincarnate what it is we have come here to observe and manifest. The human organism must, and always does, block it out in order to survive the evolution of human life.

There are other forms of divination, such as the crystal ball, chicken bones, the *I Ching*. My favorite is the Tarot. I have read the Tarot since I was twenty-one. In February 1975, I was arrested for "fortune telling" to an undercover policewoman. I was tried in court in front of a full jury and convicted as a witch. I also had to post $2,500 bail, unheard of in such "crimes" as reading the Tarot. We appealed to the California Supreme Court to remove laws interfering with practices of the Craft. The Supreme Court struck down the law in 1985. However, here I will show you this subversive science, a feminist interpretation based on a lifetime of feedback.

The Tarot

As I said, my preferred means of divination is the Tarot deck, which I keep in a Hungarian hand-embroidered pagan folk-art cloth, red with golden edges. It is lined with silk, and I believe it was always meant to be a cards cloth and not the pillowcase I found it in. What I know about the origins of the Tarot comes from a story my mother told me, and since the patriarchy has no certainties, I will share it with you. Mother said it was originally designed about 2,300 years ago, when Alexander the "Great" burned down the matriarchal libraries. Scrolls of knowledge and ageless wisdom perished in the flames, especially at the largest library, in Alexandria. The existing scientists, partially matriarchal and partially (new) patriarchal, gathered at a conference to resurrect the living knowledge still in their heads. Being from different parts of the world, they had a language problem, so they devised the Tarot deck to communicate with each other through symbols they all had agreed upon. Thus, the human condition was reduced into twenty-one forces, and later enlarged to seventy-eight pictures.

The Tarot, I suspect, comes from matriarchal origins. Those scientists didn't just make up a brand new thing in the world of divination.

The European fortune-telling deck has thirty-two cards, and though I prefer the more sophisticated Tarot deck, I use it according to European rules. My mother taught the system to me. She had learned it from an old witch, Victoria, who worked for my mother's house in rural Hungary.

I consider the Tarot primarily a tool for meditation. The Tree of Life, which is the format of the basic layout, comes from ageless times past, going back to early portrayals of the Goddess as a tree. The Tree of Life is a primary symbol of human evolution and understanding of the universe.

My method: Sit squarely and comfortably with the friend whose cards you are reading, and both of you anoint your hands with a purifying oil; Van-Van, sandalwood and myrrh are great.

I don't talk about anyone in particular while I shuffle the cards, but center myself—focus on the other person. I cut the cards with the left hand, toward the left, three times. Therefore, the first time, cut the deck in half, pick up the pile that is remaining, and place it on top of the other. Do this three times; think each time of inspiration from the Nymph, Maiden, and Crone.

Then I give the cards to the other person. She also shuffles them until they are "cooked" (feel right), and cuts the cards with the left toward the left three times, thinking about inspiration from the Nymph, Maiden, and Crone.

Now I place the cards down, one at a time. The top (first) card is always the significator. Instead of choosing a card ahead of time, the querist "creates" (through inspirational shuffling) her significator, which is indicative of her general condition. You can check this for validation with her. If the first card doesn't seem accurate, try the next card as a most discernible force around her. If it still cannot be validated, **give up the reading**. There is no shame in saying that this is the wrong time. This hardly ever happens; in my years of Tarot work, it has only happened to me twice. (Once the fate of the mother showed up instead of the daughter.)

Assuming things go smoothly, proceed to lay out the Tree of Life.

The cards can show up in different positions, which make their meaning different. I interpret reversed cards the same way as upright cards. You have to use your native wit to discern the meaning that is attached to the cards themselves, and to the position they show up in. The two together, synthesized, make a good reader.

The significator (1) indicates the general condition, also the middle of the heart, of the querist. Covering it in the next position is the force presently acting upon the matter (2). The next card's position is crossing the previous one, meaning the obstacle (3) in front of the querist. Often the covering card and the obstacle card reinforce each other; in that case, note the strength it creates. These three cards constitute the "heart of the matter."

Above this is the general sky under which all other forces are occurring (4). This position influences all other cards and indicates an overall direction of the person's endeavors.

Under the significator card is the position of the "root" of the person's life (5)—often something that has already happened, which laid the foundation for the present situation. For example, it often shows sorrows of the past that the person has not yet forgotten, not present troubles.

The past position is to the left (6). It must be the immediate past, not years ago. To the right (of the significator, as the one to the left) is the immediate future card (7).

On the far right, moving one by one, lay out four cards, beginning at the bottom. First is the "self" card (8)—what the self is concerned with. This card is a reflection, and often is a correlation to the significator card. They must make logical sense together, since they are part of the same personality.

Next is the "house" (9) where the querist lives—forces around her in her dwelling.

Above that is the card of "hopes and fears" (10): not necessarily fact, unless in the major arcana, in which case it is.

The last card is the "outcome" (11), which shows a resolving of the conflicts. If it is a small arcana card, search through the next three cards for a major arcana to see a direction predestined for the end results. If you don't have it within three cards, forget it; just know the matter is going to take time.

Patterns are interwoven throughout the layouts. Look for the "reality level." This is in the middle section, including the heart, the past, the future, the house, and the fears. See the directions of how the person deals with difficulties. Look for courses of future behavior. Count aces; count queens. Take stock of the spread before you open your mouth at all.

Small arcana are choices; major arcana are predestined forces, which are karma.

Count up the suits to discover the person's "theme" of life. Any predominant suit indicates the theme of the reading.

WANDS: work, growth, energy
CUPS: pleasure, emotions

SWORDS: struggle, challenge
PENTACLES: money, earthly subsistence and concerns

Next, look at the numbers. If any repeat three times, that is like an extra card. Check your numerology; take it seriously. Themes sometimes emerge through the numbers.

Remember, the cards are to show wisdom. Never let a querist leave without hope. There is no ultimately bad spread. A good reader searches for the silver linings, and helps the querist face bad times with good counseling.

The Meaning of the Cards (as I have found them)

Magician: Psychic talent for whoever gets this card. If the person is a witch, it is a good time to perform magical deeds, to direct psychic force. Matriarchal values overcome the patriarchy.

The High Priestess: Moral clarity; knowing what is good for you and what isn't. Teachings from the Goddess through dreams; could be the influence of a spiritual woman upon the querist; Dianic teachings (moon orientation in spirituality), woman orientation, often turning to the Movement. The querist takes herself more seriously and trusts her own judgment.

The Empress: This is the second aspect of the great goddess, Venus-Aphrodite, Lady of Plenty. She brings love relationships, but also fertility of ideas, inventions. She never comes up empty-handed; enough to eat and boogie with. She brings woman consciousness, generosity, sunny outlook, good feeling. If opposed with swords, she wins in the end.

The Emperor: Preoccupation with power, and where power comes from; how to attain it, how to use it. The type of power this card represents, if matriarchal power, is a blending of spirituality with action. People who get this card are attracted to going back to school, getting diplomas, getting into public life, running for office, etc.

The Hierophant: A most patriarchal uptight card; legal dealings, not necessarily court dealings; signing one's name to legal documents as an equal partner; sometimes marriage, but only in a captive sense; not a good influence on women's lives.

The Lovers: Overcoming all obstacles; harmony, even new love affairs. This is a love relationship among equals.

The Chariot: Balanced force within; going into battle with the promise of victory. Sagittarius energies; go-and-get-it activities. Centered people get this card. Individualism.

Strength: This is Cybele, the goddess; queen of summer. She tames wild lions, controls situations with mind strength, influence; especially good accord when patriarchy is the enemy. This card promises that all will-powered events will come true.

The Hermit: This is a Virgo card and should have a woman pictured. Spiritual guidance from within, manifested in attractions and repulsions. Go with the inner force; heavy dreams when this card comes. Analysis, creativity, insights, leadership. The effects can last a long time.

Wheel of Fortune: Karmic turn for the better; new and lucky direction of one's life, predestined good events; just lie back and let things happen. The moves here are large: direction changes, goal changes, even devotion changes, but all for the better.

Justice: Here is the Goddess Themis as a dispenser of justice. Note that her eyes are not blindfolded. Conclusions to large matters; legal dealings, definitely in court; end of a struggle; a just outcome. She ends disputes and uncertainties.

The Hanged Man: This is an inside card. The mind undergoes a major turnabout, as much as 180 degrees. It happens when the last piece of the puzzle floats in, and the woman has a "click" experience, clarified suddenly. It always precedes a major outside change; we all need these illuminations.

Death: This means death of an old way, a lifestyle, an old relationship. Only when swords surround this card does it mean death of a person. Note the dawn in the image. It is a two-way street; something dies, something is born. It usually means a radical change in one's life, even moving away from old environments. It is a positive card; women should not fear it.

Temperance: Supreme psychic management, good space, the ability to be active and balance within. Creativity, great for artists and priestesses.

The Devil: Bondage and ignorance. Often this means a voluntary bondage. Oppressive places of work are signified with this card. Also, long and uninteresting study at school—anything that takes your energies away without replenishing you. It can mean sickness, being bedridden, being emotionally bound to someone who doesn't care for you, an obsession. Only through investigation of the matter and careful decision can this be done away with. Ignorance has to be dispersed about the matter.

The Tower: A card of revolution. The cast in one's life is changing; a new act is coming in, with new players. Great upheaval, even violence. Watch out and keep calm. Life must take turns like that, for the sake of evolution. Travel is the easiest way to fulfill it.

The Star: This is Hathor, the goddess of change. The space this card brings is of spiritual and intellectual questing, creativity, and hope. This

186

is a time when the querist can influence other people, so it is a control card as well. It belongs to Aquarius, the waterbearer, and note that is is a woman. Another name for this priestess is Urania.

The Moon: The Goddess as Diana is manifested here. A very important card; it means voluntary change. It is a slow change compared to the Tower, and it comes from the querist's own decision. It can occur as character change; the person decides to incorporate new traits or discard some old ones. It is evolving a new personality from the present one, much as the dog evolved from the wolf, by human effort. It is a card of the moon, Cancer; it sometimes means hidden enemies if its position is surrounded with swords. Otherwise, it is a positive card of evolution.

The Sun: A card of Leo and the Sun Goddess Bast. A card of travel and liberation. It often means a new phase, starting with heightened consciousness; freedom is gained through understanding. When this card is in the layout, things also work out in business matters. Note the sunflowers in the picture. Sunflowers always mean business success.

Judgment: This is a card of rebirth and all that goes with it. It is sometimes confusing and even painful, but rebirth is worth it. Denied, dead parts of the personality surface and demand development. Forgotten dreams are activated; forgotten goals get the spotlight again. Memories are stirred; go along with it. The end result is a new, improved you.

The Fool: This card is great for artists. Creative thought forms are about to materialize. Outrageous plans and lofty ideas can now be created for future realities. It is not so good for noncreative people; it means foolishness.

The World: The dance of life is portrayed here, the Goddess Diana in the green circle of life. This card means affixing your name to creations (art, writing, etc.). It also means travel. A very creative space; try to use it for communication and yes, do travel with it.

As you may have noticed, my interpretations are markedly different from most books published about the major arcana. I often find patriarchal bias incorporated, especially where matriarchal images are involved. Distinctly positive cards like the Moon, Star, Hermit, High Priestess and others are interpreted as reversals.

Minor Arcana
Wands

The Wands are work-oriented and growth-oriented cards.

Queen: Magnetic personality, psychic, growth-related. It also means business success. If it is a woman in someone's life, it is an impressive, energetic woman. The Queen means the soul of the personality.

King: Fiery person, female or male; the ego part of the personality. The process of working, expenditure of energy. If it is a man in someone's life, it is an honest one, growth connected.

Knight: Change of residence, departures; the body of the personality. A young person in motion. Depending on where you find this card, the person is either coming toward the querist or leaving.

Page: Questing person; a youth, could be female or male; the spirit of the personality. A fiery young one, may be a new lover. Journey, though not a big one.

Ten: Oppression, too many responsibilities. Must have change of attitude to cope. Think more, sweat less.

Nine: Preparedness, suspicion. Having what it takes, awaiting trouble. Work on self-confidence.

Eight: Business, many goals, all approaching the goal, but not there yet. A busy lifestyle.

Seven: Courage. Feeling under siege but holding up admirably. Negotiations, bartering. Keep it up and you will have success.

Six: Victory after strife, moral victory most of all. Completion of a project where the querist has invested a lot of energy. Payoff time. Expressing oneself through a group.

Five: Strife, adversities, fights with people, competition for power.

Four: Completed work, time for celebration. Great accomplishment, prosperity, increase, felicity, beauty.

Three: Established strength, enterprise, trade. Management job, responsibility.

Two: Strength, dominion. Contemplation of worldly consciousness. Large plans.

One (Ace): A new beginning, workwise. The querist has planted a new project, which is a fortunate move. Promise of growth, creation. The beginning of enterprises; new job, new school, new relationships.

Cups

Queen: Good luck woman, loving, psychic, pleasurable, intelligent. A beloved woman, possible water sign. Artistic.

King: Calm person, but could be violent within, psychic, emotional authority. If it is a woman, it is the ego of the woman (male-identified dyke). Holds pleasure for you.

Knight: Arrival of good news; often arrival of a new lover.

Page: Beloved youth, female or male. Holds pleasure for the querist.

Ten: Happy twosome situation, contentment, children, happy home. Well-balanced couple-life.

Nine: Physical and mental well-being. The "sitting pretty" of the Tarot. All is well.

Eight: Turning one's back to success (major concern, basic old goal) in order to search for something higher. Letting go. It is a lucky card, inspired by the full moon.

Seven: Illusory success. A good card only if you are a witch who has thrown spells (spells deal with illusions). Otherwise, it shows many goals that can waste a lot of your time. Make a list of the goals and sleep with it under your pillow for three days. Each morning, try to eliminate one, and arrange your priorities that day. On the final day, the last selection is where you should direct your energy.

Six: Steady growth. Emotional growth in relationships, based on past memories. Memories become strength for you.

Five: Emotional depression. Feeling of loss of pleasure. Disappointment in love (refocus if you can on the two cups unspilled).

Four: Indecision about where your pleasures come from. Emotional blah; you have choices but none of them turn you on.

Three: The three goddesses, Graces, toasting a good turn in your life. Happy issue. Much partying. Whoopee.

Two: This is an egalitarian loving relationship. It is based on exchanging pleasures. Harmony, partnership, love.

One (Ace): This is a fertility card. Watch out if you are relating to men. Otherwise, it means happy space. Your cup overfloweth. You just fell in love. New emotional beginning.

Swords

Swords are associated with air thoughts, mental activities. More than that, swords are struggles.

Queen: This is a woman who has just been separated from her lover; a widow, a divorcee. Air-sign woman. Matriarch with might. She initiates with ideas. A good fighter.

King: Authoritative man, egoist, possessive and jealous. Bad news if it is a lover. Holds pain for you. Sometimes it means patriarchy itself, institutions that oppress the querist.

Knight: Attack, vengeance, aggressive space and activities.

Page: Initiating new projects, if it is the querist. It can also mean spying, overseeing, vigilance. If it is a youth in someone's life, it is a feisty one.

Ten: End of an illusion. Ignorance is dispersing about an obsession. Death of a pet project. Defeat. Focus on the dispersal of darkness.

Nine: Loss and tears. May be sickness. Depression.

Eight: Crisis. Not necessarily disaster, but things are at a point where they can swing either way. Indecision.

Seven: Victory after a struggle; won most, lost some. Learning new tricks.

Six: Leaving a bad space; heading for a new life but not quite knowing what it is going to be like. Sometimes a journey by water. However, it is really an inner card. Pain is left behind.

Five: Slander and disgrace. Being put down. Defeat and fights.

Four: Rest from strife, but not forgetting the pain. Deep mind is plotting the future through daydreaming.

Three: A broken heart, loss of a loved one. Separation without recourse. Sadness.

Two: Indecision, equal forces pull the querist each way. Ignorance about the issue.

One (Ace): Conquest, overcoming opponents. An aggressive new beginning in projects, with the promise of victory.

Pentacles

Pentacles are associated with earth signs. They signify subsistence and money.

Queen: Moody, intelligent, soulful woman. Money connected. May be an earth sign. She is helpful and charming.

King: Money-connected man. Also, business where employment takes place. Encounter with a reliable male.

Knight: Steady income, reliable friend, contemplation on material matters.

Page: Reconsideration, contemplation, studies, intelligent quest. A youth, female or male. Serious, quiet, studious.

Ten: Interaction with many different age levels; much society, family. It also means prosperity and material gain.

Nine: Perfected work; a healer is pictured, so it is a creative work that this woman does. Leisure and relaxation after accomplishment (you are golden).

Eight: Crisis. Unfulfilled success, but almost there. An artist building up her credits, acquiring new skills, employment. A good money card, show approach to goal.

Seven: Delay of money. Relax, it's only temporary.

Six: Unexpected money, gifts, lucky financial chances. You can even gamble now.

Five: Adaptation to new and difficult circumstances; learning a new way of existence. Also loneliness.

Four: Material possessions, property, serious money. Security, material success.

Three: Money for creative work as well as prestige. Also, building the church of the Goddess.

Two: Two major sources of income juggled. Two projects balanced against each other. The artist's way of making a living. It is a good card; existence with boredom.

One (Ace): New financial beginning. Unexpected money. New enterprise with others' help; you don't have to do it alone. Speedy intelligence.

The Runes

The Runic alphabet is all that is left of the ancient Wiccan language that existed in the time of the matriarchies; the language died out during the Burning Times, when witches were afraid to speak it. The symbols vary somewhat from culture to culture; the ones given here are Theban. It is good to write your witch's name on your tools in them; if you are really ambitious, try keeping your personal *Feminist Book of Lights and Shadows* in them. The Runes are part of our Her-itage, and we should use them whenever possible.

Astrological Birth Control

The theory of astrological birth control is based on the position of the moon in relation to the sun (phase of the moon) at the time of the woman's birth. Each month when the moon returns to the birth phase position, a second fertile period is possible. For instance, if a woman is born exactly at the first quarter, she can be fertile at each first quarter moon, as well as the usual fertile period regulated by the menstrual cycle.

To determine the moon phase at your birth, you can either consult a fairly simple paperback, *Natural Birth Control*, by the Aquarian Research Foundation, and compute your own, or have an astrologer do it for you. When you have the exact phase, you can use the information to get pregnant or prevent pregnancy.

To use as birth control, abstain from sexual intercourse for three and a half days before the exact phase and one-half day after. This must be used in addition to the rhythm method, abstaining five to seven days in the middle of the menstrual cycle, depending on the regularity of your individual cycle. These two times may coincide, lessening the total time of abstention. An alternative to abstention is to use a mechanical method of birth control during the fertile period.

To become pregnant, intercourse should take place twenty-four hours before the birth phase. If a woman was born during the period of time from ten hours before to ten hours after the full moon, she should avoid conceiving during full moon. Children conceived at that time too often have birth defects.

If a baby girl is desired, abstain altogether during the menstrual cycle fertile period and attempt to conceive on alternate months when the birth phase moon is in a feminine sign (Taurus, Cancer, Virgo, Scorpio, Capricorn, Pisces) of the tropical zodiac. This information is difficult to obtain for yourself, but an astrologist can compute it easily.

For a boy, the moon should be in the alternate signs.

The Sidereal Zodiac
by Anna Kria

Astrology had its beginnings when people watched the never-ending motion of the heavens. The sky must have provided the ancients with a drama that kept them fascinated, and sometimes fearful, because they kept careful records of events as they related to the motions of the planets, the eclipses of the sun and moon, and the steady, stately flow of the sun on its celestial path.

But now the sky is dimmed by the lights of modern civilization and many generations of astrologers have failed to notice that their tables of planetary positions no longer match the actuality of the sky. This separation occurred when the incorrect assumption was made that the sun is always at zero degrees of Aries on the Vernal Equinox. This is not true because of the wobble, like a top, in the spin of the earth. The sun's position has been slowly receding through the sign Pisces, and in 2376 AD it will enter Aquarius, thus beginning the long-heralded Aquarian Age.

The non-sky-gazing astrologers use the Tropical Zodiac, while those who place the planets in the constellations where they actually appear use the Sidereal Zodiac. Since 221 AD, when the two zodiacs coincided, there has been a precession of approximately twenty-four and one-half degrees, which means that only those people born in the last six days of their tropical signs have their true sun sign. Everyone else has the preceding sign.

As a woman with a kinship to those wise women of the past who know when to plant, bless, curse, and harvest by our moon, I practice the astrology that is based on the reality of the sky as they knew it.

Using Dreams:
Practical Steps to Dream Interpetation
by Annu

Scientific research has shown that everyone dreams every night. All dreams have meaning, and the meaning is helpful to the dreamer. The purpose here is to give the beginner a practical step-by-step guide to dream interpretation.

Materials Needed

To study dreams seriously, it helps to compile a personal dream symbol dictionary. Some use a looseleaf notebook with alphabetical index; others prefer a card file. A spiral notebook is good for writing down dreams because it's flat and easy to handle, but any notebook will do. Keep a pen or pencil handy. A flashlight is good for writing at night. Improvise in any way you wish.

How to Remember Dreams

Keep the writing materials by the bed so you can record your dreams. The average person forgets her dreams within eight minutes of awakening. Use autosuggestion to facilitate recall; before you fall asleep, repeat to yourself three times, ''I will remember my dreams when I awake in the morning.'' It also helps to write key symbols immediately upon awakening so the dream pictures do not slip away unrecorded. You may not have time to record the whole dream; reviewing key symbols usually aids recall.

How to Record Dreams

It helps to date the pages the night before and plan to record your dreams on one page, leaving the facing page free to work on analysis. It's best not to mix them because interpretations may change. Record the dream as fully as possible, including such details as people, setting, actions, emotions, colors, numbers and impressions. What seems an unimportant detail could be a valuable clue to the dream's meaning. Honesty is essential when you record your dreams.

The following step is of utmost importance: At the top of the page, briefly record important events of the day before, the main strands of thought, activities and efforts. Dreams are usually a comment on what we have recently been doing, thinking and meditating about during conscious activity. Dream content is usually limited by the dreamer's conscious focus, and the information and guidance which the individual can use constructively. Rest and physical fitness affect the recall, scope, depth and clarity of dreams.

How to Interpret Dreams

Underline important symbols, then list them separately and interpret them. Each symbol may have several meanings. One of them will best fit the context of the dream. If you can't think of anything related to the symbol, ask yourself how you would describe the symbol to somebody else, then record that description as a possible meaning. Simple dictionary definitions sometimes provide an answer. Books and symbol dictionaries also provide a takeoff point to interpretation, keeping in mind that a symbol's meaning may be different for each of us.

When you find a meaning that fits the context of the dream, record it in your dream dictionary or file. You are then on your way to learning the language of symbolism.

Another approach to finding a dream's meaning is to ask the purpose of the dream as a whole: "What is the dream trying to tell me?" This may be fairly obvious, even when you don't understand every symbol in the dream. Take a second look; a dream's meaning is sometimes not as clear as you first think.

When you find the meaning of one dream in one night, it may be a clue to other dreams of the same night, which often relate to different aspects of the same subject as do successive acts in a play. To find the meanings of the symbols, think back to the previous day. The dream is frequently related to yesterday's events unless, as sometimes happens, it is a precognitive or ESP-type dream.

Almost always, each symbol in the dream represents an aspect of ourselves and our personal situation. The main character of the dream is usually the dreamer.

Remembering what you did or thought about the day before, and knowing that each symbol is an aspect of the self, help unlock the meaning of the dream. We invent our dreams as messages from self to self, and we are each our best interpreter. Remember, you're interpreting the dreamer, not just the dream, to best determine what is most important in a particular dream.

An element of practicality is necessary for interpretation. A word of caution: If a dream seems to tell you to do something you know is not constructive, you have probably misinterpreted the dream. Dreams can be helpful tools only if interpreted correctly.

How to Obtain Guidance From Dreams

Dreams can guide and help you after you have set goals and ideals for your life. Obviously, these goals and ideals must be chosen carefully. Your choices may not coincide with those set for you by parents, mate or friends. Choices usually require serious self-examination. If you have made a bad choice, your dream will surely tell you. If you're wandering through life without a goal, your dreams will wander right along with you.

Meditation, practiced regularly, will clear the channels to receive guidance. Working to apply all the advice available in your daily life is a helpful goal.

It also helps to go over dreams occasionally after you are separated in time and emotion from them; things sometimes are seen more clearly in retrospect. Symbols gain depth, and meanings become apparent. It is best to record symbol definitions as you go along day by day in your dream dictionary. Most dreams have meaning on several levels at once, and should be interpreted accordingly. Determine the purpose of the dream.

Another aid to dream interpretation is a close friend or a group. Sometimes others know us better than we know ourselves. We may not think that we have the unused talent or characteristic that a dream says we have, but our friends know we do. A friend or group helps, not by forcing interpretations on the dreamer, but by asking what the dreamer thinks a symbol or dream could mean. The dreamer has the last word.

There are different types of dream imagery. First there is the nonsensical or meaningless imagery which occurs when the body is reacting to its own stresses during non-rapid eye movement sleep. In general, such imagery relates to problems of diet, fever or endocrine secretions. Second, there is literal imagery. Much dreaming serves the same ends as conscious thought, solving problems of outward circumstance. A third type of dream imagery is pictured and acted out. For instance, feet and shoes have to do with one's "footing" in what is being attempted. Dreams of mouth and teeth relate to what we say, such as speech that harms others. A fourth type of imagery is personal figures. Every dream has its own personal symbols loaded with shades of displayed meaning. A fifth type is exhibited as archetypal symbols that arise from mythology and ancient history, and are found almost universally.

Dreams are intended to change, as well as inform, the dreamer.

Testing the Validity of Dream Interpretation

First, there is comparison with your dream record. An interpretation which fits together all the parts of the dream is usually right. If a theme is repeated often, the dreamer probably hasn't yet gotten the point or acted on it. If a theme shows a progression in successive dreams, the dreamer may conclude that she is interpreting the dream material correctly and is making progress on the forces producing the dreams. The dreamer may validate interpretations; for instance, a feeling of release from inner panic may signal a sound interpretation. A test of your life might be how grumpy you are. Examine the quality of your relationships.

The Growth Conclusion Method

This method allows you to bypass analysis. The experienced user of dreams is aware that dreams can be consciously directed to resolve conflicts. In a variation of this, something that bothers the dreamer is identified. The dreamer then directs that particular dream to come to a growth conclusion constructed by the conscious mind.

In general, dreams tailor their content to what the dreamer can effectively handle. Dreams are usually self-regulatory and self-correcting.

As you study to interpret and apply your dreams, you may wish to consult some helpful books, such as *The Revelation*, published by A.R.E. with information on the seven gland centers; works of Carl G. Jung; or books on numerology, color, Tarot and astrology.

Information for this article was gathered from the A.R.E. Journal, *Volume III Number 5, November 1972. Also, thanks to Jim Richard, who put together an article from his personal experience and information gleaned from books and articles.*

Past Lives

I had no idea how much money people pay to hear stories of their past lives until I met somebody from the Scientology crowd. They held little tin cans and "measured" the excitement of the person if the past life was not "clear"; for a hundred dollars a session you could squeeze the tin cans in your hands and spin stories about who you used to be. Others read past lives and blamed a lot of their present problems on them. Still others actually can relax you, helping you have a journey into the old deja vu.

As a Dianic Witch living in the end of the 20th century, I am not surprised that people like to spend time someplace that's better and more decorative than our Here and Now. Still I resist the seduction. Who knows? I could be very much at home as a priestess in an old Sumerian temple, but does that help me create a ritual to march to with ten thousand women against violence on the streets? Yes, it does, but that's not my focus; I concentrate on the march.

The Here and Now is our challenge, the only part in our lives where we are called upon to act as Goddess. Everything else has been done. We have the past for a reason: IT IS GONE. The Here and Now will soon become the past and while we dwelled in our fantasies we missed making our mark on the moment. The moment of birth and death are karmic dates set before entering this existence; the middle—the growth, the changes, the richness of our experience—is the reason for living.

So don't let anybody make you believe that we are on this earth to suffer, to toil and put up with oppression, on the grounds that after we die we'll be taken care of. I have even heard a TV preacher say he wanted to come right back after the end of the world and help Jesus make his kingdom by becoming Mayor of Honolulu. Notice how the end of the world and life after death included a fully-staffed patriarchy and its good jobs intact! Obviously the Christian vision of the end of the world means further male domination of politics and TV. Woe!

This existence is most precious and important as far as we the living are concerned. Our two million years of development gave us a nice vehicle—a body—to be Goddess in. We have free will; we live in a politically interesting (if often painful and terrifying) time; we have challenge. To be Goddess means acting out our fate, participating actively in our welfare, not following a trail of tears but devoting ourselves to holistic existence. We women must work consciously to approve of ourselves, to do the best we can to turn our lifetimes into meaningful role models for our future daughters.

The religion of the Goddess glorifies the living. How much time is appropriate to spend researching our past? If there is a burning desire in your heart to go through centuries of hidden memories, and it is so compelling that you feel there is something in it for you, go ahead! If you are not intense about it, don't waste too much time, but use your resources for improving your lot in the living body you inhabit now.

Reincarnation Theories

Reincarnation in the different lifetimes is like putting new beads upon a necklace. And you know how different necklaces can be. There is the necklace that features all the same matched pearls. Then there are those with one pearl and one glass bead; some have apple seeds and some have acorns. Lifetimes can be that varied. There may be no connection between them other than the impulse to live, the thread upon which the beads are strung. Do we need to know what other beads are on the thread? Not really. If we did, Mother Nature would have arranged it so that, for example, on our 31st birthday we could recall the whole thing! Much as menstruation happens naturally to women, so would reincarnation recall. But it isn't so. Nature shields us, blocks out this information so we don't get confused about the importance of our present tense. She is wise to do so.

For artists, it's different. Those lifetimes could have information that would improve their art perceptions. Writers in particular get a lot out of past lives; many interesting books have been written about the subject.

A Technique to Recall Past Lives

Gather with a leader—you need a leader or facilitator because you cannot recall and direct at the same time. Lie comfortably on the floor, breathing in and out together, merged in chaotic meditation, which is to say no focus, no reaction: just like staring into a fire.

Once everybody is comfortable, the leader sits up and lights two white candles dedicated to memory. She burns a light incense, such as frankincense or myrrh.

> *Leader: I (name) am calling the guides to lead us back in time: Come Goddess in Your aspect of history, come awareness before our birthtimes, come and reveal the pictures in our minds, do not not frighten us but heal.*

Now the leader starts a countback in this way:

> *We are all going back to a year ago this time; meditate and see what you see a year ago this time...*

She describes each time period with a few well-known events that we can all identify. For instance, 1980 was when Mt. St. Helens erupted. The leader must be very sensitive to the space of going back, also skilled in hypnosis because you have to use deeper tools than conscious memory. She leads you back five years, ten years and finally to your birth, each time leaving enough silence to let the mind wander and recall.

After she has led you back to your birthtime, there is a strong tendency to rush the process and go to Egypt or Anatolia, where the Amazons roamed, but you must flow, not race, with your soul or you lose it.

> *We all go to the 19th century now . . . a time of revolution, a time of artistic achievements (something like that, neither too much nor too little). Where are you in 1890? 1880? 1870?*

She leads back through the years and sees if any episodes come to mind. At this point she tells the participants to allow their minds to pick up whatever messages may come forth, and go with a vision if they get one.

This is a long and patient process, requiring at least a weekend, so the leader should take a break after each century and let the people write down what they experienced. Talking is forbidden now; the silence is to be broken only by the leader. No food should be eaten during this exercise. But do not push too hard; it flows only if you remain calm.

After the exercise is complete, the participants should take a nap. At this time many more things might come to them. A modern discussion should not happen until the entire process is finished, and everybody is enriched by the experience.

Returning: When the leader has reached farthest back in the past, she tells the people it's time to return. She need not take it step by step, century by century, as when backtracking. She can simply say:

> We have reached the end of our journey. Now we turn back to our normal selves in the twentieth century. We all become as we were, a little smarter, a little more compassionate towards ourselves.

Again, light the incense and the candles and say thanks:

> Goddess of History, thank You for revealing to us pictures of our older selves; we are returning now to our times. Please bless us as we wake. We will all feel refreshed and happy. It is done.

Automatic Writing

Automatic writing is exciting and fun; it is also rapport with the dead and must be taken seriously. It is not a means to escape reality; used as such, it could set you up as a target for spirits who want to dominate you. A few simple precautions can help to create a positive automatic writing experience.

Place some cut flowers in the center of the table or floor where you plan to work. Purify the space by moving clockwise around the room holding a censer or cauldron with purification incense burning; myrrh and frankincense, or Dragon's Blood incense are fine. If others are present (three or four are good), unify first by humming, then evoke Sophia, Goddess of Wisdom. Draw a large pentagram on a yellow sheet of paper, place it under the flowers, and light a yellow candle. Now you are ready.

Use a yellow pad and hold a good pen lightly over the paper. Two women can hold the pen at once, but it must be comfortable. Feel for inclinations and go with them. At first, you will probably find yourself drawing circles. This is perfectly normal, and may be all you get for a while. Be patient. After a few moments of "loosening up," one of the participants should call for a spirit to enter the space and communicate. After a little more time, ask questions: "Is anyone here with us?" "What is your name?" "How old are you?" "What is your message to us?" "Can we help you?" These are warm-up questions, so don't rush them. Once a spirit presence is established, the circles on the paper will be better formed and less random. However, always allow for large, loopy letters and no punctuation. Continue asking for messages. Tell the spirit that it can relax and use your hand freely to communicate with you.

The communication between this reality and that one is fragile, and it depends on an almost perfect two-way connection. When it happens successfully, when the link falls into place and you can decipher the writing, when you gain wisdom from what the spirit has written, then automatic writing becomes an incredibly moving experience. It is something like knowing you will never be lonely again. Once a spirit has identified herself, you can call on her specifically. She may eventually come to be a close friend and companion. Always remember to respect your relationship with the spirits. Never call upon them for trite or trivial reasons, and never allow yourself to "lose yourself" in the excitement of the experience. Automatic writing should be done at New or Full Moon. During Waning Moons you should rest and meditate.

Chapter 7

The Politics of Food
by Mary Farkas

Good nutrition is the process of gaining our autonomy; it is the process by which we can take back control of our lives. The day-to-day decisions involved in what we eat are some of the most essential, difficult and political decisions we have to make. The understanding of food in its political context may be a new dimension for some of us.

Think for a moment about how our food is grown, prepared and distributed, from the fields to the table. How much do we know about what goes into this process? How much control do we have over it? How much personal contact do we have with it? The answer is obvious: very little or none at all. This answer is political because politics is power or control, and the control of food, the very basis of life, makes food a very political issue.

> We believe that just as it is time to fight for the right to control our bodies, it is also time to fight for our sweet woman-souls.
> We believe that in order to fight and win a revolution that will stretch for generations into the future, we must find reliable ways to replenish our energies.
> (Excerpted from the *Manifesto of the Susan B. Anthony Coven No. 1)*

Food is one of the most basic ways to replenish our energy, but in the incredibly short span of two or three generations we have lost most of our knowledge of food. Historically, women possessed the secrets of choosing, cooking, processing and preserving food for the whole community. Food facts were passed from mother to daughter and were as necessary as the ability to walk. These skills meant the survival of the group, and women were respected for this knowledge. Traditionally, women were the healers, who knew which herbs, plants and foods would cure ailments.

Patriarchy labeled these women healers ''witches'' and taught the community to fear them. In order to control a population, church and state must control the healing process as well as the crisis times of birth and death. Women healers were a threat because they were an effective alternative to the sanctioned healers—doctors.

In order to gain power for this new breed of doctors, the power of the wise women had to be destroyed. Those who sought out the women healers were accused of seeking the devil's help since it was claimed that witches derived their powers from the devil. This resulted in not only a social stigma, but the risk of death as a result of seeking a witch's help. The church and the state were as quick to murder the supporters of witches as they were to murder the witches themselves.

After many generations of persecution and witchhunts, the people slowly lost faith in natural healers and began to believe priests and doctors. The respect of the community passed from women, whose knowledge of food meant survival, to the doctors and priests who preached new and wonderful ways to cure ailments. Along with the passage of respect from women to men went the community's respect from food to drugs. They lost faith in the healing powers of readily available plants and foods. How could something so very basic and obtainable be better than the expensive concoctions and procedures used by the new male doctors? Those men treated the wealthy and the nobility; surely they knew best.

The gradual organic process of healing was replaced by "miracle drugs" that promised overnight relief. We are still trapped in the world of wonder drugs. We want whatever ails us to go away—fast. Many of us take vitamins for this reason, thinking that these pills will make us feel better—fast. We often fall into the trap of taking vitamins, believing that by doing this we won't have to put any effort into our food. We don't realize that the body can adapt itself to innumerable conditions but can only take so much abuse. Pain and discomfort are warning signs that something isn't working right; the body is letting us know that it can't adapt anymore. We must learn to pay attention to our aches and pains, and try to get to the root of their cause. Aspirin and modern drugs don't cure the reason for the pain; they merely mask the body's symptoms.

The patriarchy has taken away much that was woman's; we have lost control of our bodies, our psyches, our history, our intellectual growth. Presently we see wise women everywhere taking back control of their lives. In this process of regaining our spirit, we must not forget that the patriarchy has taken away our food and our knowledge of food. By the twentieth century, woman's faith in herself had become so eroded that she believed that the food prepared by the men of industry was better than what she could make. We must relearn the knowledge of and respect for food if the process of taking back our bodies and our spirit is to be complete.

Energy of Life

Virtually all our planet's energy comes from the sun. Through photosynthesis, plants convert and store solar energy. All of our food is ultimately derived from plants. Our food is our daily link with the energy of the universe. Food that is near as possible to its original plant form possesses the maximum amount of food value, or universal energy.

An example is the potato. When we cook a potato whole with its skin intact, it retains the most food value. If we alter its original form by peeling, we lose the skin's food value. If we cut it into cubes or strips, we lose more vitamins and minerals. If take a potato and peel it, slice it thin, fry it to a crisp, package and transport it hundreds of miles from where it was grown, we have made something almost worthless in terms of universal energy or food value—the potato chip.

This link between food and the energy of the universe was recognized by traditional peasant societies, where female fertility symbols representing the life force as universal energy were worshipped to insure a good harvest. People understood the connection among healthy soil, healthy crops and healthy bodies. They nurtured and cared for the soil. They maintained a balance of nutrients. They realized that the soil was depleted after giving birth to a new crop, so they gave back to the soil what they withdrew. They knew that careful, natural fertilization of the soil was necessary to a balance of life energy. China, the largest peasant society in the world, has achieved self-sufficiency by maintaining the practice of returning to the soil the nutrients, the universal energy, that the soil provides. China is one of the few peasant societies where hunger is not a problem. She has not committed the folly of the industrialized nations, which believe that their strength is in their industry and manufacturing. The Chinese recognize that their strength, their very lives, depend on their food base. When people are hungry they cannot work. A factory cannot produce life.

People in industrialized, urban societies have lost touch with the soil in fact and spirit. In our concrete, treeless, soilless cities, we are not in contact with the cycles of growth. We have no chance to see and help create the growth process of other forms of life—life which we help grow so that we ourselves may live and grow. Most urban dwellers are unaware of their dependence on the plant and animal world. Past societies worshipped plants and animals. Almost the entire population engaged in agriculture, and knew that survival revolved around food. They were well aware of their crops, the weather and the state of the soil. They knew where their food came from and how it was grown, processed, preserved and cooked. They had an intimate, spiritual relationship with their food. In the United States today, less that six percent of the population is directly involved in farming. We are totally unaware of the day-to-day realities of plant growth. We think that our green beans come from the Jolly Green Giant, our cereal from Kellogg's, our flour from Pillsbury, our cheese from Kraft and our milk from Safeway. Virtually all involvement with our food, except that final act of chewing and swallowing, is done for us, and many industrial foods are so processed, we don't even have to chew.

Women and Meat

The brainwashing mentality of our culture extends to the treatment of our soils, our food, our female lives. Meat has traditionally been associated with male virility; if a man couldn't "bring home the bacon," he couldn't provide for his family. The canning and food processing industry employs mostly women, yet all the butchers and meat packers are men. Meat is so strongly identified with the worst animal attributes of men, it's always a wonder to me that feminists still eat meat. But our social and cultural habits die hard. Most of us grow up as meat-eaters; we could not think of a meal without thinking of that space on our plate—often half the plate— that would be filled with meat. There is very little support from society for becoming a vegetarian. But in learning about our bodies and our health, we realize that meat is not essential to our well-being; rather it can be very detrimental to health. Most Third World peoples are vegetarians, though not by choice. The amount of meat that they can eat is minuscule compared to what we eat. For them, meat is a luxury, a flavoring for food, something to be eaten only during special times of the year. The staple food for the world has always been grains, legumes and vegetables, not meat.

Meat is a protein food, a fact we are told is "good." But meat is also 25-50% fat, a fact that *isn't* good. In the past thirty years, people in the United States have doubled their consumption of all meat products, especially beef and poultry. In this same time, the number of people dying of heart disease and cancer has also increased tremendously. The fat in meat is called "saturated;" this means it is solid at room temperature. All meat and dairy products and one plant food—coconuts—contain saturated fat. In recent studies, saturated fat has been linked to heart disease and cancer of the colon. Most deaths in the United States are officially ascribed to some form of heart disease. In reality, these deaths are due to poor eating habits: lifelong habits of eating the wrong things—sugars, refined grains and flours, alcohol and saturated fat (meat). The largest cancer killer, after breast cancer for women and lung cancer for men, is cancer of the colon. Most of the saturated fat that we eat comes from meat. We don't need saturated fat, but we need an essential fatty acid found mainly in vegetable oils, linoleic acid. Vegetable oils are called "poly-unsaturated" or "mono-saturated," meaning that the fat is liquid at room temperature. We need to eat more polyunsaturated and mono-saturated fats, because these fats have been shown to decrease the amount of cholesterol in the blood and aid in the prevention of heart disease. Safflower, corn, soy and sesame oils are polyunsaturated; peanut and olive oils are mono-saturated. We can eliminate most of the saturated fat in our diet by simply not eating meat.

All plants contain a carbohydrate, or starch, called cellulose. Cellulose is crucial to our diet because it provides bulk or fiber. This bulk is needed to move our food through our intestines. Without bulk or fiber, found only in unrefined plant foods, the food takes longer to pass through the digestive tract. Meat contains absolutely no fiber, and if one eats a lot of highly refined starches (white bread and refined grains) along with a lot of meat, there is no fiber in the diet to push the food along. Food from diets low in fiber moves half as fast through the digestive tract as food from those diets which provide enough fiber (fresh vegetables, whole grains, fruit). The increase in colon cancer in this country is due to the fact that our diets are lacking in fiber and high in saturated fats. Because of our low fiber/high meat diets, the carcinogenic toxins in the meat that we eat pass very slowly through the colon, thus increasing the risk of colon cancer.

Meat also contains some of the most dangerous chemicals used in and around our food. Pesticides and herbicides accumulate in the fat cells of land animals and fish, leaving a very high residue of these poisons to accumulate in our fat cells if we eat meat and fish. Animals are tranquilized and shot full of antibiotics, painkillers and growth stimulants. Their food is treated with preservatives and even more antibiotics. All of these drugs are present in meat even though the government is supposed to monitor the amount of drugs found in our food supply. There aren't enough inspectors checking up on the safety of our food, and the cattlemen know this. What's more, the tolerance levels set for the amount of drugs allowed to remain in our meat are established by the meat industry itself. DES is a growth hormone used by cattlemen. It was found to produce cancer in the daughters of women who took the drug during pregnancy. Recently the United States banned the use of DES, but who is checking up to see that the ban is complied with? Processed meats such as bacon, ham and "lunchmeat" contain, in addition to the chemicals found in raw meat, large amounts of preservatives and coloring agents (so the meat won't look grey) added during processing. Of this group of additives, the carcinogenic nitrates and nitrites, BHA and BHT are the most harmful.

Over ninety percent of the corn, barley, oats and soybeans, and over a quarter of all the wheat grown in this country are fed to our livestock. We import protein products from Third World countries, such as Peruvian anchovies, so our chickens and cows can get fat. We force-feed our cattle so their meat will be marbled with fat in order to be "tender and juicy," but most of the fat accumulates in layers outside the muscle, and it is trimmed off and wasted. In fact, nothing embodies our commitment to waste as well as the meat industry. Cattle do not need to eat high quality protein crops; they can convert the grasses and byproducts that we humans can't eat into food for themselves. Most Third World nations are forced to import their food because the huge corporations own the best farmland. The price of the food that they must import has risen dramatically in recent years. In 1961 Sri Lanka needed to sell 156 pounds of tea to buy one ton of wheat; in 1974 she needed to sell 663 pounds—almost five times as much. This is because as industrialized nations become wealthier, their consumption of meat products rises. Thus the grains that would have gone into the world market for Third World countries to import are now sent to the industrialized nations to feed their growing cattle businesses. The people of the Third World are literally competing against industrialized nations' livestock for food!

While on the subject of the indignities of meat, let's not forget the way in which the animals are treated. The fact that these creatures have souls, feelings and their own needs to remain healthy is totally ignored. The last few months of fattening are torture for the animals. They are force-fed and in a constant state of indigestion. In the slaughterhouse the fear, the incredible panic that they feel at the sight, sounds and smell of their own kind dying permeates their flesh and is then served to us for dinner. No, thank you.

Women and Sugar

Did you ever stop to think about all the women you know who have some sort of problem with their menses? Pain and cramps, headaches, backaches, aching feet and legs, depression, constipation, diarrhea—we have probably had them all at one time or another. Our menses are a constant by which we check our health. If we are in optimum health, we will experience none of these symptoms. If you don't know anyone who goes through a painless menstrual period, that indicates how many of us are not in good health. So what does this have to do with sugar? Simply that our health is built upon the foods that we eat.

Our bodies are made up of about forty known nutrients. If we eat whole foods, which contain all the known nutrients, then our bodies will have what they need to grow, repair tissue and bone, and maintain our health. When we eat food that is only partially complete because it has been refined and processed, its original plant shape disguised and its original life energy destroyed, we are not providing ourselves with all we need to remain healthy. The longer we eat incomplete foods, the longer our bodies will lack the needed nutrients. We then fall into a state of disease; we are missing some of the necessary links to the nutrient web. There are many different diets and philosophies of food, but most agree on some basic types of food we should eat daily to insure that we get all we need. We continue to need these nutrients all our lives.

The greatest nutrient needs come at different phases of life: when we are infants; as young children; at puberty; as teenagers; when using contraceptive pills; during pregnancy; while nursing an infant. There is another time in our lives when we have greater nutrient needs, and that is when we have our monthly menses. If we haven't taken in all the necessary nutrients, this monthly elimination will offset the equilibrium that our bodies have established, just enough that we experience how many more nutrients we need than we are getting. At each menses we eliminate blood and other waste from our body. Each month we have a chance to grow and repair tissue, and we upset our balance the least if we have all the necessary nutrients to make that growth and repair work possible. One of the nutrients needed in large quantity, to replace the monthly loss of blood, is iron. Women need almost twice the amount of iron that men do. The average diet in the United States fails to provide women with enough iron. It is standard practice to prescribe iron supplements automatically to all pregnant women, the assumption being that the woman would not possibly get what she needs from her food. If you are eating white flour products, refined grains, few vegetables of little variety, some meat, some eggs, some cheese and lots of sugar (usually in the form of soft drinks, sugar in coffee or tea, candy, sweets and alcoholic drinks) you can be certain that you are NOT getting what your body needs to maintain its health.

When sugar is digested, it actually pulls other nutrients away from your body because it does not have its own nutrients to aid its digestion. Not only does sugar lack nutritive value and rob you of needed nutrients, it adds many unnecessary calories to your diet. Our bodies can handle only a limited number of calories—approximately 2000—a day. If most of our calories come from sugar and from oils and fats, which have a disproportionate ratio of calories to nutrients, then we are leaving very little caloric room for the foods which contain the nutrients we need daily.

We have to stop eating the patriarchy's factory food, and return to eating the foods that women once knew how to make. These foods were simple but delicious because they were whole, live foods which fed and nourished. The less sugar and fat we eat, the more we open ourselves to eating foods that keep us whole.

Sugar was not a common food even fifty years ago. Today it is so pervasive that if something isn't "sweet," we feel it "doesn't taste good." Americans now eat more sugar than ever before—over two pounds each *per week*. We have let the taste of sugar make us forget other tastes. Sugar has been proven to cause tooth decay. 98% of all children in the United States today have tooth decay and over half the people in the U.S. aged fifty or older have no teeth. Sugar is a death-gift from the patriarchy. Take the power of food back from the food industry. Cut down now, and eventually eliminate all sugar from your diet. Any change will take time, so don't rush it—just do it. You will see what a difference it makes in your ability to want to eat and enjoy a greater variety of food. You will also feel better in many ways. One method of cutting down on sugar intake is to stop eating processed foods. Read the labels on things. The ingredients are listed on the label in order by weight; if sugar is a primary ingredient, don't buy that food. Get to the point where you don't have to buy canned or commercially manufactured food. You will thus eliminate most of the empty calories in your diet.

Taking Back Our Food and Our Lives

Whole foods contain all the nutrients essential for life: proteins, carbohydrates, fats, vitamins and minerals. When industry refines our food, it usually takes some of these essential nutrients away and adds chemicals so that the food will have a long "shelf life," more important by its reckoning than a long human life. Of the more than two thousand food additives currently in use, only a fraction of them have been tested for safety. The testing is often inadequate to examine the full range of effects the additives may have over a long period of time. When we eat these chemicals we eat several at a time (read the labels), but the tests are done for only one chemical at a time, and the testing is left up to the manufacturer. He gets to choose which laboratory will do his testing. In reality, the public is the testing ground. We have become guinea pigs for the chemical/food industry. As yet there is no "scientific" proof that such-and-such an additive, or combination of additives, causes cancer or mental illness or allergies; besides, who has the money to support such research—the government? No, the government has more important things to spend our money on, such as weaponry and space programs. Again, it is women who realize that food is EATEN and becomes part of our lives, part of our life process. The patriarchy is too involved in packaging and selling it.

Along with the Women's Liberation movement came a feeling among many women that they would no longer do such traditional "women's things" as cooking. So, in the name of liberation, many of us forgot—or never learned—how to cook. However, it is crucial that we remember what our foremothers knew about food. We must learn how to cook because this means knowing how to take care of ourselves. I am not against men learning how to cook, but men have traditionally not taken care of their own nutritional needs, much less anyone else's. If women do not know how to take care of themselves, the men certainly won't do it for them. We are the ones who get pregnant and whose bodies become nutritionally drained during childbirth. We are the ones who go on crash diets to look "beautiful" and stay "fashion-model slim" as we are told, thereby destroying our health.

In the food industry, as in all aspects of capitalist industry, profit is the primary concern. Sugar is added to almost all industry food, to get people hooked on the sweet taste. Valuable nutrients, the life-energy of food, are processed out. Women who understand that food is to be eaten rather than sold, transported or used as a weapon of domestic or foreign relations, are concerned with the nutritional, life-giving value of the food. Only through constant lying does the food industry make us believe that their food is better than what we can make ourselves.

Many women eat in fast food places because this "saves time" and is so "easy." We should remember that the fast food business is another aspect of our lives that is under control of the giant corporations. Every time we stop for a Big Mac, a Shakey's pizza or any other high calorie/low nutrition food, we are giving our money, our support and our good health away to the patriarchy. No one can cook as well or as cheaply as we can. Remember that the Female Principle symbolizes LIFE. Cook your own food; nourish your body. Don't eat the dead food that patriarchy serves up consistently.

Chapter 8

Witches, Covens, Shamans, Magic and Ritual

A Coven or a Grove?

Whether you will have a coven or a grove is pretty much determined by the size of the group and the inclinations of the women involved. A Dianic coven is composed of thirteen: twelve women and the High Priestess. In an open coven, if one of the members cannot be present, her place can be filled by any woman whom another coven member will vouch for. A closed coven is not open to visitors. An aspiring witch must wait until there is a permanent opening in the coven before she may join. A grove is a much larger, more open group. In a grove, there is no limitation on numbers; the only requirement is that all women be like-minded and seeking the path of the Goddess.

When the Susan B. Anthony Coven gathered for the first time, there were six women present. No one suspected that in nine short years, there would be over seven hundred initiated members! So now, technically, we are a grove, not a coven. Somehow the Goddess always organizes, and invariably there is a magical number of women present at all our Sabbats—either thirteen or twenty-six or thirty-nine.

Women often ask me how to find a coven. The answer is, if you don't have one in your area, start one yourself. It isn't difficult, and creating what you need empowers you.

Use your local women's bookstore for contacts. Write a notice with your telephone number on it and stick it on the bulletin board. Say something like, ''I would like to start a Dianic coven. Please contact . . .''

Then, when you have a few interested people, begin with a weekly study group, reading everything you can get your hands on concerning the Goddess movement.

During these sessions, hold hands at the beginning and meditate a few moments together, breathing, imagining the air filling up your lungs like wings. Breath connects us to life. You can live without food, or even water, but not for long without air. Say a few words to the Goddess of Wisdom, such as, ''Sophia, allow us to learn from each other. Open our inner ears and inner selves to Your knowledge.''

When your study group is about to finish, repeat the beginning ritual. Hold hands, breathe together, and say, ''Thank you, Sophia, Goddess of

Wisdom, for the knowledge we received today. Help us to grow in your ways and stay with us. Blessed be.''

In fact, whenever women gather together, for political meetings or otherwise, holding hands in a circle focuses the group better on the issues at hand. The touching and focusing bring diverse people's spirits together as one.

Naming a High Priestess should not freak you out. This lofty title belongs to our sacred past and therefore I maintain it. However, I found that the job of ''HP'' often resembles that of a theatrical director. The HP watches the group's energy. She has to be skillful in making sure the group raises energy and directs it properly, for healing, personal needs, etc. In other words, the energy raised isn't just dispersed in an evening of hooting and hollering. I have been in many circles where energy is hardly ever raised.

People are sedated listening to somebody read from a book. Nothing is happening. My big fear is that if we don't go beyond books, we lose the magic. Magic is an organic experience. It cannot be learned from books, only by creating it. Creating it is real. Experience becomes knowing. I am sure you will feel the difference.

How to raise energy is discussed in other places in this book, but essentially it comes from spontaneous chanting, with or without words. This method of chanting comes from the HP. I always hum first. Just hum, mouth closed, until the mucus comes off the vocal chords and a nice rich sound is floating about. Then we all open our mouths and make a nice ''ah'' sound. After that I encourage women to chant in harmony or discord, but not to strain doing it.

When this energy is raised a bit, I ask the priestesses of the four corners to invoke their respective corners of the universe. After that, I raise the energy a little more. Then the women come forward, lighting their candles and praying aloud, while we still hum below each word.

This ensures that people are constantly active on many levels, singing and listening at the same time.

When all the candles are lit, I raise the energy again, this time chanting at full force and possibly graduating into a dance, circling the altar three times. Then we bless the food and drink, still humming; then we feast. No humming then. After that, we thank the four corners of the universe after our program, and resume the humming.

Never read in the circle. Memorize the lines if necessary. Improvise. Trust yourself.

Who is the High Priestess then? The woman who can raise the group's energy. Somebody with a bit of theatrical background, as well as Goddess background. The High Priestess is often the one who started the group.

Next, we have the Maidens, the Nymphs and the Crones. Traditionally, the Maidens do everything the HP does, like assistant directors and players as well, since they do invocations. Maidens help with the altar, carrying the sacra up and down the mountains, making sure everyone is heard, and protecting the circle from disruptions.

One of the most outstanding Maidens I ever worked with was Helen Beardwoman, who could easily replace me when I was out of town. I was certain the Susan B. Anthony Coven No. 1 would continue just as I had built it from the start.

Nymphs have a cultural role. Being the youngest in the group, they are depended upon to make sure the Coven has fun. Yes, fun! They collect appropriate songs, sing nicely, dance well, and laugh easily.

The Crones of the coven are the eldest women. Crones are not called on to work unless they want to. They can choose what they want to do. They can sit down if they get tired, or just sit in the middle and be revered as the Goddess in Her wisdom aspect. Crones are often prophets. Oracular sayings might pass their lips or they might be impish or more rambunctious than the Nymphs. However, you never interfere with your Crones.

A coven is recognized if it has celebrated the holy days of the Earth for at least one year and a day. A coven has more than three people in it. In olden days, thirteen was a workable number for a coven. It still is, but it shouldn't be a rigid rule. Don't close a coven's ranks just because the membership has reached thirteen. Let the coven breathe. Closed covens don't last very long in my experience. They become like ingrown toenails; they hurt at the end.

Today, the purpose of spirituality is not to imitate what went before, but to facilitate the future by bonding as souls.

The Laws of the Craft

Many people are disappointed to find that we have no Ten Commandments, but only one Golden Rule:

DO AS THOU WILT AND HARM NONE.

How easy this sounds! However, it is a much harder rule to follow than a set of rules and regulations, and it requires much wisdom and your complete consideration of all those with whom you share your planet. All living beings must be considered in the ''harm none'' clause. It is impossible to go through our lives without hurting others, willingly or unwillingly. We know that. We all have disappointments and wounds, and we deal out our own fair share.

The law does not refer to normal living, the usual ups and downs. It refers to the magical spells we weave. Those are what we truly have to examine, to make sure we do not attack the innocent.

Besides this major law, there are some minor ones. For example, the law of the tenfold karma. If you are good, it will come back to you. If you help others prosper, others will help you prosper. The same applies for harming others; that too shall return. So there is no wisdom in manic hexing, for example.

There are also expectations and requirements of behavior in the Craft. I will try to sum them up.

1. Honor the High Priestess. One of the most despised "sins" is "stealing a coven." This means that if a High Priestess has welded a group together, nobody should usurp her and take over the coven. Before a new High Priestess is chosen, a High Priestess must be absent a year and a day from the activities of her coven. This "rule" comes from ancient times, when the coven leaders often had to hide from the Inquisitors, and plenty of time was therefore allowed for the High Priestess or Priest to return.

2. Honor the succession of teachers. This means that if you were lucky enough to have a spiritual advisor who first opened your eyes to the Goddess and Her religion, this teacher counts as a "mother" to your soul, and deserves the same attention and gratitude you give your natural mother. It is not noble behavior to take without giving. If you take knowledge without putting something back in energy and services, you will earn the same fate; someday you too will teach somebody who will not give anything back to you.

3. Relate back to the mother coven on Midsummer when all the tribes are gathering. It is custom to return, process and have some fun with the original coven from which you were hived. If your path was a lucky one, you were educated and then "hived" with your new coven with the blessings of the mother coven. We honor this connection once a year by returning to celebrate Litha.

4. If there is dissent in the coven, make a new coven. This is one of the oldest rules, which aided the Craft, instead of disrupting it. Not everyone gets along with everyone—we are witches, not saints. So when trouble comes, just see if it's not a sign to make a new group. Then part amicably and try to maintain respect between the two groups.

5. A coven's loyalty is the coven's luck. Do not hex anybody within your group, or mess with her psychically, but rather go to the High Priestess or Priest and use regular methods of problem solving. Avoid irrational anger! Then follow the coven's advice. If that doesn't work, leave the group.

6. Hexing is generally avoidable. If you attack the innocent, the ban returns tenfold. This is an old rule, so witches take care to come up with imaginative solutions and to be sure the person with whom they are angry is really the culprit. On the other hand, rapists are fair game to hex; witches have to practice this somewhere.

When you have absolutely resolved to create a hex, leave the name out, saying, for example, "He who broke into my apartment" or "He who raped me." The Goddess knows whom you are referring to, and while you may miss the mark, She won't.

When the hex goes out to general purposes, such as "enemies of women," the Goddess makes historical changes, which you may read in the news. There is no retribution for standing up for yourself; you need not fear hurting somebody unnecessarily. For example, Christians pray against gays, yet more and more gays come out of their closets. Obviously, the Goddess has veto power.

7. You are as secure as your own psyche allows. If you imagine that some witch can really harm you, you give a lot of power to that person. But if you don't, you can just fly above it all and let the vibes fall back where they came from. Men often try to make women "lose" their heads, so they can "have" them. It may work on a non-initiate, but once a woman is her own possession, she is secure against self-serving kitchen witches with lust on their minds. Male witches manipulating women are not much different from society's patriarchal pig messages, in which women internalize and participate in their own slavery. A witch bows to no man.

A woman with Goddess consciousness is stronger than any patriarchal messages, and can change her life and rid herself of unwanted demands.

8. The High Priestess represents the Life Force in the coven, and the High Priest her consort and lover. The High Priestess is supreme. Her consort is sacred to her but is never her Master or Lord or Guru.

9. Many covens have couples in them; others have singles. If you have a consciousness where jealousy is not a threat, sex within the coven and new sexual alliances are blessed events. But experience has it that when sexual relationships break up in the coven, the members must stop worshipping together as well. That is not blessed, and must be avoided through preplanning and agreements. For Dianic groups, there must be a clear understanding of what to expect. It is women's strength to bond with each other (we are so new at it) but worship should not suffer on account of sex. Worship is a higher form of bonding, and should be regarded as more than just a social get-together. The bonds already formed should be protected, not threatened. Then the coven will stay together for years and form a powerful psychic circle that can take care of the needs of all who participate. (In patriarchal religions, male celibacy is simply a denial of bonds with women. There is plenty of sex, both homosexual and heterosexual, among priests.)

Ethics Within the Coven

The only law is that you cannot steal a coven from the High Priestess. If a priestess started a group, and she led, taught and grew with the coven, a new member cannot just come up and say, "Let's leave our teacher behind now, let's get rid of her." If there is disagreement in the coven, the one who is in disagreement must leave. She may start her own group. In fact, this is a good way to propagate the Craft. But she cannot destroy a group that is already present.

The Craft is not a political organization. We operate on an ancient honor system. The High Priestess is seen as a female Elder, and therefore has powers others don't have. The High Priestess, for example, can ask members to leave if she feels they are disrupting her psychic space.

When the group gets too large and new priestesses emerge, it is wise to hive the whole group. Hiving rituals take place at Candlemas (February 2). The new group stands in the middle of the mother group and gets blessed. The new High Priestess may give a short haggle about her purpose with the new coven and their common goals. Then each year, if possible, the new group rejoins the mother group on Midsummer's Eve. This is a traditional time to gather all the tribes together.

The best all-around policy is to practice *politeness* to each other. That's when we can use the old titles; they breed respect. Lady Medea, Lady Circe, Lady Persephone. The word "lady" means "she who makes the loaf;" it isn't a class title. Use each others' witch names. Practice calling each other names different from your regular ones. This language will help you have dignity and confer honor upon each other.

Finally, a word about power. She who puts out more work will accumulate more power. Work and power are in balance in the universe. So if you want to reorganize the next meeting, summon the people, write a poem, recite a verse, dance or sing, you should tell the High Priestess, the Maidens or the Nymphs. Volunteer a lot. Be active. Whining about not having power usually gets you nowhere. Contribute and see how your power grows.

Seven Sibylline Sayings
by Erika H. Sophia
(reprinted from *Thesmophoria*)

1. Pain is the primordial evil. Therefore, the *First Saying* is: Actively interfere with avoidable, meaningless pain, wherever and however

217

possible. (But in this, as in all things, first examine the total context, being sure that you keep all things in balance.)

2. Pleasure is the primordial good. Therefore, the *Second Saying* is: Promote your own pleasure *as long as* it causes no pain either to yourself or to other feeling beings.

3. Balance is the mainspring of the universe. Therefore, the *Third Saying* is: Seek balance in all things, sparing no effort to search for the deeper, more hidden balances of life and reality.

4. Creativity is the secret of life. Therefore, the *Fourth Saying* is: Be creative *in your own way*, with your body, mind and spirit, and with whatever resources come your way.

5. Courage is the cardinal virtue. Therefore, the *Fifth Saying* is: Be courageous in every moment and area of your life—especially in fulfilling the first four Sayings.

6. Consciousness is what makes us human. Therefore, the *Sixth Saying* is: Increase consciousness, your own and others', whenever this is compatible with the other sayings—and even sometimes when it is not.

7. Celebration is a necessity for the spiritual life. Therefore, the *Seventh Saying* is: Rejoice that you are a woman, and celebrate your feminine nature in all things small and large, hourly, daily, and on special occasions.

Dianic Ordination Ritual

When a woman studies a year and a day with a coven, she is entitled to be initiated. When the new initiate has worked and helped facilitate circles of the coven for a year and a day, she is entitled to be ordained.

A specialty is required for her, and there are many. She can be ordained as a priestess of teachings, healing, management, prophecy, scriptures, poetry, weather, fire and earth. For example: I am a priestess of teachings and ritual; a therapist friend of mine is a priestess of healing; another friend is a priestess of herbology.

The time for ordination is the same as initiation: Candlemas (February 2). After your coven initiates the new members, the ordination follows. The tools of the craft are collected from the women, to be given back to them during the ceremony. Ordination is an acknowledgment of magical works well done, and a group blessing on the individual who achieved it.

The new priestesses are called by their magical names, such as Medea, Penthesilea, Ea or Circe; these names signify the guardian spirits the women have chosen for their path.

All stand in a circle and hum. Feel for the jelling of the soul-group. When meditation is deep enough the High Priestess speaks:

We are the continuation of long lines of ancient women who were dedicated to the Goddess of Life. Tonight we are lucky enough to have new priestesses to ordain. In the Dianic tradition we have initiation and ordination; we leave the individual free to choose her own process and excellence. Within our coven we like to recognize the contribution of new sisters.

Four ordained priestesses stand at the four corners of the Universe in the circle, each invoking her favorite goddess she sees with the four elements. Examples:

(Priestess of the East:) Come great teachers of the East, priestess of Isis, shaking Your sacred tambourines, come Ishtar, come Lilith!

(Priestess of the South:) Awake and fly to us, teachers of the South, Firesouls, winged like cherubs, sun Goddess Arinna, oh come!

(Priestess of the West:) Awake and rise to us, o lovely Goddess of the West, come to us Love, come to us Aphrodite, on Your shell float to us Tiamat, Queen of the Dolphins.

(Priestess of the North:) Gather together Your gifts, o Goddess of the North! Foodmother, greenmother, come teach us all Your ways.

The High Priestess calls: *The temple is created. The Goddess is here. Who are the priestesses seeking the recognition of the teachers?*
One by one, the women answer: *It is I,* (each using her magical name).
The High Priestess: *Come* (name), *to be presented to the Universe.*
In the middle of the circle the High Priestess steps out; she holds her hands palms open, feeling the radiation from the initiate's hands. She and the new priestess turn to the east.

I (High Priestess's magical name) present to you (name), a priestess of (her specialty) who has completed her ministry with us. Bless her, o Goddess of beginnings, with new powers, new energy, new ways of communication.

By "presenting," I mean the High Priestess physically and gently rotates the body of the new priestess with her arms held in Goddess position. Now she turns her to the south:

I, High Priestess of Dianna, Medea, present (name) to You, o Firemothers. Infuse her with Your vitality; give her Your

*passion to accomplish all the works she is to do. Bless her
with magnetism, endurance and fierce power.*

Turning again:

*I, High Priestess of Dianna, present to you (name), o guar-
dians of the West. To bless this new priestess with Your love.
Let her heart be glad in your service. Let her soul arm the
hearts of others and let her ally always be You, Aphrodite.*

Turning north:

*I, High Priestess of Dianna, present to you (name), o God-
dess of the North, Foodmother and Fooddaughter; bless
this new priestess with nurturance and information,
powers of organizing and powers of just and fair conduct.
Blessed be.*

Then the High Priestess takes a small bottle of oil (I use ''Priestess'')
and anoints the forehead, saying:

*I purify you from all anxiety; I purify your eyes to see her
ways; your nose to smell her essence; your lips to speak
of Her; your breast for courage and beauty; your genitals
for pleasure and happiness; your feet to walk in Her path.
Finally I bless your palms to do the Goddess's work.*

Turning to the magical tools gathered at the beginning of the ceremony
and holding her hands over them, the High Priestess blesses them:

*All the tools you used and loved, bless them all with the
Goddess's love.*

Now she hands over the ring, putting it gently on the new priestess's
finger. She gives her the cord to wind around her waist, her wand to hold
in her hands, her knife to invoke the powers, and she places a necklace
for immortality around the ordained priestess's neck. When this is complete, all say:

It is done. The Goddess blesses Her new priestess.

The newly-ordained priestess can now offer a few words of statement,
or just meditate to herself, and participate in the ordination of the woman
who follows her.

Celebrating and feasting follow, with laughter, music and stories about
how these women found their Goddess and how and when they first felt
called to serve her as priestesses.

Practicing "Solo"

To practice "solo" is something all witches do, usually in greater number than those who act as part of a coven. "Solo-witching" should be an integral part of one's daily life. Many covens have come into existence of their own "organic" accord in the last few years, and this phenomenon is largely due to the natural tendency of women to explore spiritual needs and feelings with one another. The woman who is lucky enough to find like-minded women to commune with still needs to work at her private altar, just as does the woman whose private altar is her sole spiritual possession. At her altar, every woman is her own priestess.

Often women's homes already have a special space set aside for valuables, family pictures, jewels, oils and other personal mementos. The woman is usually not conscious of the fact that, by natural inclination, she has created the beginnings of an altar. A solo-witch deliberately elaborates on this special space, making it more practical for her purposes by removing all objects except those which aid in her meditations.

The most important difference between coven-witching and solo-witching is the attitude of the practitioner. In a circle of women (or women and men if it is a "mixed" coven), the witch is usually dependent upon facilitating priestesses who are responsible for guiding the ritual toward the most appropriate rhythm, content and intensity. In her own home, the woman is totally dependent upon herself to create a psychically conducive environment in which to do work. She has a responsibility to establish a "temple" space in which to act and interact. This process is not quite as easy as showing up for coven celebrations of Sabbat. During ritual a home needs to be "cleaned out," telephones unhooked, visitors discouraged and interruptions ignored. It is also important to gather all the tools of the Craft in one place and take a ritual bath of purification before doing any altar-work.

The purpose of coven-craft is to build and strengthen the natural female bonding between Sisters as it occurs on a Divine level, while solo-practicing serves to enhance and enlarge a woman's personal power over her own life and circumstances. To do both is to be a practicing priestess. To do either is a matter of Divine choice.

Witches fortunate enough to be able to conduct their own worship rituals in an outdoor, natural environment have little need for extensive preparation or stringent precautions, but an urban solo-witch needs both, as well as an active imagination, in order to transcend the pervasive vibrations of the city. Rural witches have the luxury of choosing a natural setting in which to worship; groves, lakes, meadows, rivers, woods and hills are excellent temples which provide contact with Nature at Her most elemental. City witches may find that they have more need of ESP, the fifth dimension and ancestral spirits to provide contact with these same elemental forces.

Solo-witching is a constant exercise in ingenuity, but secrecy regarding your work is still one of the cornerstones of witch-wisdom and power. Knowing when to keep quiet about an issue is as important as knowing when to struggle for one. Love-spells in particular are never disclosed to anyone, but it is a good practice in general to avoid telling other people what you have done at the altar. If you know a strong priestess of divination, check with her in regard to your spells, and she may suggest an approach or alternative spell. Doing this is not breaking secrecy. Secrecy adds intensity to your work and acts as the vessel in which you hold your spell. Breaking secrecy can damage or ruin a spell.

In covens, secrecy is not as imperative, and the collective consciousness holds the spell as securely as the vessel of secrecy. A witch does not, however, tell uninitiates about coven work or ritual unless she is teaching them.

Witches' tools become doubly important in the practice of solo-witching. For example, your red cord, perhaps worn with coven members in a Circle, can be used to cast a protective circle around your private worship space at home. It will provide you with a "natural centering" space, and will serve you fully as well as a magic Circle drawn on a sacred mountaintop.

Witchy tools such as athalmes and swords, worn openly, will ward off attack. Pentacles on necklaces are important because they are recognized by the dead and spirits who respond only to such symbols. This is one of the strengths of ancient symbology; signs are part of the collective consciousness, whose universal language is symbolism.

Having a special chalice or altar-cup is very important, and this chalice should only be used in your sacred rituals. The altar censer or thurible can follow you anywhere, and be part of daily activities, indoors or out, at worship, work or recreation. It should be regarded as a very good friend.

It is best not to cut corners when practicing solo-witching. The witch's home is a temple, and there is an ongoing maintenance job to be done; purification as well as cleaning must take place. Purification of psychic space can be aided by keeping sacred herbs in the corners of the house (Angelica is traditionally used for peace and harmony, for example), and candles burning in fireproof jars. Taking care of houseplants is a good idea. These plants are much more than decoration—they are coworkers. This applies to pets as well. When addressing Athena, Diana, Brigid, Cerridwen or Artemis, it helps to involve cats, dogs, owls, snakes, or some other representative of the animal queendom.

Bless your entire house at New Moon or Full Moon by walking around it three times, carrying a thurible of burning incense, preferably frankincense and myrrh. Invoke the Goddess Vesta and the Muses to assure good times, creativity and security in your living space. Throw the circle of invisibility around your home and pronounce it invisible to all evil. This is particularly important for witches practicing in urban areas where the high crime rates inherent in patriarchal society are of special concern. Witch-sense decrees that we take no chances or shortcuts in the areas of self-protection and self-preservation.

"Targeting" is a very important concept in the art of solo-witching; it is the process of choosing the intent and ultimate target of your spell. Solo-witches must be particularly cautious about throwing spells of reversal or attack, or hasty revenge based on assumptions. Spells thrown in anger are capable of going much too far and may be heartily regretted later. Personal power ill-directed can be a frightening thing. Before using your powers to throw reversal spells, it is best to sleep on the issue for at least one night, preferably three, and to strengthen and purify yourself through ritual before taking any action.

Harm is most often corrected by inevitable Karmic Law, and you may not have to involve yourself in a situation at all. Hexing the innocent is punishable by the gravest of consequences: Your hex returns to you tenfold. For these reasons, most wiccans studiously avoid hexing, and concentrate instead on a fair and karmically just outcome. Forget the "how" and allow the witch-Goddess Aradia to take care of the problem. Chances are good that a perfect solution will be arrived at when a witch gives the Goddess free space in which to act, without trying to limit Her by providing specifications born of a finite mind.

Specifically, "targeting" must be done only with a conscious commitment and a background of research. Spells should generally be devised in such a way that they remain open and flexible.

Panic-witching for a solo practitioner occurs when a spell doesn't seem to work. Some do and some don't, but we must remember that karmic "debts" and "assets" accumulate over lifetimes, and provide the landmarks for today. Engagements, appointments and commitments made previously may remain hidden in the subconscious. A witch might actively pursue a particular solution or individual only to miss a karmic "appointment" with someone very important.

It is possible to "stall" your karma, but it's best not to, because sooner or later the inevitable must occur. Spells that don't work are also valid in the sense that an answer has been provided. Sometimes it is necessary to stop throwing a spell and await the inevitable Cosmic intervention. The Goddess will make Her plans known to any witch willing and able to listen. Letting go of a spell is not easy, especially if it has become an obsession, but it is never healthy or desirable to nurture an obsession anyway. The key to this is Will. Meditation and maintaining a "white" altar will help.

Solo-witching encompasses the entire lifestyle. It means consciously cooking healthy foods for yourself and your loved ones, and it definitely means not eating much red meat. A witch should take care to provide the physical body with the best care possible; natural sources of vitamins for health, and exercises to strengthen muscles and develop the body are good. The practice of Kundalini Yoga is traditional for many witches, since it originated with ancient women as the concept of serpent-power as power of the Great Goddess. But there are many different disciplines you can enjoy. Sports, games, dance—all offer spiritual-physical exercises.

At all costs, avoid slavery of any kind. A slave-witch is not much good. The Goddess insists on the total freedom of Her worshipers, and often demands full nudity at the altar in order for us to prove the concept. Only free beings are able to feel comfortable when uncovered. The naked body represents Truth rather than lewdness, and it is important in rituals as a signification of the purity of the prayers. Of course, slavery doesn't disappear when we take off our clothes, so the work is social consciousness. Affecting social change becomes a religious activity when it's done against slavery of your economic or spiritual well-being.

A solo-witch would do well to subscribe to some kind of pagan publication or purchase pagan reading materials for the home. These will provide support, encouragement and motivation for continuing practice of the Craft. Constant education and knowledge exchange provide fertile ground for the growth and development of a creative witch.

It is also imperative that solo-witches keep a meticulous *Book of Lights and Shadows*, which records in detail the work performed at the altar. This Book is not only a yardstick for measuring how much growth and change have taken place, or how many spells worked in certain ways, but also as a document of practical witch-lore for the benefit of future generations. The *Book of Lights and Shadows* is the witch's prayerbook.

Solo-witches can be found everywhere. They belong to every profession, age level, economic status and ethnic group. Some are conscious, some not. Some acknowledge affinities with the psychic world, while others exhibit completely unacknowledged potential. There are witches who are politically conscious and see connections between religion and politics which have existed since time immemorial. Some witches are involved in the psychic workings of people in the here and now, while others are "backyard" pagans who love a good celebration with friends and neighbors. Many males prefer solo-witching, while women tend to be involved more easily in a group.

Ethnic minorities cannot afford to give up their magical rituals and practices, but must use them to preserve their genetic souls. Among whites, only oppressed groups such as women need to resort to magic. Men often pray to a patriarchal god in one form or another. Women most often pray to a Blessed Virgin, the Queen of Heaven, Queen of the Moon, whose serpent indicates that She is the ancient Great Goddess, Dia Anna.

Finally, don't hold back as a practicing solo-witch, but create and give birth to as many new spells, chants, rituals, challenges and endeavors as you can. Designate creativity as a major focal point in this life, and make a conscious effort to walk the five points of the sacred Hexagram: the "top" point of the Life Force, connected with sexual energies; the "right side" point of individuality and survival, indicative of the principle that we belong and survive in our ecological niche; the "left side" point of the Self as Divine spark, cultivated through devotions, meditation and rituals; the "left bottom" point of passion and an excitement for life which balances the "right bottom" point of power, natural in origin, learned through development, strong as a foundation for standing or building on. The solo-witch who keeps all this in mind will certainly thrive.

Two Decades Later— My Goddess Ministry

To belong to a witches' coven is still very scary, elusive as well as dearly desirable to many women. I would like to share my experience of several years of high priestessing.

I wasn't born a polished priestess; I grew with my coven. When I started coming out as a spiritual feminist, the term was considered contradictory. Religion and politics were not seen as one and the same. Women thought of politics as leaflets, speeches, rallies or even guns. But religion controls the inner woman and her thoughts, which then govern her actions, so you can't get away from the fact that the Inner Woman is Revolution. I made a decision to add my talents and heritage to the struggle to liberate the religious woman inside, and help her create a faith system which would ultimately serve her and her children.

For all our victories in the Seventies, it is obvious that we failed to win the masses of women away from the male-dominated churches. It's still ninety percent women who support ANY church today (Mormon, Catholic, Jewish, Protestant, fundamentalist, you name it). Why? Because women have a greater spiritual need than men. Yet men capitalize on this instinct and set themselves up to govern women through religion. When we break men's stranglehold on women in religion, we can consider the revolution of women won. Everything else will be evolution compared to religious indoctrination.

What do we need to offer women to make it easier for them to satisfy their religious needs and leave the male-glorifying churches?

Results. Space. Peace of mind. High self-image. Universal meaningful work. Love and acceptance.

Do they get all these from male churches?

Patriarchy has invested heavily in nice, quiet buildings to go sit in, where women can at least be temporarily safe from male sexual harassment on the streets. They have incense in some churches (stolen from the Old Religion) pleasing to the senses. They have confessions that give relief and some acceptance. They have activities where women can find friends. Some churches even reach out to gays. All without changing the basic concept of Christianity, the all-powerful male god.

For this women have to donate money. Women have always supported churches with donations and labor. They have to subjugate their sexuality. But most women don't really care about that; they are not heavily into sexual experimentation. They only want peace. They get to sing songs with other women and feel like they're living in a community.

Can we give women all this and more?

Feminist women's religion cannot promise large cathedrals to worship in; women find themselves poorer than ever in this century. But we can promise to build up the inner temple—it's portable, and we all have one. This alone will keep us busy for a while. We can recapture the culture, the rituals, the sounds, the feelings of community. We can have the incense and candlelight which make religion so attractive; we can have peerless poetry of divine inspiration; we can have pomp, circumstance and dancing.

What is required from women to get all this?

A willingness to study is a must today when so much has to be reclaimed. Women's religion can be orally transmitted, but there are few able to do this. The media are not yet ours; our books are mostly self-published and our resources are limited. The responsibility to study and follow up is certainly required. Years of teaching often exhausted me, and when a new woman demands that I tell her all I know in one breath, I cry out in desperation, I can't help you if you won't read! Only three percent of Americans today read, and the majority of these are women. Women read naturally more than men. So we are in hopeful shape, but we must make this conscious devotion and continue to READ.

Donating money is a must. Nothing is free in a revolution. As women and consumers, our spending power is the only power that we have always had. Being conscious consumers, putting prices on sacred things, is new to us. The world tries to sell us deodorants and washing machines, never our own good graces. We must pay each other, and learn to trust each other with our money, to make a flora of information possible. I am not taking about adoring one "leader" and ignoring the others. In my personal experience this is not a problem. I have not seen anybody ignored.

Nobody is having her silk slippers kissed the way the male gurus are. But somehow we went overboard with the fear of creating hierarchies among ourselves, to the point of ignoring an honor system without which we are mute in dignity.

We are mute because we have no way to say thank you. We are only saying Gimme, gimme that Old Time Religion. But we never make it more graceful and honorable, for it is ourselves we honor in religions, and nobody else. For example: There are several pagan festivals in this country where the feminist religious presence would be invited and needed. I cannot afford to travel to them because it would come out of my own pocket and I have not grown rich in my years of spreading the faith. Yet strategically, it would be very good if I had a travel fund for the Goddess. Not millions but enough for airfare, publicity, accessibility.

So how do you begin?

First, you assemble and meet for a year and a day doing nothing but study, read and rearrange your heads. You may also stop reading men authors for a year. Did you ever do that? It is a great way to cleanse your mind! Saturate yourself with lore about the Goddess, and try to observe the eight Sabbaths even if you just sit in a circle and light a candle for each of you.

In this book, I have described in detail the Sabbath proceedings and given the traditional poetry; you get a lot of guidance there. In almost every chapter I have repeated that this religion is improvisation. There is no one way to contact the Goddess. This religion is not a one-book religion like Christianity, and not a one-mantra religion like the Krishna cult, but a body of knowledge which revels in variety, creativity and joy. It is a pleasure-oriented religion, where kisses and pleasures are seen as sacraments.

Who shall lead the rituals?

Let's look at what specific "jobs" are to be done concerning a Goddess ritual. You need a group; more than three make a coven. You need to invoke the Goddess from the four corners of the Universe, which means you can share this with four women right away. You need a recitation of the traditional Great Charge, or Invocation of the Star Goddess, or some other poetry appropriate to the season. This requires yet another woman who can do this well, a women who has a passion for reciting poetry by heart.

Then you need a High Priestess in charge of the communal energy's rise and fall. This is the trickiest job of all. How can I teach you to listen to the communal energy? The best way is when you are all doing the hum, the vibration which we use to raise power/maintain energy. This is done by all in the circle, and is not a drone. It is put out on the outgoing breath. If the top of the head vibrates, you are doing it right. This is the barometer by which the leader feels if the group is "cooking" or "sleeping." Your instinct will tell you which.

Don't be overdemanding. There are lulls in the energy flow, and that's okay. But if some women shuffle their feet and look around while the women with the chalices go unheard and ignored, you have to stop the circle and do something that restores attention to the sacred work at hand.

You can say, "The energy has dropped—let's raise it again, sisters!"

Group leaders need a repertoire of songs and power-raising dances, chants and improvisational techniques. I have been trained in improvisational theater, and I have many such natural skills. Those of you who don't, look into it. The Second City School of Improvisation was my teacher. Viola Sills wrote a book about it. It is good for circle training. You just use its essence, not verbatim. (Viola never dreamed that she was training a pagan priestess instead of an actress. There is a big difference.)

An example: You cry "The Goddess is alive!" when you feel her presence (never when she isn't activated). The group answers "Magic is afoot! Athena is alive!" You continue, "Magic is afoot! Dianna is alive! Magic is afoot." Encourage the women to contribute names of goddesses they know about. That keeps them thinking, and they have no time to be bored.

When you run out of Goddess names, you substitute your own. "All that is alive is the Goddess." So then each woman gets to say her own name and the group blesses her with the response, "Z is alive! Magic is afoot!"

Another example. If you are outdoors you must dance to keep warm. Standing in one place is boring and unhealthy. So you do the traditional spiral dance. Face outward; leading the group in and out, make snaky patterns around the altar singing a song that all know (see this book for songs).

You can do it until you feel you have had enough, then all fall down to the ground tumbling and laughing. You can gather them again to stand still, now that they have had a good workout.

In the beginning, try to find a mountain and climb it for a warmup exercise. It is spooky at first, ladies foraging out alone in the night, but it will increase your sense of personal freedom. My coven and I practiced at least seven years almost exclusively in nature, in any weather. Of course, Southern California is balmy even when it's wet. You can see how the gentle Goddess Religion originated in the Mediterranean region, the cradle of high culture and good weather.

It's harder to maintain high energy at an indoor celebration. There is the distraction of familiar surroundings; there is less space for dancing. The blessing of the indoor practice is that you can be skyclad, which is certain to make any space appear ancient and natural. Skyclad celebrations are very special because there is an extra freedom lived out, which is not permitted by present-day society: ladies worshipping themselves in the buff.

Always be crowned, skyclad or clothed; wear wreaths of flowers and green things on your head and you are transformed into an ancient symbol of the Goddess. Wear your bracelets, necklaces, rings, gowns, wands, silver knives and red girdles.

As a priestess, give yourself permission to do this as soon as possible. In patriarchy, adoring yourself with Revlon products is encouraged. The entire cosmetic industry mythically started from ritual adornment which Goddess people spent a lot of money buying. The painted faces of Egypt and the rouges of Crete were ancient sacred ritual tools, late to degenerate into making women desirable to men. We must take back vanity's mirror as a sacred tool of women in worship. We are beautiful for ourselves and our sisters. We are beautiful because nature is beautiful. Women are nature. This becomes obvious at a skyclad sabbat.

My way

Sabbaths physically begin a few days before the Dabat date. First we find a safe place to go. This takes phone calls, organization, carpools, advertising in *Themis*, our newspaper.

When the group assembles at the Feminist Wicca, they are already crowned, bejeweled, ritually clear. No other talk disturbs the meditation on the colors of candles involved and the women thinking over what they want out of this sabbat.

I usually show up around 8 pm, thirty minutes before time to leave. I greet participants; we embrace, kiss a lot and tie up loose ends. We take a collection for the church, namely the Susan B. Anthony Coven No. 1, explaining that we need to continue publishing and raising funds for a permanent site (sigh).

I am looking at the women, see some new faces, some old friends. I distribute the maps. Last call to get on the road in a caravan.

When I arrive I take in the new site and decide where to set up the altar. We make a large circle holding hands and counting heads by running numbers from one to another, each calling out our number: One, Two, Three...

I like to contemplate what the number means when I begin. We appoint the youngest woman present Nymph. Her job is to keep an eye on the chalice when it is passed around, and refill it with wine when needed. She is getting excited—she has never nymphed before. Another young woman laughs gleefully in the corner: I'm glad I don't always have to be the youngest! We choose our Crone, the oldest woman in the Coven. She simply Queens, and all her wishes are served.

We appoint the priestesses who will evoke the four corners of the Universe. Back in the early Seventies, I had circles of sixty or seventy women, but I had to do everything myself: all the corners, all the dismissals.

Times have changed, praise the Goddess Durga. Priestesses ordained now are present to volunteer for corners. I usually take North. The priestesses assume their positions at their posts.

In the meantime there is a last call to the bathroom. Nobody is allowed to leave the circle during rituals. This is most serious. A woman can have enough discipline to stay in a circle for about an hour. If there is a dire case, we can do an emergency symbolic opening of the gates to honor the women's experience which is held in common: being in a closed circle.

Make sure the food and everything else you need are in the circle. Children are not required to follow the same rules. A small child wandering among the women is not breaking the circle.

Drop your clothing and put it in the corner; memorize where it is. You will want to be able to find your belongings after sabbat.

Now we form a circle and breathe together in and out. When the breathing is synchronized, you start the hum. The witches' hum is our chanting basis. It is improvisational and can be produced by all, simply vibrating the vocal cords gently together without strain. When the top of the head vibrates, you are doing it right. Sound unifies the body. The group becomes an entity, a thought form, a vibration, sometimes with intensity, sometimes lulled, always moving. The women's bodies undulate; there is a sway to the circle. This vibration is kept up during all the magic work.

Priestess of the East picks up her place with arms stretched facing outward toward the East, raising her voice above the general hum and invoking the Goddess. The women turn to her and say "Blessed Be" after she is finished. Now South, West and North. Back to East—otherwise the circle "leaks." It is an old custom. Just do East twice. Then the Crone says, "The circle is closed. The Goddess blesses her women."

This is when the serious power praying happens. A tapestry of sound can be woven, a prayer of sound, not words. I've heard some moving power-raising sounds in my time! Singers who flew with their voices straight at the Moon. Choruses of women in temples of old come alive. The temple descends on us, and we are transported to the presence of our divine creativity.

You don't interfere with that energy. You don't stop it. You know when it stops. Then you step to the middle of the circle and explain the holy day in an informal speech, not some formal churchy-sounding preaching. Let there be humor anytime it wants to happen. Respect without formality. Pick up the sacred chalice, pour the finest wine you have and place it on the altar. Bless it with your hands, then hold it aloft to the Moon if you are outdoors. (Note: The Catholics hold up the Holy Ghost over their chalice just like the Full Moon lands and sits in my chalice at esbats.)

The first cup is yours. "Goddess of all Life! We welcome you and ask you to join with us in our celebration." Libations on the ground if you are outdoors; a sprinkle with your fingers on the altar if indoors. Then pass it from woman to woman, from East to South, and each toasts the Goddess for her own reasons. This is usually acknowledgment of the sacred designs, such as "Thank You, Goddess, for fulfilling my plea last sabbath and giving me this new opportunity to love!"

When the chalice goes around once, depending on the group's mood and how long all have been standing, take some time and stretch, making the body warm again. The "Breath of Fire" exercise is fast and efficient for a quick warmup. Then you can send the chalice around once again for those who want something to help them this season. If there are too many women to do it twice, have each woman both praise the Goddess and ask Her a boon.

Now rekindle the incense burner, put in some very fine quality incense and recite either the Great Charge (usually the Maiden) or the Invocation of the Star Goddess (my favorite). All listen within for guidance.

You may choose to chant more songs, but it's well now to bless the food and wine, and sit down for a feast. You feed somebody else, saying "May you never hunger" and offer a drink, saying "May you never thirst." In this way you are free to eat and drink to your heart's content.

After the first munchies, entertainment is usually in order. Women sing songs and read poetry. Informal behavior during performances enhances the party atmosphere.

There must be one person in charge watching the flow of energy, and another tuned in to her. Whenever "everybody" was High Priestess, the circle fell apart. Responsibility can be rotated, of course, creating a great training ground in your coven for all women.

Just before the high energy wanes (you must stay tuned in even through the partying), get up and thank the spirits (East, North, West, South, East again) for attending. Hail and Farewell!

The Story of the Danaids

At the water festival called Hersephoria, the true story of the lovely Danaids comes to light. This festival was held at any time the rains were needed for the people's food crops. Carefully selected Maidens who had no deaths in their families that year, or whose parents both still lived, had the honor of bringing in the blessing waters. Large urns with tiny holes in them were filled with water and the Maidens carried them around the town they were serving. Of course, the water flowed through the holes and sprinkled on the thirsty ground. These water nymphs were worshipped for making Argos fertile. They had their own temples and their own honoring festivals. Of course they were the daughters of Dianna, the soul of the Wild.

Their story suffered perversion at the onset of patriarchy. In order to discourage the power of the Rainmaking Maidens, a new story was pinned on them. They became the daughters of Danau (masculinized form of Dianna) and were forced to take husbands. They killed their husbands on their wedding night, and as punishment they were given leaky urns to carry endlessly around to the wells and back. The story is transparent. The fifty Maidens represent the fifty weeks in the matriarchal year, and the function of the leaky urns was their normal ministry. Listen to their song and understand why the marriage didn't work for them:

> *We, the great seed of the Holy Mother, ah we!*
> *Grant us that we, unwed, unsubdued, from marriage to men*
> *   may flee!*

Possession by Christian Demons and Devils

In the news recently was the tragic story of a young woman who died of starvation while being "exorcised" by Christian priests. They were charged with murder and their defense produced a tape recording of the young woman, speaking in a male voice and hurling obscenities at them. The possession, not the exorcism, was to blame, claimed the defense; the Devil made the woman starve to death. The inquisition was satisfied.

This particular case is one of many in which we see the emergence of a frighteningly ignorant thought-form, the relatively new idea of a "Devil." Christians, Muslims, even Krishna people pay a lot of attention to the concept of evil incarnate. The Christian devil, like their god, is male. The same holds true for Muslims. Hinduism differs in that it offers female evil in the person of Kali.

The truth is that duality religions (something Wicca is NOT) need a "bad guy" from whom their "good guy" can save humanity. Their gods are usually warrior types, fashioned after heroes and military figures. Television reflects this duality in the good-guys-in-white-catch-the-bad-guys-in-black theme.

In essence, the patriarchal gods and devils are exact flip sides of each other. If you have one, you get the other. Patriarchal duality: good-bad, black-white, god-devil, man-woman. There are other ways.

Kali is quite different, representing a fossilized belief in the ancient trinity of the Goddess. Within the natural cycles of all life, Kali brought change, transformation, rebirth and regeneration. But in contemporary India, Kali's shrines are virtual slaughterhouses. Kali does not "possess" people's minds. In Her cycle She has no flip side. She is round. The destruction in Kali is the death necessary for rebirth. Future-oriented death is not evil; it is natural. It is part of the Round.

Frankly, my cure for "diabolical" possession would consist of an intensive program of education, prevention and removal of all the negative and harmful myths the person may have absorbed.

In case a witch has to attend to a person who is possessed by the Christian devil or patriarchal demons, remember that the Great Goddess is LIFE. She can be stimulated even in the most brainwashed mind.

A trinity of priestesses should first purify the room with frankincense and myrrh, making invocations to the Four Corners of the Universe. Enclose the space with a protective magic circle.

Walk slowly around the room with a censer, holding it up in front of you. Pause at the East while the High Priestess says:

> *Watchtowers of the East—Ea, Astarte, Aurora, Ashtoreth—come into this house. Come through the doors, through the walls, through the ceiling and the windows. Permeate this room with Your healing energy. Initiate (name) into Your Mysteries. Blessed be!*

If at this point a new name for the ill person comes to you, accept it and use it. Initiation means a new name, a new identity. If you don't find a new name for your friend, wait until one comes. Cure could depend on whether the person absorbs the new name.

The other two priestesses follow each invocation with affirmations:

> *The Goddess is here. The Goddess has come. She is present in us. Blessed be!*

Pause at the South and say:

> *Watchtowers of the South, Spirits of the Fires, Sacred Fires, come permeate this place. Burn away all anti-Life energy. Let Your work be done through the heart, through the blood. Come now and heal (name). Blessed be!*

The accompanying priestesses:

> *The Goddess has come. The Mother is here. The healing be done. burn away all ills. Blessed be!*

Pause at the West:

> *Watchtowers of the West! Goddess of Cleansing, of the Waters of Life, come and wash away all ills. Equalize as only the Waters can. Permeate this place. Flow through*

(name), work through the muscles, through the fluids, blend in the blood. In, in comes the good! Out, out goes the ill! Blessed be!

The other two priestesses say:

The Goddess has come. Welcome! The Goddess of Love is here. Welcome! She washes away the ignorance like rain. So welcome! Blessed be!

Finally, pause at the North and say:

Watchtowers of the North! Great Earth Mother Whose destination is the darkest of space. Earth-Mother, Earth-Daughter! Make a new manifestation of (name's) thoughts. Bind the ills with Your assured hand and take them to the underworld. There lock them up under seven keys, and seven-headed serpents of Sacred Duties will keep them there for seven years, only to release them into the VOID. Blessed be!

All priestesses chant:

The Goddess is present. The Goddess is here. The Goddess is blessing all here who participate. She blesses (name of one priestess) who is fair and strong; She blesses (name next priestess) who is valiant and loving; She blesses (name third priestess) who is nurturing and generous. Blessed be!

This may be chanted repeatedly for strength and blessing.

Turn inward and hum to raise inner power. Holding a cup of clear water sprinkled half-and-half with honey, sprinkle it over the room and the ill person. This is the Mother's Holy Water. Have everyone drink of it if possible; if not, the priestesses drink for good luck.

Invocation of the High Priestess:

Hearken to me, Old Mother! You Who preceded all the gods! Astarte, Ishtar, Ashtoreth, Lilith, Havla! Come and aid (name) to find peace in Thee! Out, out, bad thought, imaginary devil, entity of ill fortune! Come in, come in, Mother of Cure, Mother of Love, Blissful Mother. Blessed be!

The trinity of priestesses should develop a rhythmic musical tune, using a bell, flute, cymbals, even sticks. The rhythm should be kept together and the invocation chanted over and over. You may change the mantra as you wish, but always keep the emphasis on the Mother Goddess aspect.

Also, tones of E are very healing and might be useful. If you can blow or hum an E, do so. Don't expect an immediate cure. The mind became ill over a long period of time, subjected to an incredibly bad mythology. It may take several sessions of hearing about the Goddess before the woman is able to see Her, feel Her, and have Her awakened within.

When you notice the woman is calming down (even the toughest cases have "rest periods"), try to give her an acupressure massage. Follow this with a scrubbing, using sponges in lukewarm water, then anoint the body with Priestess oil or rose-scent, and give a cup of Valerian tea for sleep. Make a circle of salt around the bed where she lies, and place large pentagrams overhead or under the bed. Keep freshly cut flowers at the bedside for guiding spirits.

If after receiving such loving care the person is still unresponsive the next morning, bring a big brass horn, the loudest you can find, and blow it into her room. Expose the body to sound vibrations so strong that the thought form can change.

Each time a repeat performance is needed, blow the horn as loudly as possible. Repeat purification of the room and continue chanting ancient imagery of the Goddess into the room. Use slide projectors, musical instruments, everything.

Repeat this treatment five times, once for each point of the Pentagram, but no more. If it hasn't worked by the fifth time, save your energies for yourselves and don't absorb any more of the sad madness that comes from an overdose of Christianity. Even witches have their limits.

Chapter 9

Shamanism
Throughout Herstory

Shamanic Roots of European Traditions

O mighty Goddess of the Seven Rays!
O mighty God of Seven Rays!
I offer you the great Stag sacrifice!
I place it under your Tree of Life.
Bless me with years worth living!
Bless me with days worth living!
Give my daughters long long lives!
Give my sons long long lives!
Give my arrow powers of the seven good luck!
Give my spear powers of the seven good luck!
(Shaman song from Osztjak tradition)

Before white people were Christianized, before Europe was taken by the sword of the great Byzantine Empire, before Rome extended its imperial grasp around Western Europe, white people followed a native European nature religion. This was a varied and ethnically diverse form of shamanism that related to the earth as a living god. The very word "shamanism" originated in Europe.

Constantine ruled the Roman Empire during the fourth century AD. His empire included most of the population of the continent. He opened the door to Christianity by making it a state religion and decreeing that Christian churches could hold property. This imported Middle Eastern religion had a feature very similar to what Europeans were used to at the time: a god who dies and is reborn. This was the old story of the Nature God of many names, the son of the earth, the Green Man, Pan, Zagreus, the corn god, and Dionysus. Europeans simply went on with their old practices and added the new.

But there was a significant difference in the new faith. Its followers shed the meek and mild attitudes of the original Christians, and developed a spiritual-imperialist theology. This new spirituality said, "If you do not worship our god as we tell you, you are of the devil and therefore we are justified in killing you and sending you to our god for punishment." Europeans didn't know how to repel this kind of reasoning. Like Native Americans, Native Europeans couldn't understand a Great Spirit that would force anybody to become a follower, or that this Great Spirit from the Middle East would be cruel, possessive and jealous. These attributes were not divine; they were the qualities of the church lords' imperialist thinking.

So the peasants reacted by going underground, practicing their Craft on the nature holy days and going to church Sunday mornings. But then came the awesome, consolidated power of church and state. During this period, which lasted from the eleventh to the seventeenth century, the church had the power of the state. The Christian hierarchy could arrest and torture anyone to extract "confession". The peasants, whose land the church coveted, were often the target. This is known as the "Burning Times"; the shamans were renamed witches and their nature worship labeled Satanism. True Satanism didn't even exist until the seventeenth century, and then only as a backlash to the Inquisition, which tortured and burned its innocent victims over "the Devil," a concept foreign to pagan mythology. Nine million men, women and children were burned alive in Europe to rid the land of the last vestiges of nature religions and gain the property of the accused.

My family has painful records of how my ancestors were tortured and killed: how they had to dig their own graves and lie in them, buried alive, only their faces showing, which the Christians then bashed in with iron rods. My heart is filled with eternal distrust toward a religion that sanctioned that genocide. Europeans killing each other over a book from the Middle East!

When they ran out of witches, the Christians looked to the "savages" of Africa and became slave traffickers. Then onward to the New World, where they became Indian killers. Today they own television stations and preach the "gospel" of imperialism. Their new activism has taken them to Central America, where they hope to subdue with New Right evangelism what the USA can't conquer with arms, contras and death squads.

Let's look at our own heritage. We know more about Native American shamanism than our own. We have honorable spiritual roots, so let's reclaim them! White people worshiped Life and the elements of nature; they prophesied by the birds and the winds; they practiced rune magic. Most significantly, they used song and dance as magical tools. For example, they used song to gain the love of a man or woman, and they danced to invoke the favors of the earth for healthy crops and children. They even used music to commune with ancestor spirits. The only relic we have from those times is our Goddess embroidery, worn by brides at country weddings and folk dances, often ending up in the National Folk Ensembles. Take a look at visiting folk dance groups from Hungary, Poland, Bulgaria, Russia or Yugoslavia. You will see how the principles of the Old Nature Religion are acted out in sacred dances which survived centuries of persecution. The four corners of the universe, the four elements and the center are very clearly danced in these performances. Women perform the dances of puberty rites, blessing the brides and the mothers. Both sexes dance out the divine wedding in an ecstasy of women's whirling red skirts, and the black pants and white shirts of the men. There is no shortage of dances celebrating flirting and finding a partner. Competition between the sexes— trying to outdo each other in difficult dance steps—is another favorite theme.

A shaman was chosen in the womb. There was often something physically unusual about the baby and the family knew they had a special child. Sometimes the babies had an extra bone in the form of a tooth, or as the children grew, they displayed a special talent for dancing or singing, or perhaps wild animals gathered around them without harming them. Sometimes a shaman child was sickly; there are many tales of great shamans who spent their entire childhood in bed, weak and coughing. These children were harder to recognize, but by the age of seven (a lucky number to shamans), the invisible world came and "stole" them to educate them in shamanism. The family was expected to let the child go without a fuss, because it was a great honor to be chosen. The shaman child was returned to the community at age thirteen, another lucky number of old Europe, and found her or his function in the tribe.

What did they learn from the shamans? They all reported a common story, of being taken up the Tree of Life, step by step, and introduced to the masters of the elements air, fire, water and earth. They learned from each master how to use their powers to serve the people. Then came the last step; the young shamans reported having been dismembered, torn limb from limb, without pain. When they had experienced total annihilation, their teachers pieced them back together. Those children who had been sickly became the healers, and were never sick again.

In the old nature religion, shamans were of both sexes. However, the paths of female and male shamans were very different. Male shamans often had to wage duels over territory while great thunderstorms raged over the land and the people hid in fear. First the shamans would shift shape and battle each other in the form of great blue bulls, their clashing of horns audible for miles. Then they changed into snakes, wolves, eagles or falcons. The victor retained the duties of community service, while the loser had to move on and find his own territory. Male shamans did not kill each other. A fatally injured shaman died and was reborn because his knowledge included the skill of traveling to the realm of the dead and back.

A female shaman had a different task. After returning to her family, she often became the herbal master. Female shamans tended to live on the outskirts of their community, where they erected a spirit house. In this house, they prayed to their guides, the great Mother Bear, the Heaven's Queen, Chief Woman, or Grandmother-on-the-Moon. If a female shaman asked a male shaman for help, he was obliged to give it to her and her people. If she asked him to leave, giving up his hardwon territory, he had to do so, because her status as Spirit Woman included this power. Spirit Women from the great plains, mountains and rivers of Europe maintained tribal unity, happiness and wealth.

There was rarely more than one shaman per tribe. It was a very special position, supported by the entire community. The relationship between shaman and people was not as it is today between clergy and parish. The shamans were not rich. They were responsible for the weather, the bounty of the hunt, the health of the babies, the culture of the people, the dances and songs, and the shaman drums and wolf lyras.

European shamans had many important magical tools. Their spirit wand, usually of birch, oak or alder, came from a tall branch on a sacred tree. These sacred trees had several "steps" on them so the shaman could climb up and speak directly to the spirit world. She would put her spirit wand in her spirit house, climb the tree, and go into a deep trance. Each step served to deepen the trance state, and once she was on top, her face portrayed the altered state of consciousness. Her head bore a shaman crown. A woman's crown was often made from wildflowers, herbs and feathers; men's were made of bones, animal heads, feathers and branches.

The most appreciated European shaman instrument was the lyra, made of five strings from gray wolves' intestines. Each string belonged to a world of the unseen. The lowest string belonged to the earth, the highest to the sky. When the lyre was played, people and beasts were healed and the rain was controlled. After a healing, the shaman would proclaim her most powerful talents:

> *Rightly people say*
> *I am a knower of magical songs*
> *Rightly people say*
> *I am a knower of magical words.*

Song of the Holy Women

> *I am singing a shamansong! I am singing a shamansong*
> *Dwelling in seventh heaven*
> *living in the sixth heaven*
> *My Mother created me.*
> *Round formed lakes like water-rings*
> *like heads of the wild rooster-round*
> *I Spiritwoman descended.*
> *Into a golden cradle I descend*
> *I Spiritwoman.*
> *Dangling from a golden chain*

I descend into the depths,
I Spiritwoman.
Upon a mound built by dippers
I descended, I Spiritwoman.
Upon a sleigh with double corners
I embarked, I Spiritwoman.
The cornered sleigh I embarked on,
I Spiritwoman.
The darkest of night's dark center
Of the Crone Spirit
with the hearing divine
I Spiritwoman.
Over to the south of the river Ob
The big-shouldered Bear queen
they celebrate her holyday in feasts
I hear, I Spiritwoman.
Black fur-lined rich nest
Red fur-lined rich nest
I hold up my white head
my proud hundred-locked head
I Spiritwoman.
Upon my five-fingered foot
I fasten my reindeer boots,
I Spiritwoman.
Upon my six-toed foot
I fasten my reindeer boots,
I Spiritwoman.
Black wild prayer lucky jacket
Red wild prayer lucky jacket
I threw upon my holy shoulders,
I Spiritwoman.
My girdle lucky at black prayer
I fastened around my hips,
I Spiritwoman.
Red girdle, lucky at red prayer,
I girded myself with, I Spiritwoman.
My moonbeam-spotted magic veil
I placed upon my hundred-curled white head,
I Spiritwoman.
My sunbeam-spotted magic veil
I bound my hundred locks of hairs

I Spiritwoman.
From the village away
I am stepping away, I Spiritwoman.
From the cities away
Stepping away, I Spiritwoman.
I am the keeper of
a hundred stags and herd
I Spiritwoman.
I am the keeper of a hundred reindeer
I Spiritwoman.
I am the soul of the woods
I step the three steps
of the sacred Nymph spirit girl
I am stepping the four big steps
of the maiden spirits
I Spiritwoman.
My names are:
Black Cat-formed Priestess
Black Cat-formed Priestess
My other names are:
Hissing like a she-sable Priestess
Hissing like a she-sable Priestess
Such fame is spread about me
I Spiritwoman.
After all this
The woodspirit girls' three steps I step out
I Spiritwoman.
The woodspirit Maidens' four big steps I step out
I Spiritwoman.
In the fish-rich bays of the river Ob
Prosperous bay
I leave behind the seven big cities
I Spiritwoman.
The dwelling of the geese-feathered men
the dwelling of the traveling shaman
on the reindeer-beaten path
I go there myself, I Spiritwoman.
The seven-woodbeamed roof
The six-woodbeamed roof
Encircle the dwelling
Seven times in the daytime

I encircle the dwelling
six times in the nighttime
I Spiritwoman.
This ancient woman built
from redwoods carved door
from forestpine carved door
I open up with my five-fingered hands
I Spiritwoman.
I enter the house filled with boys' happy noises
I enter the house filled with girls' happy noises
I Spiritwoman.
The people there bring me fresh tinder fire and fresh musk
So they welcome me, I Spiritwoman.
Bless you women, filled with gifts of laughter
Bless you men, filled with gifts of laughter
To your daughters I wish long long lives
To your sons I wish long long lives
I Spiritwoman!
On my five-stringed instrument
I play the lowest string
The lower Crone spirits sing, let them sing!
I play the highest string
The highest Queen spirits sing, let them sing!
What can I leave you with?
I leave you my lucky dance for the rivers' fishes
I leave you my lucky dance for the forests wild
When I leave you
No sickness shall touch you!
My wide inner lining of my sacred cape
enfold you with protection!
The sleeves of my sacred cape
bless you all with, bless you all!

Initiation of the Shaman Drums:
Invocation to the Fire Mother

Shamanism in my own country was the dominant pagan ministry. Both sexes could become shamans. This chant is one of the lessons taught shamans on the astral plane. The shaman would drum and chant under the full moon, beating her drum as her feelings dictated. From then on, the drum served as a direct line to her guardian spirits; whenever she played her drum, they would respond to her with help.

Blessings! Blessings! Blessings!
You are the white nights' fire blessing!
You are the Queen's pure blessing!
You are my six-humped white Mare!
My six-eyed speckled Tiger!
Thirty-headed Fire Mother!
Forty-headed Virgin Mother!
The cooker of the raw things!
The thawer of the frozen things!
The fanner of the green flame!
Robed in green whooshing silks
She who descends on seven slopes
She who dances the seven dances
She who plays the seven games!
You are the Mother of the Triple Flame
Woven pearly horns upon your forehead!
You are the keeper of the stone hearths!
Thirty-headed Fire Mother!
Forty-headed Virgin Mother!
Immaculate Purity!
All wise scientist Mother!
Let our eyes see no evil
Let our hearts know no evil
Descend holding the white flame aloft
Descend encircling six times
Descend blowing forth blue flames
Be our Mother o whirl...
Be our Father o swirl...

Shaman Invocation to the Goddess of Spring

Upon my back my children sitting
pressing my back, protect me!
Upon my shoulders my children
protecting my shoulders, protect me!
Before the Moon is full
At the sight of the Sun
At the beginning of the year
The fruit trees' blooming time
At the cry of the she-cuckoo
The Earth opens and green appears
The trees open and buds appear
I'll be there for you, don't fear!

Weather Work

The witch's space in society, her value and usefulness, developed out of a need for her ability to make rain. Rainmaking always figured prominently in agricultural matriarchies, and even today shamans are called upon to make rain for their communities. Each country thus developed its own brand of shamanism, and all of these are valid. In Japan, when a shaman wants to make rain, she picks some flowers and then throws them away on the road, so the skies will presently open and weep. In ancient Greece, the priestesses used to make water on a bullhide in order to bring rain. Among Indians, ringing cowbells and performing certain dances to the rain gods seem to do the trick. Dianic witches work with a circle, where power is raised and the Goddess of all organic life, the Fair Luna, Selene, Helena, Diana, the Moon is addressed for all the healing rains.

Gather at least five sisters and go to a parched and wild place where nobody can see you. Create the circle as usual, but when invoking the Four Corners, call the Goddess of Water and Her clouds from all directions. This is because it may not be known exactly how the Lady will accommodate the circle, and She may have to be called in from all sides.

In weather work it is very important to remember that rain is made to fill a need. Witches do not go out practicing rainmaking just to see whether they can or not.

The Goddess of All Life is apt to defy you if you try to interfere with Her works out of pride. Her real work is not to drop everything (volcanoes, earthquakes, rivers) just because one witch is summoning. Weather work performed consciously, as a service to the community, is what the job is all about. However, you must still accept the possibility of failure without sadness or getting an attitude. The Lady may have better things to do, or decide that no rain is a better plan.

But in case of dire need of the people, priestesses brought the rains down with enough regular success that the Goddess appears to have taken notice of the people's wishes.

Understanding all this, take a purifying bath, adding a handful of salt to the bath water, before going to the circle. Anoint your body with Priestess oil, sacred to the Moon Goddess. Secure a flower, preferably a white or yellow rose or lily, and place it in the middle of the circle. Take deep-sounding drums, cymbals, cowbells, and if you have cowbones with which to make rhythm, bring them. Use willow wands—willow loves the water best—rather than athalmes in this ritual, especially for drawing the sacred circle and the pentagram of protection in the air. Bring a bucket of water into the circle, and let the flowers float in it. Raise power by looking up at the Moon and imagining a cone which rests on your shoulders and rises to Her face. Begin a unifying hum.

Shaman, turning to the East:

> *Hail to Thee, Goddess of New Dawn!*
> *Hail to Thee, powers of the East!*
> *Bring us Your protection and blow*
> *Your clouds here to rain! Blessed be!*

Shaman, turning to the South:

> *Hail to Thee, Powers of Great Fire!*
> *Witness our rites and blow*
> *Your water-laden clouds overhead!*
> *We need the gentle drops to heal our fields*
> *And grow the substance of life. Blessed be!*

To the West:

> *Hail to Thee, great Goddess of Waters!*
> *Corner of the West!*
> *Aphrodite, Goddess of Life!*
> *Lift Your heavy clouds,*
> *Your vast western waters,*
> *And blow them toward our lands!*
> *We await Your rain as we await rebirth!*

To the North:

> *Hail to thee, Demeter!*
> *Whose Earth is parched in this place*
> *And whose daughter, Persephone,*
> *Is growing old before Her time.*
> *The greens are yellow and life is thin.*
> *Reach out Your mighty brown arms*
> *And embrace Your lover, the Winds.*
> *Squeeze from Her arms the life-giving rain we need.*
> *So mote it be!*

Now begin to dance around the bucket of water. Burn frankincense and myrrh in your cauldron. These are favorites of Isis.

While the dance is growing in energy, first slowly, then faster as the spirit is captured, and from East to South to West to North, one of the women chants this very old rain-making rhyme from Asia. I have translated it from the Hungarian.

Kajrakan![1] Kajrakan!
Blessings! Blessings! Blessings!
Give a handful of space for waters in the sky!
Give a needle-sized space in the waters of the sky!
I am the daughter of the Shaman!
I am the willow on the river banks!
My people are shouting for you!
Demeter is waiting for you!
Be the earth's navel in the sky!
Be the sky's navel in the earth!
Spirits of our mothers, I invoke you now!
Open up the shutters of the sky!
Give a handful of opening for the rain,
Give a needle's point opening in the sky,
Burst forth from the Mountain Mother's back!
Burst forth from the lap of the River Goddess!
Great Luna, manifest yourself!
Waters, waters, waters coming down.
Blessings! Blessings! Blessings!

While the music-making and dancing continue, pick up the bucket of water and splash each other liberally with it. It is best to do this naked, splashing water on each other's fronts and backs, shrieking and hooting and making wild. Let the flowers fall to the ground, and do not pick them up. Now dance over the wet area until you are exhausted. All fall down on the ground, still calling for the rains. Wait until the energy slows, then thank and dismiss the spirits. The rains will come.

Parting Clouds: Whistling Up the Winds

Weather work, like personal work, is witches' work, and parting clouds is a good way to start practicing it. Pick a nice place outdoors and contemplate what you are going to do. If possible, you should sit with your back against a tree, since your aura is magnified when combined with the tree's energy, and the magnified waves get larger and higher all the time you connect with the tree. If possible, sit in the Goddess position.

Choose any cloud you want, and visualize it as it separates. Work on this only as long as it feels good and you are successful. If it doesn't work the first time, stop before you reach a point of frustration and resentment. Just let go of it for a while, and then check later to see how it's going. Parting clouds can make your whole day.

---

1. Old name for the Moon Goddess

Another good exercise to do as long as you are outside learning weather work and there is no wind is "whistling up the wind." This practice is useful for bringing in the clouds or cooling the weather if it's too hot. You can whistle yourself, or use a pipe of some sort, but you must whistle. Think of yourself as the wind, and do a little dance as you identify with Nature. With your hands, make pulling motions as you dance. Reach out for the wind and pull it to you while you whistle and dance.

The Song of Amergin:
A Round of the Year

Translated from the Celtic by Robert Graves and Chris Carol. Music © Chris Carol 1979. © 1948, 1966 by International Authors N.V.

> *To my mother, Gwendolyn*
> *Lady of the White Circle*

INTROITUS

> *Gone is our history, burned to ashes;*
> *Our poetry forgotten as time passes;*
> *Return deep memory, root of our dissension;*
> *Nurture the tree of present invention.*
>
> *Gone are our dignities, gone our powers;*
> *Once in freedom we blossomed as wild flowers;*
> *Life moved among us, like a loving mother;*
> *Sharing her wisdom, we care for one another.*
>
> *Without our mother, how shall we start living?*
> *Without our mother, how shall we seek beauty?*
> *Without our mother, how shall we die peaceful?*
> *Without our mother, how shall we be reborn?*

BETH-Birch
I AM A STAG OF SEVEN TINES

> *Welcome, welcome, welcome all ye here;*
> *Welcome, welcome, welcome in the year.*
>
> *Dark is the night and chill the winter wind,*
> *Crisp the snow on the barren furrow;*
> *Bring in the Yule Log, make the fire bright,*
> *We shall wish for a warm tomorrow.*
>
> *Over the fire the branches dangle*
> *Of holly bright that is King tonight;*

Red is the berry, green the prickle,
The sacred mistletoe glowing white.

Now we may feast and pass the Wassail Cup,
Sing the ballad with joy and mirth,
Soon we shall sleep and dream the night away,
Gathering strength for the Spring's rebirth.

On the earth, on the air,
Through the fire, by the water,
I am STRENGTH, the first month's daughter.

LUIS-Rowan
I AM A LAKE ON THE PLAIN

All on a plain there stands a lake,
A magic mirror doth it make;
And gathered on a wintry night,
Ye may behold a wondrous sight.

For in that lake reflected are
the Lady Moon and Morning Star;
Across the sky they journey on,
And to her son she sings this song.

Cradled in my loving arm,
Your dream unmarred by fear of harm,
Swift be your ride in the heavenly Boat,
As on the Milky Way we float.

Where turns the Crown of the Northern Wind
A silver island shall you find
And on that isle a castle white
Wherein is peace and calm delight.

Inside that castle's silver wall
There stands a dark majestic hall,
And in that hall a Lady fair,
The end of all desire is there.

So slumber deep thou Heavenly Twin,
And so thy journey soon begin;
For they who in Lobe's flames will die,
Shall rise again, I promise thee.

On the earth, in the air,
Through the fire, by the water,
I am BREADTH, the second month's daughter.

NION-Ash
I AM A WIND OF THE SEA

In the moonlight, the crystal bright
Of our names is glowing clear;
Dragon stones stand alone
On the sand as we draw near...
Wave on wave, wave on wave,
Wave on wave of the sea mares rave,
Tides are high as we ride by,
Embrace the tide and with the sea mares ride.

Foaming, frothing at maddened mouth,
Hooves churning in the brine,
Tails flailing, ranting, raving,
We gather line on line.
Wave on wave, wave on wave,
Wave on wave of the sea mares rave,
At the spring tide, swell with pride,
Embrace the tide and with the sea mares ride.
Mighty now, we too must bow
To Time's mightier hand;
Comes the ebb tide, we subside,
And graze the golden sand...
Wave on wave, wave on wave,
Wave on wave of the sea mares graze;
One and all heed Rhiannon's call,
Embrace the tide and with the sea mares ride.

On the earth, in the air,
Through the fire, by the water,
I am DEPTH, the third month's daughter.

FEARN-Alder
I AM A TEAR OF THE SUN

Weep, weep for the sparkling stream,
Weep, weep for the great oak tree;
Weep, weep for the bright blue sky,
Weep for the memory.

Weep, weep for the sacred grove,
Weep, weep for the peaceful years;
Weep, weep for the fruitful field,
Weep for our present fears.

Weep, weep for the endless fight,
Weep, weep for the vengeance night;
Weep, weep now with all our might;
Weep for our birthright.

On the earth, in the air,
Through the fire, by the water,
I am CLARITY, the fourth month's daughter.

The legend of the Rollright Stones

Once there stood in this sacred place an alder grove, beside the stone circle. The alder buds spiralled on the twig in the dance of life; the flowers bursting green sang of the mystery of the waters; the red bark sang of the flames of fire; the brown twigs echoed the color of earth. . .

The circle now lies silent, each dewdrop a tear of the sun, sorrowing until the prophecy shall unfold. . .

That when the labyris is laid to the altar and her blood is shed, then shall the King Stone move, and the dance begin anew.

SAILLE-*Willow*
I AM A HAWK ON A CLIFF

I am a hawk on a cliff
Poised before the fray
In the dance of death, dance of life,
The hunter and the prey.

Flashing feathered streak, wicked beak,
Swift as the eye can see,
Straining every nerve, downward swerve
In glorious artistry.

Bright the open sky in my eye,
But blood is on my breath,
Thunder shakes the sky, as I fly,
In all of life is death.

On the earth, in the air,
Through the fire and water,
I am SKILL, the fifth month's daughter.

UATH-*Hawthorn*
I AM FAIR OF FLOWERS

I am fair of flowers,
Blossoming today,

Scent of women's sweetness,
Sprig of magic May.

Snowdrop white in beauty,
First of all the flowers,
Winter cannot bow thee,
Nor the darkness hours.

Sunlike shines the crocus
In the lengthening hours,
Wind and rain caress thee
Through the springtime showers.

Crimson bloom the roses
Fragrant past belief,
Scent the summer breezes
Bringing sweet relief.

Fairest of all flowers
Crown our roundelay,
Scent of women's sweetness,
Spring of magic May.

On the earth, in the air,
Through the fire, by the water,
I am BEAUTY, the sixth month's daughter.

DUIR-Oak
I AM THE ONE WITH CROWN OF FIRE

She is awakening
(Magic is afoot)
She is arising;
She is dancing;
She is glowing;
She is radiant;
She is brilliant;
She is beauty;
(Turn back the wheel lest we burn)
She is splendor;
She is shining;
She is setting;
She is fading;
She is dying;
She is peaceful;
(Magic is afoot.)

On the earth, in the air,
Through the fire, by the water,
I am MAGIC, the seventh month's daughter.

TINNE-Holly
I AM AN AVENGING SPEAR

I who heal may also hex,
The good enhance, the evil vex;
I am an avenging spear.

The rich and powerful know no fear,
Though the seasons change throughout the year;

But I'll speak up and make them hear;
I am an avenging spear.

For peace and love we ever yearn,
But some do wrong and never learn;
This time it won't be us that'll burn;
I am an avenging spear.

I'm tired of promises, tired of the lie
Of a better life after I die,
We take what's ours and touch the sky;
I am an avenging spear.

What goes up must soon come down,
So wipe your tears and mend your frown
Their time is up, go claim your crown,
I am an avenging spear.

On the earth, in the air,
Through the fire, by the water,
I am VENGEANCE, the eighth month's daughter.

COLL-Hazel
I AM A SALMON IN A POOL

Swiftly flows the river
From the mountain to the sea,
The rapids as they flow
Teach me what they know
Of strength and grace and speed,
And flashing as I go
I ever learn and grow.

Gently winds the river
Through the plain down to the sea;
The still and silent pool
Makes a wise one from a fool

With depth and calm and peace
And flashing as I go
I ever learn and grow.

On the earth, in the air,
Through the fire, by the water,
I am KNOWLEDGE, the ninth month's daughter.

MUIN-Vine
I AM A HILL OF POETRY

Hey the gift, Ho the gift,
Hey the gift of the living.

Queen of the dawn, Queen of the clouds,
Queen of the planet, Queen of the star;
Queen of the rain, Queen of the dew,
Queen of the welkin, Queen of the sky;
Queen of the flame, Queen of the light,
Queen of the sphere, Queen of the globe;
Queen of the elements, Queen of the heavens,
Queen of the moon, Queen of the sun.

On the earth, in the air,
Through the fire, by the water,
I am ECSTASY, the tenth month's daughter.

GORT-Ivy
I AM A BOAR

I am a boar on this high place
In the first fresh frost
On autumn's face;
The hunters call to sound the chase
But I am bold
I will run this race.

For many moons we roamed this land,
Where others fell
I learned to stand;

The old and great join in the dance
Courage and cunning are my inheritance.

On the earth, in the air,
Through the fire, by the water,
I am VALOR, the eleventh month's daughter.

NGETAL-Reed
I AM A SOUND OF THE SEA

Calmest cold of deepest deep;
Sinuous swishing of sea snake sidling;
Baleful bark of sorrowing seal;
Shrill shrieking of temerous tern;
Bounding breaker on ragged rock.
On the earth, in the air,
Through the fire, by the water,
I am TERROR, the twelfth month's daughter.

RUIS-Elder
I AM A WAVE OF THE SEA

I am a wave of the sea,
Rolling on forever onward,
Gathering strength
Pausing for none.

Sunbeam riding on the ocean wave,
Firefly riding in the sky,
Amazon riding on the ocean beach,
Old moon rising up on high;
Everything is beautiful
In the earth and sea and starry sky
Old moon fades and young moon grows
Our life will never die.

On the earth, in the air,
Through the fire, by the water,
I am FLOWING, the last month's daughter.

ENDING

I AM THE WOMB OF EVERY HOLT;
I AM THE BLAZE ON EVERY HILL;
I AM THE QUEEN OF EVERY HIVE;
I AM THE SHIELD TO EVERY HEAD;
I AM THE TOMB TO EVERY HOPE;
BLESSED BE MY NAME.

Chapter 10

Masika's Book of Life:
A Hungarian Heritage

Masika Szilagyi

Introduction

My mother, Masika, was the result of an immaculate conception, the facts of which are strange but true. Grandmother lived outside the small town of Jaszentandras, on a farm used for livestock and various crops. Through seven months of the year that Masika was born, Grandmother had no idea that she was with child. She had not been fertilized by a man, and menstruated regularly every month. However, she put on weight, and when her back began hurting a little she went to the doctor for a checkup. To everyone's astonishment, Grandmother returned home with my mother, all wrapped up in a baby blanket. At birth, Masika lacked nearly everything necessary for a healthy baby, and weighed a mere 170 dekagrams. Truthfully, nobody expected her to survive.

But this baby showed extraordinary endurance, and Victoria, an old woman who worked in Grandmother's house, adopted Masika almost as her own. Constantly vigilant, Victoria kept a close watch on Masika, cooking very special foods for her while nursing her into health. Victoria was a very well-known witch from Transylvania.

From Victoria, my mother learned all the arts of witchcraft: how to bless and curse; how diseases are cured with natural herbs; how to understand the language of animals; how to read cards and omens; how to speak with spirits.

One time Mother became seriously ill, and doctors were imported from the capital, Budapest, to heal her, but nothing they did made her any better. The illness spread to her kidneys and eyes. She was at her end.

Late one night, as Masika lay dying in bed, she awoke to find Victoria in her room. The old woman's hands bade Masika to keep silent as she brought two containers into the room—one filled with thirteen eggs, the other empty. Then Victoria pulled open the curtains of the window, allowing the full Moon to shine brightly into the room. "The time has come," she said, as she took Masika's nightgown off and sat the child in the bright beams from the Moon. Mother's skinny little body trembled in the cold as Victoria began her cure.

One by one, Victoria took the eggs from the basket, stroking each one gently and fully over a part of Masika's body. She left not one inch untouched. She placed the eggs in the empty basket after she used them.

Victoria prayed constantly as she did this, chanting rhymes for power and healing, mixing sweetly the Pagan with the Catholic, according to Universal Imagination.

"I am going to take this illness away from you," promised Victoria. She then went home to build very special nests, placing the healing eggs in them. Later, she cleverly left them in various places on the dirt roads of the countryside, as if they were stray nests left by some wandering hen. Daily she visited the nests, watching to see how many of the eggs were still there.

Then one day Victoria whispered to my mother, "Only two nests are left, and when they have been picked up, you will be well."

The physicians from Budapest just looked on, waiting for the child's death, but instead, Masika's fever broke. "All the nests are gone!" Victoria told Masika on another day, and Mother got up and walked, acting fully cured. Years later my mother said she had been healed because she believed Victoria more than she believed any other human being.

There were occasional nights in Masika's childhood when Victoria would lift her out of bed and walk a long way in the dark with her. They would march steadily through thickets and bogs until they reached a grove, thickly shaded from the eyes of outsiders, where other people of all ages were assembled around a fire. Masika remembers such groups gently singing of ancient shamans, who could be invoked when people in trouble needed help. Sometimes, at the end of a song, the members of the group would spit into the fire so that it sizzled. They invoked Boldogaszony, the Glad Woman, Great Lady of the Hungarians, and Special Mother to our nation. Although the State and its religion attempted total domination of the peasants, so that no one dared miss a Sunday at the Church, underneath the Hungarian "subas" (sheepskin coats) the hearts beat Pagan.

Victoria excelled in telling moon-tales. "There are mountains there," she would say, "and valleys, but not one flower, not one tree grows there. This is the land of the sad, sad spirits who are searching for peace. Lady Luna flies sorrowful through her once-blooming realms. She perches on the edges of the Moon and looks out from there into the great starry Universe, thinking about the Golden Times—when waters and trees, flowers and beings lived there with Her. But today it is the Land of the Dead." Thus did the old Transylvanian weave her tales.

Victoria could not even write her own name, but she was often seen carving signs on a willow branch, after which she would wrap the branch up and send it to someone—a witchy letter.

For fourteen years Masika lived in the same house with Victoria. During this time Victoria constantly taught my mother all she knew about everything. She spent time teaching Masika how to recognize the marks of death around people. Masika recognized such marks, invisible yet touchable, when visiting one day. ''We shall not see this woman again until her burial,'' Masika informed my grandmother, and soon the woman suffered a fatal heart attack.

Such incidents brought Masika quite a bit of attention from her family. ''How does this child 'know' such things?'' they wondered, agreeing eventually that it must have been coincidence. However, Masika's knack for prophecy grew, and her accuracy was amazing. The family, however, was concerned about this strange child, and especially about Masika's habit of talking to spirits all the time, giving the impression that she was forever talking to herself. Eventually, Grandmother took my mother to the nerve-doctor.

The doctor spent an entire morning with this skinny 14-year-old tomboy. During the examination Masika told the doctor, ''There is a woman standing beside you, and she is one who loved you very much. It is too bad you cannot see her, for she is very beautiful.''

''Describe her to me,'' demanded the surprised doctor.

With complete accuracy, Masika then described the doctor's mother— the hairdo, coloring, clothing and the single red rose she wore over her breast (the rose the doctor had given her at their last goodbye). Masika knew it all. The doctor was impressed. His diagnosis of my mother's condition was that she had an overly sensitive nervous system, inclined to neurasthenia, and able to sense what the average nervous system could not.

''She is by no means ill,'' the doctor reported to the family. ''My advice to you is to ignore her when she makes these predictions, and when they come true, make nothing of it, but act as if it is the most natural thing in the world. Do not act surprised or afraid around her. She will grow out of it.''

The family tried to follow these directions. The unexpected became the routine. For example, on her way to school, Masika might turn to someone and say, ''Cousin Miklos just stepped on the train to Karcag. He will be here by eleven.'' Nobody acted surprised. The family simply told the cook to prepare one more portion for dinner—company was coming. Everyone now knew that Masika was a ''seer.''

Masika's education in the old ways continued. When Victoria read the cards for someone, she would teach Masika her secrets.

''They think I watch the faces of the cards alone,'' confided Victoria. ''The pictures only serve to take my mind away so that I don't see the lamps, the furniture or the person whose cards lie before me. I only listen, and I hear, very clearly from deep inside me, the story which the person must hear from me. Then I speak aloud what I have heard within.'' Victoria believed that card readers had an obligation to refrain from passing into a deep trance in order to rise above immediate circumstances, allowing the inner voice to flow undisturbed.

Victoria taught Masika to bless, to attract, to suggest. If Victoria wanted to see somebody, she would repeat her "special names" a few times, encouraging my mother to say the names too. Then she mentally told her to put her coat on, open the door, walk through the streets to the home of the chosen visitor, and ring her bell. "Then," directed Victoria, "take her by the hand and don't let go, but lead her home to us. Mentally open the door again and let her in. Gaze into her eyes very deeply and say, 'We are expecting you! Come and visit.' " The spell worked in three days, and Masika had fun "bewitching" reluctant boyfriends with her newly-found charms. (When you work this on somebody a great distance away, expect a letter or phone call rather than a personal visit, unless the finances of the person are abundant.)

I once visited Masika in Budapest. I found her in her studio creating masks of ancient women, shamans and folklore figures. She was a happy woman. She was finally able to build her own house, in which there was room for her art as well as her family. Since she was among the mere two percent of successful artists in Hungary who are women, I was very proud of her. I asked, "Are you still practicing witchcraft?" Mother was taken by surprise. "How would I have the time," she answered. "I am much too busy. Besides, I gave all that up years ago."

The next day we were outside looking at Masika's garden, and she complained to us about the highrise that was under construction across the street from her beloved new home. Intended as a college for international students, the edifice solidly blocked Mother's otherwise perfect view.

"So what?" I shrugged. "Why don't you brush up on some of your powers and erase a few stories from that building?"

"No, I gave that all up," Masika replied seriously, but I could see her eyes sweeping the top two stories of the building with new perspective.

Then, about the time when the first star, Venus, became visible, and the Moon was rising in a crescent over Budapest, my mother got up from her studio workbench and washed the clay from her hands. Walking deliberately to the garden, she stopped and faced the highrise, crossing her thumbs and stretching her arms out to the Moon. She whispered the names of four Hungarian shamans, one for each corner of the Universe. Then she waited, motionless. Soon a small wind woke up and began to rustle the rosemary leaves in her garden. "They are here," noted Masika with satisfaction.

"My curse upon this building ahead of my view," she said. "Curses upon each of its four corners so that they crack. Curses into each molecule. A curse upon the whole edifice, that it may fall! This is my wish. Do it for me, spirits!'' Then she returned to the house, washed her hands once more and set about preparing dinner.

Nearly a full Moon cycle went by. I had forgotten Masika's emphatic curse until my brother, who was also aware of it, brought me an interesting item from the newspaper. The article told of problems with the new college building across from Mother's house. It seemed that cracks had inexplicably appeared in the walls and foundations, and sewer water had flooded the basement. Moreover, the corners of the building appeared to be out of alignment. The building's engineers had been thrown in jail. Building a faulty structure in Hungary was a politically punishable act.

"That crafty witch," I laughed, as my brother looked at me warily.

Soon after, the construction workers and engineers removed two floors from the building—just enough to remove the obstacle from my mother's view. Feeling a little guilty about the episode and her obvious part in in it, Mother decided to make it up to the students who moved into the college. She began leaving slightly imperfect or cracked ceramic art pieces in her yard. The students appropriated every one and held a successful fundraiser with the treasures.

Clairvoyance in the Family

My stepfather, Imre, was a physician who came from a long line of healers. He was the seventh son of a seventh son, and a sensitive of the good sort. His life was completely possessed by the fates of his patients, and he stayed in touch with them even after they left the hospital.

One night, as Imre was sleeping at home, we were all wakened by the sounds of his yelling and screaming. We found him sitting bolt upright in bed, frantically pointing at his forehead. Mentally, he was back at the hospital.

"Try it on the temples, Zoltan, try it on the temples!" he yelled, obviously calling to a doctor at the hospital who was not noted for his brilliance. Then Imre flew into a rage, shouting, "Damn you! You've killed the patient with your incompetence!" He fell back against his pillows.

Masika woke Imre, demanding to know who had died. "One of my patients in the children's ward," he groaned. "Zoltan was on duty and failed to give the child a blood transfusion."

The next morning Masika accompanied Imre to the hospital, where the porter took off his hat to my father as he entered—a sign that there had been a death during the night. Imre questioned Zoltan directly, acting uninformed because he didn't want to have to explain how he had "seen" all that had occurred the night before. Zoltan became very nervous at Imre's probing, and tried to convince Imre that he had done everything possible.

"Did you try on the child's temples?" prodded Imre.

"Oh, I tried that, yes. I tried everything!" Zoltan lied.

Imre threatened to have Zoltan's license taken away, and Zoltan finally confessed to everything. Imre fired Zoltan from the city's hospitals anyway.

Another time, when Imre was operating on a surgical patient, a colleague noticed that tears were streaming down his cheeks onto his white mask. Concerned, he asked Imre if he was all right. Continuing with the operation, Imre paused only briefly to say, "My father has just died." Then he finished the work successfully and went home to find a telegram announcing the sudden death of his father.

Imre's mother also possessed this ability to "see". She was a curious woman, a teacher by profession, whose great sorrow in life was that her husband slept around with various patients in town. As a protest, she refused to leave the house for many years. I would visit her often in her home, and she would tell me, "Little Joy, why don't you go down to Maiu Road? Five yellow roses just opened up on the right-hand side. Pick them for our table." I would obey and find the five yellow roses just opened, exactly where she said they would be.

The day after her husband's death, Imre's mother received an urgent call from the school in town. The regular teacher was ill and they needed a replacement immediately. This amazing woman, who hadn't left her house in twenty years, suddenly picked up her purse and a few books, and left to teach school as if she'd done it every day. She taught as a regular teacher for the next ten years.

And then, of course, there was my mother. She once saw a German airplane crash in the vicinity of home. She spoke with the wounded soldiers, ran home for first aid, and returned with her father to administer it, only to find that there was no plane, no crash, no wounded soldiers. This was before the Second World War had begun, and Masika's father rebuked her strongly, saying, "You must need a cold shower, saying such things!"

Exactly one year later, at the same place, Masika again witnessed the crash as she had seen it earlier. She convinced her father to go with her, after he threatened her with the spanking of her life if she had made it up. This time, however, it was all horribly true—even the war with Germany.

"Hey, do you know I was talking with Mrs. Y last night," Masika might remark one morning as she told us about her latest dream. "I had a few jokes with her before I remembered to ask why I was talking with her when she wasn't dead yet. So Mrs. Y said, 'Oh, haven't you heard, Masika? I passed away last Tuesday.' So, what do you think about that?" Talking to the dead was Masika's favorite nighttime entertainment.

Often she would call up other people after breakfast, to relay messages that she had received the night before. "Hello, this is Masika. I talked with your mother last night, and she said she is in favor of you sending her granddaughter to college. And one more thing, she said there is some money in the hollow pickle jar in the basement. You'll have to look through the rubble to find it, but she wants you to use it.'' The beginning of a normal day in my mother's house. And Masika was always right.

Fortune telling was a specialty Masika practiced a lot, sometimes simply for her own entertainment. While riding on a crowded bus in which there was no seat for her, Masika would address a rider lucky enough to be seated: "Hmmm. You are going to see about that new job. You have an appointment with Mr. Kieuz's firm. Well, don't worry, you will get a job with that firm, but not the job you are applying for today.'' As a result, Mother usually received a seat and the eager attention of a busload of passengers, reluctant to disembark until they had their fortunes told.

The Hungarian Olympic team used to visit our home before each Olympic Games to have Mother tell them how best to use their energy and how to win the most medals. Behind the Iron Curtain, winning is a political must and failure is not safe. Masika would read the cards and then tell the competitors what to watch out for, what to do and where to go, and even what foods to avoid. After the Olympic Games in Helsinki, in which Hungary won sixteen gold medals (unheard of for such a small country), the winners returned to our home and gave Masika a trophy for her help.

Masika's most spectacular achievement probably was speaking Egyptian while in a trance. Only some university language professors could understand her during these times. It is believed that Masika was once an Egyptian priestess of Hathor, the Maiden Goddess of Egypt. Masika thinks she must have disobeyed the rules of her order by consorting with men, and was removed from the order as a result. Perhaps the Order of Isis would have been a lot easier on Mother's karma, since the Mother Goddess does consort with men, but such are the Fates.

Masika belonged to several psychic groups, the first of which was the so-called "Paris Nine.'' She was still very young, an art student who joined as the group's only female member, and she became the group's medium. When she returned to Hungary, she belonged to another secret society that practiced tele-transportations, quite a difficult thing to do.

Book of Superstitions

Out of the fertile field of Hungarian Pagan culture comes the *Book of Superstitions,* grown from religious, ethnic, cultural and individual roots unlike any other, and indicative of my own roots.

1. If you receive good news or are healed of disease, don't say, "Thank Heaven, I am healed," or "Thank Heaven, I have money," or things of this nature, because the evil spirits get jealous and mess up your good fortune. If you said something like this by mistake, knock on wood three times with your left hand, moving from the bottom to the top of the wood.

2. If your dog is sitting on her hind legs and howling, it means that she senses death and is announcing the approach of Hecate, the Death Queen, whose sacred animal is the dog. This could concern anybody who belongs in the house, or somebody on a journey to the house.

3. If you are traveling to visit someone without an appointment, and a bird flies across your path, forget the visit; the person will not be home.

4. If a bird shits on you, you will have good luck all that day if you don't wipe it off until the following day.

5. If your nose itches, you have adversities.

6. If you bang your elbow into a corner, an unexpected visitor will soon arrive. If the elbow hurts a lot, the visitor is from far away.

7. If you place a loaf of bread upside down on a table there will be fights in the home.

8. If salt is spilled from its container, let the one who upset it clean it up. Otherwise poverty will strike the house, bringing great fights over money issues.

9. If your left palm itches, money is coming to you; if the right palm itches, you will soon spend money.

Note: Masika doesn't really have too many superstitions. She says that this sort of thing is really for the Christians rather than witches, and that witches have too much studying to do to bother much with superstitions.

Book of Dreams

1. If you dream of stepping in animal excrement, that means good luck. If you dream about stepping in human excrement, that's an omen of bad luck. Dreams of stepping into your own excrement are usually omens of disgrace. If you dream of somebody else stepping into excrement, it means money will come to you.

2. If you walk in mud in your dreams, it means illness. If the mud reaches your heart, death is near.

3. If you step next to mud in a dream, you have escaped illness. If you step out of mud, your escape will be a lucky one.

4. If you dream of feeding strange children, it means gossip which is adverse to your own life.

5. If in a dream you brush your hair and lose many strands, troubles are coming. If you see white hairs as you comb you hair in your dream, the one you love will leave you.

6. If you dream of getting a haircut, shame is coming to you.

7. If someone in a dream braids your hair, it means a journey is coming to you.

8. If somebody cuts off all your hair in a dream, leaving you bald, you will die a violent death.

9. If you dream of bathing in clear waters, your life will take a turn for the better. If the waters are dirty and muddy, then troubles, illness and sadness are ahead. *Note: My experience has been just the other way around, but dreams are shaped by many variables, not the least of which are the dreamer and her culture.*

10. If in a dream you swim in a river whose currents take you farther and farther from shore, it means that the plans you are making will be difficult to achieve. If you dream of reaching the shore, you will overcome all difficulties.

11. If somebody is trying to drown you in your dreams, you have a strong enemy who envies your luck.

12. If you dream of taking a trip by train, car or ship, this means you are lagging behind in your work or plans.

13. When you dream of pushing through a dark tunnel, it is a birth memory.

14. If you dream of going for a walk while wearing a hat, it means your sex life isn't very active.

15. If you dance in your dreams, you are doing far more than necessary.

16. Crying while you dream means you will have a lighthearted day.

17. If you dream of lovemaking, you are not getting enough physical pleasure when you're awake.

18. If you are chased by wild animals in your dreams, it simply means you ate too much dinner.

Note: On the whole, only dreams that occur at dawn are fit for prophecy because the rest of our dreams are likely to be the product of stomach action, and they may interfere with true psychic messages.

Book of Cures

My heritage boasts a wealth of healer-women. The following is just a sample of Masika's folklore remedies and does not constitute a modern compendium of either diagnostic or treatment techniques.

1. Sickly child: If your child is skinny and pale, yawning more than playing, perform this thirteen-apple cure. Stick one iron nail in each of thirteen

apples. Place the apples out in the window to keep them fresh. Wait seven days, then take the nail out of the first apple and let your child eat the apple in two portions after meals. Follow this up with the other apples, always eating each apple in two sittings after meals. Replace the apples already eaten, thus feeding your child iron-reinforced apples throughout the winter. This will strengthen the bones and increase weight, vitality and stamina. *Masika's note: Isn't it wonderful how the ancient witch cures spoke to the need for adequate iron in the blood, far ahead of the medical doctors who had not yet learned even to read blood-counts, or wash their hands?*

2. Eye care: If your eyes begin to discharge, gather chamomile flowers and throw them in boiling water. If it's summer, use only fresh flowers. Boil the flowers for five minutes, then let steep for ten minutes, letting the mixture cool to room temperature. Using a clean white cloth cut into strips, wash your eyes with the liquid, then throw the cloths into the fire and burn them. Use each piece of cloth only once, and when you throw the third piece into the fire, say:

> *Queen of the Flames,*
> *Mighty Mother of Fire,*
> *Take away the sickness from the eyes.*
> *Protect me from illness!*

Do this three days in a row, in the morning and at night, and your eyes will be free from disease. *(Masika: This cure has existed for at least 350 years. The doctors then had no idea of bacteria, but the witches, by throwing the used cloths into the fire, prevented reintroduction of bacteria into the eye. And who taught the witches? Other witches.)*

3. Beautiful woman's skin care: Clean your skin carefully every night by washing it in lukewarm water and using a mild soap or fresh flowers to scrub the face. When your skin is clean, take the fresh urine of a pregnant woman and rub it on your skin. The next day, cook chicken soup (without paprika) and strain all the fine fat from the top. Using just a little of this, rub it well into your skin every night. Every Tuesday and Friday, lean over a hot tub of boiled chamomile tea and let the vapors enter your pores. The chicken fat is for use every night just before retiring. On Saturdays, when you wash your face, use rosemary leaves to scent the water. Mint may also be effectively rubbed into the skin. *(Masika comments: In the Old Days, vitamins were not yet discovered—only in the 20th century did scientists find that the urine of pregnant women is loaded with vitamins, and is used in the manufacture of many medicines. This skin care might sound laborious and disgusting to the squeamish, but it is still practiced with fine success in the country.)*

4. Love potion: Go to a tree which has Spanish flies swarming around it. Using your LEFT hand, pick up three handfuls of flies. Count them, marking every third one for your will. Kill them so that their bodies remain in one piece. Dry the flies slowly, taking off the hardest parts of their bodies and powdering the soft parts. Put this powder into hard liquor and let it stand for three days, then strain it and give a very short drink to the one you desire. Do not give her more than one drink, or the one you desire will become ill—the kidneys and the bladder could be harmed by too much of this drink. Do not be bashful after giving this drink, if you were not bashful about preparing it.

(Masika's note: Love must be easier than this. If you have to go through all this simply to have sexual pleasures with someone, maybe you should reconsider your lifestyle. I give this recipe for curiosity only.)

5. Backaches: If your back hurts very badly and you can only walk while stooped over, this is what you can do to get better. Prepare a clay bench for yourself, built with three rows of bricks—plaster it all around and make the surface as smooth as polished wood. It's good to build this in a place that's protected from the elements in all seasons. When it is completed, lie on the bench on your back. Fill red cloth sacks with fine sand. Have your helpers hang some from your ankles. Do the same to the shoulders, hanging the bags down from just above your head as you lie on the bench. Do this every day for about an hour, and use the bench afterwards whenever you want. Be careful and wise. A backache can appear to be gone, but when you catch a cold or otherwise get weak, it may come back again. If you cannot build this clay bench, put a strong, heavy board in your bed and sleep on that.

6. Cold sores: If your mouth has broken out with something nasty, it usually means you have eaten the wrong thing. Smear the sores thickly with your earwax on a swab. This makes the sores go away faster than any salve the pharmacies can give you.

7. Advice to men: When a young man has pimples, it's advisable for him to sleep with women. But when that's impossible, take large leaves of the comfrey plant and wash them thoroughly; this is important because dogs love to urinate on comfrey and dog urine is terrible for your skin. Once clean, the comfrey leaves are ready to put on your face overnight. The leaves work best when crushed in a cloth with a hammer, because then the juices are more available for absorption into the skin. This cure works for young women as well, of course, but women are not advised to sleep with men for their own skincare purposes.

8. Arthritis: This is a very old cure, and a rather painful one. Soak your body, the joints in particular, in hot water so that you feel warmed all the way through. Prior to soaking, gather a bunch of fresh so-called

stinging nettles and soak them in a large bowl with a small amount of vinegar added to the water. After your bath, let your helper take out a bunch of the nettles and strike them against your skin, paying special attention to the joints, the back and the knees. It is a stinging and painful cure, but the ancients swore by it.

9. If you have a boil, do not touch it, scratch it or bother it. It will go away. If your rheumatism bothers you during the winter, when all the nettles have been frozen, mix strong paprika with some chicken fat and apply it to the hurting joints. It will bring new, healing blood to the parts that need it. This cure is sold today in pharmacies, in heat-producing salves.

10. Earaches: If you have an earache, chop up a bunch of red onions. Put some cream in your ear and then stuff your ear with the finely-chopped onions. Lie on your good ear so that the vapors from the onions have a chance to cure your earache. Lay with this onion cure for at least an hour, and overnight if you can manage it. Repeat the treatment daily until the earache is gone.

11. For a headache, grind up some horseradish. While you grind it, inhale it, which will make you sneeze. Put some apple cider vinegar on the horseradish and eat it slowly. Don't do this on an empty stomach; it shocks the system. Let it steep in the vinegar for a half hour for a more potent effect.

12. At childbirth, the umbilical cord should be cut with a freshly sharpened, birch-handled knife. The knife is made by the expectant mother. She dresses the knife up in a baby hat, but nobody is allowed to see it until the moment when the midwife needs it to cut the cord. This practice of hiding the new knife and keeping it clean in baby clothing was one way the ancients used to assure good hygiene.

13. If your lot is good, such that you have gotten fat, and the dark blood in your face is making you purple, watch out! You could get a heart attack. Before this happens, call your local healer and let her bring three leeches. Take off all your clothing and lie down on your back for treatment. Let the leeches be put on your ass or your arms, but never on any major arteries! They will relieve your condition, used properly. The leeches suck the blood until they get enough, and then they fall off. If you desire to have them fall off earlier, put some salt on them. During the course of a month, you should only have five such treatments, allowing a day between treatments.

14. The wound which will not heal is still a medical threat. Scientists are still lost as to a cure. But in olden times, wounds in general were not considered necessarily a threat. If there was a hole in somebody's stomach, the peasants made that person fast and pray for three days, only permitting her to take milk internally. Then the healer-woman would prepare a drink with a mild solution of copper sulfate in lukewarm water and have

the sick person drink it. This made the patient vomit up everything from the bottom of the stomach, including ulcerous tissues, and the copper sulfate acted as a disinfectant on the freshly cleaned lining of the stomach. This was especially effective in early days because they didn't operate, and was an excellent way to remove sick tissues from the body.

15. In olden times, fresh wounds were treated and dressed with spiderwebs or mildew (which we know today to contain penicillin). If there was an inflammation or infection somewhere on the body, one remedy was to slice a ripe tomato and place it on the sore with a large comfrey leaf. All this was then tied to the body with red cloth. In treatments such as this, the bandage was often red, the color of vitality, and was considered important to the cure. Yellow, the color of the sun, was also popular in healing spells. In transferring sickness from a patient, the curing objects were often left for others to pick up and take away, but such tools were distinguishable by their yellow cloth, yellow leaves or yellow flowers. Those of the Wicca never picked up strange money, nests, eggs, or any strange items found on country roads, especially if they contained a yellow object. This always meant a transfer-cure.

16. If you have a weak stomach, or have stomach pains often, here is a treatment that has worked for many. Take three healthy potatoes and grind them slowly to a pulp. Let stand for fifteen minutes, then strain them into a cup—it will look like juice. Drink the contents of the entire cup before breakfast, then go back to bed. Toss and turn, lying on your stomach, your back and your sides, so that the juice gets to coat all the stomach. After this, eat some breakfast. This helps the stomach endure the input of the day's food.

Note: This last recipe was a major item in the charges against a healer-woman during a witch trial in 1570.

These very recipes have been modified and refined into what is modern medicine, especially in the part of the world where healers and physicians cannot afford chemicals. The cures of the witches are still the bases for many preparations sold in Hungary and other socialist countries today. In Third World countries, herbs and natural remedies are known from the core of medicinal treatments of the people.

From Mother's *Book of Sorrows*

My mother and I come from a long line, a great circle of witches. I am the last branch of an 800-year-old family tree, although I consider myself the first on the tree of the New World. Ever since I can remember, Mother kept a book about witch-burnings, intending to pass it on to me one day.

It was not easy getting this book from her. For years she claimed to have lost it, and other times she denied ever having it at all. Finally, Mother sent me her book. She called it her *Book of Sorrows* because it depicts the torture, burning and murder of witches—all with terrifying accuracy. I believe it to be a timely and powerful reminder of what was done to women in the name of Christianity not very long ago. Many of the archaic and repressive laws resulting from this period of mass hysteria are still on the books, and the persecution of the Goddess's children has not stopped to this day.

The following is excerpted from Masika's *Book of Sorrows*.

In Hungary, King Kalman declared a complete halt to any witch-persecutions, trials and tortures in 1175. In spite of this order the Christian churches still held legal witch burnings with no interference from the King. The total recorded number of witches burned at the stake was about 10,000 women. Since records were only kept by the Church, the actual number can be understood to be at least ten times that.

The victims included anyone performing any pagan act; carriers of herbal lore and cures; midwives, priestesses and prophets; any person with a witch's paraphernalia such as chalice or wand in the home; any women pointed out by a man who claimed he was hexed by her.

Accused witches were brutally tortured. To force confessions from the poor women, their tormentors would prick their bodies all over with hot needles. If the accused did not cry out, she was lost, since the devil obviously had his mark on her. After hours of torture, women were stripped naked and displayed in the middle of the town, usually in chains. They were then ridiculed and offered as frightening examples of what happened to pagans.

Meanwhile, the executioner would begin negotiations with the family of the unfortunate victim, soliciting a bribe for a fast, death-dealing blow. He met with each family in this way, sometimes taking every last possession from the house. If the victim's family could not meet the demand in some way, the woman was left to die a slow and wretched death.

Often this barbarism provided entertainment for the town. Every cry and scream was discussed by local observers as the Catholic priest held his crucifix high over the woman's burning flesh.

In spite of the intense tortures, the people clung to their old religion, refusing to give it up.

The last witch burned in Hungary was Margit Salka, who lived in Szeged on a small island in the river Tisza. Margit was an herbalist who had learned the skill from her mother. In 1869 she was accused of poisoning a man from the town and, although there was no evidence against her, she was burned to death. She was thirty years old. Even today her island is called "Witches' Island" in her memory.

This is an excerpt from the account of one particular witch "trial", that of Erzsebet Galantai in February 1761.

Judge: Do you confess that you made love potions and let young men from Csongrad drink of it so that they all became enamored of you?

Erzsebet: No. I know nothing of such a drink.

Judge: Do you confess that sitting on a wand you flew up and became a bird?

Erzsebet: No, I don't.

Judge: Do you confess that you spat upon the wheat-fields and thereby caused a great drought?

Erzsebet: No.

Judge: Do you confess that you gave birth to twins and then buried them alive?

Erzsebet: It is true I gave birth to twins, your Honor, but they were dead. I had to bury them, otherwise I would be suckling them, since my milk is oozing after them.

Judge: You had better admit to the rest of the charges or you will be tortured.

Erzsebet: I cannot, your Honor, because I have not done these things.

Erzsebet was then given over to be tortured. The sadistic men could do anything to her that they wished. The priests were eating lunch and dinner while the poor woman screamed from pain. The torturers poured hot water into Erzebet's mouth, and she finally confessed to everything. At that point she was sentenced to death.

Erzsebet had to dig her own grave. Then she was put in a casket that had the head end sawed off. When they placed her in the casket, her face was looking through the hole into the ground and the rest of her was buried alive. Then the men poked at Erzsebet's face with hot irons until she felt no more. At last, they chopped up her skull so that she could not rise by night to haunt them. All in the name of Jesus.

Another case took place in Transylvania in 1550. Anna Apor was a Transylvanian noblewoman. Her father was believed to be friendly toward the Turks; therefore he was beheaded and all his goods were confiscated. Later, when the King himself began making pacts with the Turks, it was feared that Anna might get back all her land. Gossip about her being a witch soon began.

Anna's supposed crimes include the charge that she turned people into wolves and dogs. She denied this, of course, stating that she would love to turn herself into a fly and leave her shackles behind. The judge hastily claimed that Anna had lost her powers because she had been sprinkled with "holy water" and smoked with incense. The judge further charged Anna with knowing the power of trees and herbs, which Anna acknowledged she did indeed.

Anna's fingernails were torn out. She was stripped naked and her beautiful hair was chopped off. Still she did not confess to being a witch, so they ordered the "water test" in the belief that witches always float and never sink. The whole town turned out as Anna was stripped naked and heavy chains were fastened around her waist. Slowly they lowered Anna into the Tizsa. It was December. Anna knew how to swim, unlike most women of the period, but she was so exhausted from the tortures that she sank and embraced the cooling waters like a mother.

The judges then declared Anna innocent, and one of them commented that her pain in this life would come in handy in the next world, facing her "lord". However, Anna was apparently swimming underwater, and soon surfaced. Her waist was bleeding from the chains. She was immediately judged guilty of all charges. Her death sentence was to burn at the stake, but a Transylvanian uprising occurred coincidentally with her pending execution, and the records do not show what actually happened to her. We believe that she died of hunger, forgotten in the dungeon, as the ruling class busied itself saving its property from the revolutionaries. Some say Anna was freed by her people.

There were instances of men also being executed for witchcraft. One such man, a leader of his town, was found guilty of witchcraft and his body was quartered so that each piece could be taken to a corner of the country as a warning to others disposed toward the practice of paganism.

Mother's *Book of Sorrows* has many "sister" books all over the world. In Tier, a city in France, only ONE woman was left alive. There were days when hundreds of women were burned, so that the stench of burning flesh would dissipate by the time Christmas was celebrated!

The worst persecutions took place in southern France, southern Germany, northern Italy and southern Austria. When the mother or father of a family was declared a witch, the children up to a year old were taken as well. Entire families were burned to death because of the fear of paganism. Later, Christians softened this stance, and only drove children of convicted parents around the burning pyres three times, flagellating their naked bodies. What cries, what memories must we all carry in our collective unconscious!

Many witchhunts were the direct result of greed over land and property rather than religious zeal. Whoever pointed a finger at a witch, resulting in her conviction and execution, was rewarded with ten percent of the murdered woman's goods. The Church received the rest. In Salem, in colonial America, the intent was the same. Cotton Mather had lands adjoining those of Goodie Nurse, and he wanted hers. He managed to acquire almost all the property of all the witches who were hanged.

The budding medical profession was also hungry to rid itself of the herbalists, who rivaled it. To cure was a bigger sin than to curse as a result of this deep jealousy.

The persecution of witches may be best explained as a desperate attempt on the part of the newfangled Christian churches to establish themselves with the peasants and the townspeople, and to accumulate wealth. All this took place during a period of warring which went on for decades, and terrible plagues which the Church could not combat. During times of economic depressions, the ruling class often finds an outlet for the people's anger by pointing the finger at minorities upon whom anger may be safely vented. In essence, they scapegoat a particular minority in order to save their own tenuous position, and divert attention away from their own ineptitude and impotence in the face of real enemies and problems.

This shows what Judeo-Christianity has done to my religion. It indicates the tremendous suffering and pain that are the heritage of Women's Religion. Every woman who embarks on the Path must allow herself to feel rage for the millions of women executed. This atrocity must not be allowed to occur again.

Where I come from in Europe, we suffered tremendous losses. Four of my aunts were killed during the Burning Times, but very few, if any, European families cannot find at least one female member who was not murdered. These women were killed because they were women. They knew something that the patriarchal religions considered "sinful". They knew how to deliver babies without giving the mother "childbirth fever," how to attract good fortune and heal the body. These women could take care of a community all by themselves. They didn't need the advice of the struggling new medical profession, which was still quite ignorant. They were prime targets for scapegoating.

Thus, a full-scale political and religious war raged against the Wicca. Women were tortured, burned and hanged regardless of whether they had ever been to a Sabbat. Women were slaughtered on a massive scale, often without any evidence whatsoever that they were actual witches, priestesses or pagans. To the eternal shame of the Christians, nobody stood up to stop this 300-year massacre. Even today there has been no calling for an accounting of responsibility around this issue. Witches are still being scapegoated and "burned" today.

We must move on, but we must not forget. We cannot.

Chapter 11

The Goddess of the
Ten Thousand Names

C ome with me to the Temple, close your eyes, and then open them again. I will show you images of the Goddesses created before us by Goddess-worshiping people. We are not the first, nor the last. And even if we are the first women to turn to worship themselves and their own creativity in the Goddess, then more glory to us.

I will not attempt to convince you of the authenticity of what you see. You must trust your own eyes and common sense, and learn to look. It is important to see these images without being distracted by what they are called, classified, or thought to be by archeologists. Archeologists are not witches who yearn to see the Goddess. Her guises often mislead them. We don't have many allies among scientists today. The Craft threatens them; their jobs may be in real danger if they start telling the truth. The possibility that there was ever a society where women ruled, or the belief in women's inherent ability to be superior, is abhorrent to them. The temple is for those who are excited seeing Her in a different light. The temple can be entered through your mind with a clear affirmation of life. Come now...

Images abound of the Mother Goddess, Female Principle of the Universe and source of all life. This imagery is much more important than we have been told. She lives in clay, in stone, in ancient tools, in modern paintings. She has been changed almost beyond recognition by patriarchal militaristic forces, but She survives.

Here is a Great Corn Goddess of South America, Lady-Unique-Inclination-of-the-Night, giving birth. Her delivery is painless because She knows nothing about a "curse" from a jealous Christian god. Women knew how to lessen the pains, and expel the afterbirth, through herbs. They didn't think of giving life as a punishable crime. The Great Corn Goddess gives birth to Herself.

The Goddess Mother Demeter is often seen sitting on Her throne. She is the fertile earth, from where all bounty comes. She is the lawgiver, and the protector of women.

Kore (Maiden) corresponds to Persephone, daughter of the Earth. She represents all that is above the ground, and is usually portrayed with a sacred flower or the "apple of dominion" held in Her hand. It is the same apple we later see Mary holding in Christian temples. The apple Eve sank a healthy bite into was always Her apple!

The Egyptian Maiden-Goddess is Hathor, Whose law is change. She wears a headdress with a disc of the sun and disc of the moon as Her crown. Since She invented writing, Her favorite plant is the papyrus, which She usually holds in Her hand. Hathor is the Maiden-aspect of Isis. One of Hathor's holidays is a time when everybody gets drunk. Another of Her festivals is when She is angry and tears patriarchal men apart, reveling in the sea of their blood. She is a passionate Goddess.

The Great Goddess Nut also comes to us from Egypt. She is the Universal Goddess, encircling everything. The Sky Goddess and the Earth Goddess are represented as part of Her trinity, and between them is a calendar of planting cycles, considered sacred wisdom to the followers of Nut. The concept behind this is that if you know when and how to plant, then you will consistently create enough food to nurture your body, with time left over to engage in the creation of beauty. Nut became a symbol for women marching to "Take Back the Night" because She rules the Universe and the Darkness.

Goddess Hygeia holds a boa constrictor, a symbol of Her regenerative powers. Statues of Her show a real, seemingly familiar, black woman's face. Many artists of the period used the faces of real people in their creative expressions of the Goddess, so we know how these people looked. Images such as those of Hygeia probably came from the women physicians who believed that their towns should have statues of the healing aspect of the Goddess in order to stimulate healing in themselves.

The Goddess Bast comes from Egypt. She is the sun, powerful and able to effect the growth of living things. She was generally seen as a black cat or lion-headed Goddess, very much involved with dancing and expressions of pleasure. Egyptian physicians often were recognized by the symbol of the black cat, who was worshipped for its symmetry, its disposition, and its strong relationship to Bast.

In Europe, Bast became Dianna Lucifera, Moon and Sun Goddess. Lucifera appeared a mere century away from the concept of "Lucifer" as a "fallen angel." Lucifera was in reality the Goddess Lucina, brilliant Sun of Healing. Lucifera is the Maiden aspect, usually shown holding the torch of the Sun. Later on, this image recurs in the Statue of Liberty. We see the Sun Goddess, crowned with a crescent, holding up the torch of life.

Kali the Terrible is the Goddess of Death, greatly resented by men because of Her awesome power. This concept embodies the philosophy of our ultimate return to the One Who gave us life—in this case it is not our human mother, but her kin-spirit, the Female Principle. Kali always has a young-looking body, very fit, trim and powerful. She is often portrayed with a beard, a symbol of wisdom and power not confined to males. Beards and garishly protruding tongues are aggression gestures.

Black Kali had a very big impact on Indian culture. Many of the ancient temples of the Goddess and Yoni shrines are decayed and overgrown with grass, but Black Kali's are still intact. Even the modern Hindus in the Krishna tradition refer to this as the Age of Kali, suggesting that we are in a period of great evil and wickedness. Kali is Goddess of Death and Regeneration, but She is not evil. As the Indian representation of Magaera, Kali is often shown dancing on the body of Shiva, one of the male gods, indicating Her dominance over all life, particularly the Male Principle of the Universe. Skulls hanging from around Her neck usually symbolize the many generations who went before and will follow after, as well as the inevitability of death.

A painting on a vase containing a woman's remains shows the attitude towards death. The priestesses are instructing the soul of the departed, which is represented by the Ka, or bird. On the other side, the Goddess is beckoning for the soul to reunite with Her. No cruel fear or the horror of Hell is seen here. A calm and almost cheerful passage from one life to another is depicted.

The worship of the Goddess Athena goes way, way back. She is actually an African Goddess, though the Greeks "whitened" her considerably. Athena is credited with the invention of writing, music, spinning and the sciences. She is usually shown holding Her sacred sceptre of rulership in Her hand. Athena in Her African aspect is still very young, but strong. Legend has it that Athena had a best friend called Pallas. Pallas fell from a cliff during their Amazonian games. In her sorrow and love, Athena affixed Pallas's image on her breast as a spirit of protection, and her name in front of her own, hence Pallas-Athena.

An Asian Athena stands assured in her power, able and spiritual. She holds her tortoise-shell shield. Tortoises symbolize wisdom and endurance. They live for hundreds of years.

Athena is a very important Maiden Goddess. She never consorts with men. In the trinity of the Goddesses, there is always this Virgin aspect, the Maiden as a lesbian Goddess. This is the Goddess of Freedom, exemplified by Athena, Diana, Persephone, Artemis and Kallisto (some of the more recognizable Virgin-aspect names). In the Goddess pentarch there is a lesbian Goddess as well. This leads us to surmise that sexuality in the matriarchies emphasized pleasure rather than procreation, and that lesbianism was a natural mode of interaction among women (a natural birth control), while heterosexuality was chosen seasonally for the purpose of breeding or attraction for men.

Some Yoni priestesses anoint themselves to prepare for their rituals. Their intimacy and freedom contrast sharply with the lack of freedom of our sisters in the Orient today. They certainly seem lesbian.

Athena is the force binding humans to their societies, giving social feelings. She is NOT a Goddess of war. Patriarchs demanded that Athena be reborn from a male or the people would no longer be allowed to worship Her in any way. Thus, an artificial "birth" was contrived, and out of Zeus's headache over what to do with all these maiden Goddesses, Athena supposedly sprang, fully armed. Times were so bad for the Goddess and Her people, Athena was fully clothed at Her "birth," rather than being proudly naked as before.

Athena holds the Goddess of Victory in Her hands, because Athena never loses. Once there was an election in Athens to rename the city. The new patriarchs wanted it to be "Poseidon." After the votes were counted, the patriarchs lost because the women turned out in record numbers and voted for their Goddess. This cost the women the right to vote and name their children after themselves (changed over to naming them after the fathers). And the institution of marriage was introduced to subdue the women's civil rights.

Athena was widely and reverently respected. Her sacred bird is the owl, and Her mother is Rhea, whose name means "Flow of Life." Rhea was considered to be the Supreme Queen of Heaven—Queen of All.

The Goddess Ngami is from Africa, a Moon Goddess like Diana. The Voodoo tradition is related to Ngami, but the word "voodoo" simply means "little god." Think of this when you are forced to hear all the negative teachings about Voodoo, and take them as a religiously ignorant, racist, ethnic slur against the African Old Religion.

Aphrodite, Goddess of Love and Fertility, suffered the worst rape at the hands of patriarchal rule. The Goddess of Death was written out and never spoken of again, and the Virgin Goddess survived in modified form. But the Goddess of Love and Sensuality, "She-Who-Binds-Hearts-Together," was made a whore, a deliberate incorporation of all that is "evil" with all that is "female." Her name used to be Marianna or "La Mer", meaning "the ocean." She is a Goddess of the Western corner, usually shown holding an urn or seashell, and pointing out Her genitals as the Source of All Life.

Aphrodite is the Virgin Mary before appropriation by the Christians. Ancient stone statues depict Aphrodite with Her Sacred Child, Eros. The Child is not turned away from Aphrodite, but faces Her in a posture of security, familiarity and tenderness. There is an awareness here that the Child will grow up to be treated differently, unlike modern patriarchal societies where males are treated as children all their lives, nurtured and cared for first by their mothers, then girlfriends and wives, and finally daughters.

Mary is depicted in many ingenious ways. First of all, the Lady of Guadalupe appeared on the very spot of an earlier Goddess shrine, and requested herself a new temple. When the peasant to whom she appeared asked for a sign to make the bishops believe him, she gave him roses. Roses are always a sacred flower of the Mother, especially red ones. This image is very reminiscent of a vagina. If you squint your eyes, the pagan idea shines through the door of life, and the yoni appears. The emanations are the labia and hairs. The red is the blood coming out, and the head is the clitoris. The blue has always been the mantle of the Queen of Heaven.

Early depictions of Aphrodite show Her to be strong, sturdy and proud. She has all Her muscles and stands erect. In later representations, however, Aphrodite loses all Her lovely muscles and the bodily strength that goes with them. Because patriarchy found these particular attributes to be distasteful, Aphrodite was modified over time. She crouched a little at first, then bent over, and finally reclined. The postures portrayed thus forced Her image to drop from an assertion of strength and power to a languid passivity.

Priestesses of Aphrodite served the fertility-aspect of the Goddess, in contrast to the Maiden aspect served by the Virgins (lesbians). Priestesses of the Love Goddess were known as ''holy women,'' or ''Qadishtu,'' and lived in the temple complex. These women extended the Goddess' Grace to impotent men who were fathering no children. Usually the wives brought the men to the temple so they could be cured of their impotence by lying with a Goddess manifest, the ''sacred woman.'' Later, when the child of such a union was born, the happy couple would leave a generous gift at the temple for the Priesthood. These gifts became part of the temple property, passed down from woman to woman, and a factor in the continuing independence of the Priestesses. Very often the ''sacred children'' were brought up to assume the temple roles of Priestess or Priest, as extensions of the Goddess.

Lilith is an original Hebrew Goddess, mentioned only briefly in Judeo-Christian sacred texts and later written out completely. Lilith is the Female Principle of the Universe Whom the Jews had to overcome. Generally a religion which is superseded by another religion, through military might rather than conversion, suffers a reversal. The first thing that happened to the original religion was that it became totally masculinized. The religious names were changed; then the functions of the deities were subverted or completely eliminated. This is particularly obvious in the case of Lilith.

She is accompanied by the owl, whom She shares with Athena. She is winged Herself because She too is a spirit. On Her head are snakes, a familiar Goddess symbol of regeneration and wisdom. Lilith was originally associated with life, the birth process and children. She was protector of all pregnant women, mothers and children.

Statuesque portrayals of the Three Graces, the Three Muses, the Three Mothers, are familiar to most of us. Their names must be spoken only with great reverence because if They are taken in vain or abused by the patriarchal forces, the Mothers become the Three Furies. Their names are Alecto, Goddess of Beginnings; Tisiphone, Goddess of Continuation; and Magaera, Goddess of Death and Rebirth, whose name means "Schism" or the "Abyss." These three concepts form the cornerstone of Women's Religion. They were later stolen from us and integrated into the Judeo-Christian religions as their own trinity, when the patriarchs were busy masculinizing the Goddess.

Hecations, where the sacred Nymph, the Maiden and the Crone hold the torch of life, stood at the crossroad sacred to Hecate the Three-formed and represented the circle of life. Imagine walking by hecations every day. Hecate is the priestess to Persephone; She is the Witch Goddess. She can change forms and ages; She can rejuvenate and kill. Her chariot is pulled by dragons, and her favorite witch is Medea, whose name means Priestess. (Legend has it that Medea didn't die, but Hecate came for her on Her chariot and swept her away.)

The Goddess has 10,000 names, shared by women around the world. Her name is Diana, Holy Mother. Her name is Tiamat, Her name is Hecate. Her name is Isis, Inanna, Belili; Her name is Sapasone, Belladonna, the Great Corn Mother; Her name is Alaskan Bear Mother, Artemis, Brigid, Io, Morrigan and Cerridwen; Her name is every woman's name—Carly, Doris, Lily, Catherine, Sharon, Susan. All of the personal names of women derive from Goddess names, as all women without exception are the expressions of the Mother—Goddess-on-Earth-Manifest.

Three In One

Patriarchal theology has purposely fortified the misbegotten impression that the Trinity is male and inherent in Judeo-Christianity. In reality, the concept of a spiritual triumvirate of deities was understood and respected by religions far older than the young Christian upstarts.

Goddess-worshipping people had little use for perfect dualities—in theory or practice—believing, quite accurately, that such a precept was by definition simplistic and limiting. The children of the Goddess saw Her as the Three-In-One. All the Goddesses were either triads (as three-formed), pentarchs (five-formed), or ninefold (Muses).

The Nymph begins the Thread of Life; the Goddess of Continuations weaves the Thread into a Tapestry; and Magaera is ready to cut the Thread with Her Shears. The Three are the Maiden, Mother, and Crone. Beginnings, continuations, endings and constant regeneration are thus symbolized.

The Trinity relates to the three major cycles of womanhood: Nymph as pre-menstrual daughter; Mother as life-giving creative force; Crone as the post-menopausal wise woman. Each stage of womanhood was worshiped as sacred in itself. All transitions are celebrated with appropriate rituals.

Here is the sacred Nymph in all her playfulness. She is representing the fun and play aspect of the Female Principle. The perfection of the Nymph emerged to be hailed in recent Olympic Games when Olga Korbut and other young gymnasts showed their control and skill. They would be considered the sacred Nymph manifested. The Nymph also has a position in the coven; she is responsible for the fun parts: food and drinks, music and songs. In our coven, she makes sure that the chalice never goes dry, and refills it from her wine jug.

The image of the Crone perhaps suffers from the longest abuse and greatest misunderstanding. Every Goddess, Maiden or Nymph has the "terrible" (as in awesome and frightening) aspect, often referred to as the Hag. We see this aspect in abundance on Halloween, and it is an important part of the female Life-Force; in Her cycles, as in Her rituals, there is death before rebirth. But the Crone must not be discarded as a useless, ugly hag who shrieks and hoots on Halloween. This modern image of our sacred Crone is deliberately derogatory; reviling what is feared is typically patriarchal.

The Crone was revered in Goddess religion as the Carrier of Wisdom; She had lived long enough and well enough to be able to share Her knowledge, thus making "tuition" a little cheaper for the young ones. We don't all have to go through the same problems, since there is such a positive thing as learning from another's mistakes. When a culture discards its elderly, each succeeding generation has to suffer through the same traumas, never learning a thing. Such an attitude keeps us from following the natural flow of information, and it is very sad for our species.

The concept of the Trinity relates to the three phases of the Moon, as well as to the three major cycles of a woman's life. The New Moon brings beginnings, introspection, inner wisdom to make a start; the Moon grows as beginnings are continued and the energy is heightened; then the Full Moon brings fruition, completion and ripeness, and the endings follow to the next New Moon, thus completing the cycle and beginning another at the same time.

The theme of trinities is carried out in jewelry, in necklaces, in braids of hair, in Nature, clothing and art. The Pentarchs, the sevens, the nines, all hearken back to this original concept of the Goddess as One, as a sacred Trinity, as Three-Times-Three, as Multiple (multi-racial, multi-functional, etc.).

Luna

Some people think that Goddess-worship is merely some cultic Moon-worship, but that is not true. We worship the Moon not for her light but for Her awesome power—what she *does*. The Moon controls the ebb and flow of the Ocean's tides. Without water there is no life. Because the Moon has this special relationship with the Earth, She receives a lot of our attention. We respect and revere what She is able to do; we worship the ways in which She influences and manifests life; and we attempt to learn from Her the healthiest and happiest, most spiritually fulfilled way to live. The Great Huntress, Diana, is Goddess of the Moon. She regulates wildlife, menstrual cycles and conception of babies, and is therefore of particular relevance to women.

Signs and Symbols

So-called "traditional" religions have developed symbology by taking original pagan symbols and integrating them into the newer religion. They have accomplished this over the centuries by deliberately misinterpreting and mistranslating ancient records, and by consciously writing the Great Goddess out of the picture altogether.

Nothing can be more unnatural than life without the Mother. However, patriarchy succeeded in selling the world the concept that a Father God created himself. Never in the history of life has there been an instance of male giving birth to anything, let alone a universe and its people. There has never been an instance where humans issued from anywhere other than a mother's womb. That is how all life works.

This is also why the naked female form is revered in witchcraft as the Source. The Goddess, in statues, pictures and drawings throughout history, is often shown pointing to Her genitals. She is not being coquettish, but indicating the Source of Life. Naked figurines such as this, found all over the world, have been dismissed by archeologists as very minor parts of fertility cults, lacking in importance. Try to live without fertility and you will find that nothing goes on. Fertility is your food. Fertility is your pleasure.

One of my favorite ancient Goddesses is 13,000 years old. The more abstract a Goddess representation is, the less it appears humanized. Her rectangular arms are symbols of manifestation. The hole in Her legs is the universe. When She was created by some loving hands, male gods were worshipped nowhere on the earth. Her breasts are barely indicated, as they are not important. Her femaleness is evident.

The earliest representations of the Goddess portray Her as a bird. She is the white dove, the wise owl, the vulture in Her death aspect, the sacred heron of Aphrodite. Early Anatolian findings interpreted the bird as signifying a Holy Spirit that gave life, healed, and could be activated in people.

The dove seems to be the one religious symbol left virtually intact. Picasso's dove became a worldwide symbol for peace in the 1960s, and the dove still represents the "Holy Ghost," left almost totally devoid of personality. Even as the symbol of Aphrodite, Goddess of Love, the dove has generally survived the worst of patriarchy. (She is spread wide-winged on the Vatican's ceilings). The dove was always sacred to Isis and Dianna.

The religion of the Goddess is joy-oriented, life-focused: a celebration in music, dance, poetry, singing, and constantly in tune with the process of promoting Life. The religions which destroyed us had to do something very different, because otherwise there would be no reason for the people to change. Even military controls were not as effective as had been thought. Thus the concept of "sin," newly invented by patriarchy and introduced with religious and military fervor, was reinforced by the reversal of all the positive symbols of the Goddess into negative ones (in the sense of "sinful," "bad," or "evil").

An obvious example of this is the Tree of Knowledge or Tree of Good and Evil, growing in the mythical Garden of Eden. Originally, wisdom and knowledge were symbolized by a tree from which they came. A Goddess was often depicted holding an apple in Her outstretched hand. In the Adam and Eve story, however, the apple and the Mother Tree are slandered as vehicles of deceit, shame and a blinding awareness of the naked human form. Western civilization is still paying for this pathological concept.

In reality, trees are very psychic beings, capable of magnifying the human aura countless times and directing it sky-ward. Joan of Arc had her personal "faith tree" just outside of town, and when she stood under it she heard her "voices"—they were all female voices too! Napoleon used to lean with his spine against a tree when he was especially fatigued, believing that the tree would renew his energy. It is a very good idea to develop a close relationship with a tree. People who worshipped the Goddess believed that trees cure ills, relieve fatigue and give new energy. They considered it well worth their time to establish deep and meaningful relationships with trees. Although this has been dismissed as tree worship, it was not. Pagan celebration of the powers of trees pays homage to the Life-Force as represented by the Tree of Life.

Very often the Tree symbol has four arms, symbolizing the four seasons and four major Sabbats. In other areas of the world this Tree/Wheel of Life has eight arms, indicating the eight sacred Sabbats. The Wheel of Life is today better known and recognized, perhaps, as the swastika, but it originally had absolutely nothing to do with such an absurdity as "white supremacy" or Hitler's demonics.

Statues of Yugoslavian Goddesses have been found painted with the Wheel of Life and sacred birds. Furrows on the bellies of such Goddesses symbolized the farms of the worshiper or Her community, and were used to invoke fertility of the land. Some statues even sport sensible, brightly striped socks. She is a Goddess who knows how to dress for cold weather.

This Hungarian Great Goddess, about 8,000 years old, is very dear to me. There are drawings of the fields on Her belly. Diamonds usually mean rain, and her snaky arms, regeneration. She has a penis head, but it broke off. Fragile things, penis heads, they don't stand the test of time.

Of course, nakedness to Goddess worshipers has never been seen as evil or shameful. The body is a temple, a shrine for the Goddess, and as such is not separate from our souls. We are whole persons. Pagans never promote the separation of body from soul as the patriarchy does. The patriarchal dualism of good and evil, black and white, leading to a law of sin and shame for which there is a promise of redemption, is religious poison, a poison carried over into the dangerously foolish practices of building nuclear reactors where people are trying to live; of selling health-damaging foods and medication; of forcing concrete buildings and roads onto every available space on earth; of poisoning our air and our waters. This is only possible when the people have no concept of their bodies as sacred, worthy of spiritual and physical attention, or needing protection from their own inventiveness.

Many statues of the Goddess show Her with proudly exposed breasts. In matriarchal society there was no shame about exposing the female breasts, because the Goddess as Female was revered as women were revered. The exposed breasts of the Goddess-images were not erotic symbols, but wholly indicative of Her femaleness; the Force that gives Life and Nurturance.

The famous 25,000 year-old Venus of Willendorf, a seven-inch statue, is another example of what kind of art people created before the rise of so-called "civilization." I think it was held in the palm of the hand, while prayers were offered to the Goddess of Plenty. She looks abundant. She has it in Her to give. She has no face because She isn't human, but a Force.

In this scene, we see the Cretan Woman's Mysteries dance. Crete was a capital and last resort of Goddess worship. Beauty, jewelry and high culture held the people's attention.

Today's taboos against the exposure of female breasts, while allowing males to freely expose that small anatomical area, has to do with ancient symbolism. Symbols of nurturance are the most powerful in that they remind men of their dependence upon the Mother—the Female. Patriarchy does not like being reminded of this on a daily basis, but earlier cultures did not mind facing the natural facts of life. They knew how the Great Mother worked, and it was considered healthy and fine for women to expose their breasts, taking pride in the fact that they were the carriers and nurturers of living beings. A society in which women have to hide and cover their breasts is a society in which nurturance is neglected or despised; a society more in touch with suffering and death than mothering. The naked female breasts, as symbol of women's power, deeply frighten men. Breasts are covered for that reason alone, not because they arouse sexual passion.

The same holds true for the vagina as a Goddess symbol. It is not because of lewdness that the vagina is such a prominent feature of many Goddess images, but because of recognition and reverence for the supremely important Source of Life.

Some images of the Goddess show Her as a Toad in the position of conception. Often the Goddess of these images has rounded breasts but no head. There is often a sheaf of wheat shown to indicate that She is a Force, and to show how the people personalized this Force just a little in order to better relate to Her.

Another symbol of note is the depiction of Lilith with claw-like feet. Pagan symbols are composites, and such feet are meant to be very animalistic. Again, She is a Force, not solely human. She has wings, claws and perhaps hair made of snakes. Like Isis, "She is that is."

A bronze mother is 13,000 years old, strong and tender. She stands on a lion, the great Yin animal often accompanying the Goddess. Her head is a penis.

The penis-headed Goddess may be found all over the world. She is one way women have included the penis in representations of life-orientation, as a part of Her sacred creations. This illustrates how inclusive matriarchal religions were. The women recognized that all life comes from the Mother, that Her statues and images generally emphasized Her breasts, vagina or belly as symbols of plenty and abundance. Men were not excluded; they were sons and lovers. Thus, the representations of the Goddess would include the male procreative organ as a part of Her. Some Goddess images have penis-heads, others were made with the penis symbol as a necklace or belt, but the Male principle, while secondary, is not forgotten in representations of the human connection with the Female Life-Force.

The premise behind this was that a true religion will benefit people's individual lives, as well as all humanity. Any religion which excludes any part of humanity, therefore, was deemed inferior and a vehicle for political oppression.

Associating the serpent with the female in particular and evil in general has been terribly exploited. In the Bible, the serpent is already suffering from a bad image as an instrument of Goddess worship. So, of necessity, patriarchy masculinizes the snake to the point where it represents a "male force" in an aggressive, even phallic sense. They made that up; we didn't.

The snake is actually a positive, healing concept, embodied in much of the Old Religion. The serpent beautifully symbolizes regeneration. It is a wondrous thing to watch a snake go through the process in which an entire "old" skin is cast off and replaced by the brilliantly-colored new skin beneath it. This is an awesome reminder of Nature's ability to renew Herself.

Snakes are not only symbols of regeneration. They had practical usage in ancient times. They were used to keep vermin out of the community sewers and storehouses. Some snakes were specially trained to Priestesses to gather herbs. This is yet another example of how Mother religions work cooperatively with Nature. Rather than fighting Her elements and life forms, and treating Her creatures as pests, we put them to work with us. Snakes were thus kept sacred in the temples, and may still be seen in pharmacies and medical centers as symbols of healing.

There is absolutely nothing evil about the snake. The projection of the serpent as evil came from the patriarchal projection of all Goddess symbols as evil, of the Goddess religion as evil, and the assumption that anything women were involved with must be inherently evil.

Spells and Creativity

There is much more to "creation" than making people. There is the creation of harvests, good feelings, good health, song and art and culture. What is left to us from the matriarchies is mainly in stone, Alexander "the Great" having seen to it that the libraries were burned. Our foremothers have linked themselves to us through their enduring pieces of art, depicting much of their essence in clay or stone.

Goddess worshipers were constantly slandered by patriarchs who attacked them as idol worshipers. We know that Goddess-worshipping people created art, not "idols." Worshipping the Goddess as a Force, the people were never guilty of mistaking the representation of the Force for the Force Herself. This is particularly well demonstrated in artistic images of the Goddess without faces. As Goddess-worship developed, we see more varied and detailed representations of the Life-Force. Where She was revered, Her images looked like Her people.

289

Small clay figurines represent Ishtar, Ashara, Isis, all the Goddesses. These small "idols" were the "abominations" later described by followers of Yah-weh, because they were such an integral part of the Goddess religions. Made by the women, figurines such as these were representative of different aspects of the Goddess, as well as graphic expressions of the women's prayers. They always have at least one symbol in common.

These are the creations of the people. The clay figurines were made at home and then carried to the temple as a "votive" offering. There was no interest in sacrificing living beings in Mother's worship. The people made religious art because creativity was understood by all to be cultivation of the Divine, and was therefore regarded as a form of worship. Creativity was spell-casting.

A statue holding a child may have represented prayers for an easy childbirth or a child needed in the family. Statues holding their breasts are pleas for nurturance, for sustenance. Fat bellies with carved furrows were petitions for fertility and abundance of food and health. Simple, instinctual folk art; expressions of needs presented to the Queen of Heaven.

Such statues have been found which are up to 8,000 years old. Large ones with back-to-back crescents represented a major petition, the crescents being another universal symbol of the Goddess, used by many witches as a sort of "signature" in their work. The meaning of the crescents used in this manner was "She Who Shines For All."

One Goddess image from a cave in France holds the Horn of Plenty. Her hand points to Her belly in a familiar gesture. This was created in a period during which we are told cavemen clubbed women over the heads and dragged them into caves. That is pure fantasy. In these caves are walls and walls of Art—more than we could have used in many centuries. People were constantly creating spiritual images to help themselves understand and cope with life, and their artwork was all centered around the Great Goddess.

Yoni shrines were very special places, built and used by the ancient peoples as temples of worship. Within these shrines Her people would sit or stand, sing, dance, read poetry, or meditate on the Source. Some people even stayed in the shrine overnight in order to facilitate prophetic dreaming. Several of the yoni shrines show the Goddess in a birthing position. Imagine going to pray at such a shrine. Imagine anyone failing to develop a reverence for the Mother as Source of all Life if, from the time men were tiny boys, they were taken to such shrines to burn a little incense and thank the Great Mother for giving them life. The female anatomy in many yoni shrines has been closely observed. Even the outline of the clitoris is right where it belongs. There was no need for a denial of sexuality among the children of the Goddess, since it was considered a powerful gift that the

Goddess gave to Her people. When female and male worship at shrines depicting the Source of all Life, there is a chance to experience true spirituality. This is where common sense blends with mysticism. You know where life comes from, you have a healthy respect for it, and you build your entire life around it.

This natural stone stands in nature, a shrine. You can tell how often the sides were rubbed for good luck. The shape is unmistakably female.

At this Yoni shrine, people whispered into her middle and burned incense at the door.

Here is a meteorite; you could climb into it, and chant and meditate. This is a natural spiritual resource.

One misinterpreted ritual of the matriarchal women, recorded in a wall painting of Knossos, was the sport of bull leaping. The idea behind this was that no one should be hurt, even though a bull would sometimes trample an acrobat in the excitement. The bull, however, was a sacred animal, never meant to be killed. He signified the Male Principle of the Universe, and was very dear to the Goddess. The entire bull leaping dance was performed as a ritual, symbolic of the Goddess mating with Her male consort and exercising gentle control over the raw power of the male animal. Today, the macho ''sport'' of bullfighting is a direct reversal of this beautiful and ancient ritual. Bull leaping took much more skill than wounding and killing trapped bulls, and the contrast between matriarchal and patriarchal customs could not be clearer.

The Oldest Profession

Priestessing, not prostitution, is the "oldest profession." Part of Aphrodite's worship called for a Priestess to lie with men to insure their fertility, but that service to the Goddess lasted only one day out of a woman's life and was not prostitution by any stretch of the imagination. Once a woman had done her service, she could spend the rest of her life priestessing in any way she chose.

Ritual Priestesses often ate sacred mushrooms to increase their physical strength because women of old took their religion very seriously. Celebrating and dancing for three days and nights was not at all unusual.

Ethnic dances of all kinds have come from these sacred dancers and their religious rituals. Sacred ritual dances were taught by Priestesses and used liberally to condition the minds, bodies and souls of the entire community. Dancing was considered a form of spiritual as well as physical exercise, and appears today in such forms as Yoga and Tai Chi. The law is: What does not move, dies. This holds true for everybody. In the Old Religion it was customary for the people to go to the temple for a ritual celebration or a Sabbat, and to dance and move until they could go home feeling fresh and renewed. All this was a part of the cultural heritage, considered absolutely essential for the well-being of the community.

Basically, a Pagan Priestess in the tradition of the Wicca can do anything from blessing mothers for easy childbirth, to blessing the newborn babies. Women's wisdom included not only the proper blessings, but the proper herbs to administer to people in need of healing. The High Priestess presided over such rituals as "trysting," the pagan counterpart of patriarchal marriage. The Priestess was also responsible for blessing the fields for abundant harvest, for bringing on rains if there was a drought, and performing the proper spells to rid the town of disease or pestilence.

The Priestess was the "fortune-teller" of the community, well-versed in all manner of divinatory techniques and skills. The Tarot is one such tool of divination, but there are numerable others: "augury," divination by omens; sensitivity to the voices of the animals; communication with plants; interpretation of stars and planets, numbers and colors. Whatever the Priestess touched, the Goddess of Life would touch. So the Priestesses of ancient times were also known as "Goddesses on Earth," a concept which further separates us from the other religions.

With the advent of militaristic patriarchal rule, the spiritual leaders of the matriarchies were an awesome power which had to be dealt with. Priestesses of Athena, Artemis and Diana were promptly hung from oak trees by their hair, with anvils tied around their ankles, to force them to renounce Rhea as Supreme Goddess and accept the new male god (Zeus) as omnipotent. Through tortures which have continued to the present day (clitorectomy, electric shock, etc.), these patriarchal usurpers perpetrated the most massive cultural and religious coup in the history of the planet.

Today, as the results of that tradition of patriarchal religious zeal mount, we see that it has brought us death-worship and ecological destruction. TV preachers jubilate over the world's pending disasters as "proof" of their faith. In the meantime, 90% of all churchgoers are women; the true battleground for spiritual liberation is still in the temples.

Here is a relief from the temple of Ephesus again, showing that women can defend themselves. The scene is the revenge of Thermadon Amazons on Athens, because Theseus kidnaped their queen. The Amazons' existence, so often denied by scientists, looks so very real on these statues! Men don't get ideas of defeat by themselves, and certainly don't then put it into stone! But here we have fine examples of womanhood. The Amazons were strong and beautiful at the same time. Weakness was not seen as feminine.

A local Amazon, Califia, gave us the name California. The story has it that she lived and ruled with her sister and co-queen in the Bajas. They lived a prosperous but unadventurous life. They kept griffins (flying mountain lions) and trained them to tear apart any men who might land on their islands. One day Califia decided to go find adventure and help out the Pagans in their fight against the Christians, halfway around the world. When she arrived in Turkey, the Christian crusades were on. She whistled for her helpers, the griffins, who proceeded to eat the men of both sides! To make up for this, she promised to personally lead the Pagan troops against the Christians the next morning. In the battle, she was separated from her sister and captured. Part of her punishment was that she had to marry men whom she had bested in battle. This was a big disgrace for Amazons. But the women didn't give up. They kept talking about their golden places and silver chalices, telling their new husbands how much gold they had back in the old country. Greed got to the Christians (bet on it every time!) and they set out to go to their wives' country, in hopes of cleaning them out. This never happened, because nobody knows anything about the husbands after they left the harbor. The sisters returned much wiser to Baja, where they reigned in peace, no longer even missing adventure.

The original sin was matricide. The toppling of the matriarchies and the rape and murder of the mothers was, and still is, the greatest of all sins. No purging of our culture has occurred since the Inquisition, no public accounting for the sins of the "fathers." A major contribution to the continuing hostility and alienation of males is their deep core of guilt. Men continue to be guilty of matricide. No amount of purification will take that blemish away. Matricide is punishable by eternal unhappiness and the Goddess punishes in different ways. There isn't a heaven or hell someplace "out there;" we create both right here where we live.

The punishment for matricide is foul air, poisoned food, ecological disasters (earthquakes, famines, hurricanes and drought). Mother is not happy, and She will not take this anymore. She has lots of time. Every hundred million years or so, the entire earth gets reworked when the Queen decides that this particular spaceship has to change. That is the Law—Change. What does not change, dies, and even in death, continues to change.

Men harbor the constant, sneaking suspicion that they are wrong after all. As the day of the End nears, they feel their anxiety grow. Sadly, this anxiety is misdirected in their death orientation, so that they cause the eating of their own young. Young men were and are used in aggression-expression, which is supposed to solve problems. Kronos eats his own son—the old man drafts the young man to die in war. When nations are convinced that the only solution to differences (usually economic) is to kill other people, we obviously have nations led by men who no longer think, and where the life force is no longer healthy.

A very important evolutionary note here regarding humans and the other beings who share the planet with us: Every time the male of a species begins to attack the female, that species is on a suicide course. In fact, no male animal but the human attacks the female, and he does so with astonishing violence and regularity. Human males are therefore hurtling toward a final retribution—the extinction of their species and their planet—a course of self-destruction that began in earnest approximately 2,500 years ago.

The Fall

The question of how the matriarchies were taken over, destroyed and rebuilt into patriarchal societies remains unanswered. What made men so hostile and angry that they rose up against their own mothers, the life-givers? We still don't know for certain, but one likely cause is the fact that not everybody "made it" in the matriarchal cultures—causing the problem of power.

Matriarchy was deposed mainly because of our lack of suspicion about our sons. We really did not deal with the possibility that they would rise up against us and kill us. Imagine living in a society where it was customary to run around all day bare-breasted and free; where rape was practically unheard of and punishable by death should it ever occur; where women were worshipped by their children if they had any, and worshipped as an expression of the Goddess whether they had children or not. In such a society there was no fear that the sons would turn on the mothers, and no one spent any time or energy building weapons to defend against anyone, much less the community's own offspring.

Matriarchal women had no defense systems. They didn't even have swords, although they did use wands. All they had was superior sewer systems, elaborate baths, beautiful wall paintings and exquisite jewelry. They were beauty-oriented, not war-obsessed, and thus were easily overrun and sacked in the cruelest sense of the word.

In matrilineal society, superior males were chosen as mates by matriarchal women. Men not selected as mates were unable to gain any of the status, property, wealth or recognition associated with a woman's family. These males banded together outside the communities. Soon they found that if they had their "own" women to breed like cattle, they could produce their own people and become more powerful. These men on the outside did whatever they could to bring women into their possession.

The mythological rape of the Sabines was an example of such beliefs carried out in reality. While the Sabine men were away, patriarchal soldiers marched into town, raping all the women and impregnating most of them. The "logic" of it was that if each man impregnated at least one woman, who then bore a child, the original males would double their numbers. It was a small step from there to possessing women, breeding like livestock and keeping them pregnant as much as possible. Soon the patriarchs had their armies. This same right is defended today by the "right-to-life" groups who desire to keep women pregnant and poor.

Children of such practices grew up in a totally different power structure. Women were merely chattel, breeders and servants. Males called all the shots, and violence, brute strength and aggression became attributes to be admired and worshipped. Within a fifty-year period, patriarchs produced entire armies and continued to escalate such degenerate activities as ransacking cities, raping and murdering women and female children.

Because history occurs simultaneously, this sort of thing happened all over the world at about the same time. Patriarchs were not a collected and organized group attempting to bring civilization to a "primitive" people. They were hordes of males reacting violently to their position vis-a-vis matriarchal cities and matrilinear families.

The first patriarchal religions had to contend with cultures based on female supremacy. Goddess shrines and temples were all around them, and it was obvious that the matriarchal identity would not easily be squelched. The people of the Old Way did not accept the idea of a patriarchal society with its death-blood-sacrifice focus. The patriarchs, the northern invaders in particular, had to bring in their own god. Since even military force and widespread propagandizing had a limited effect on the Goddess worshipers, it was obviously time to introduce little "dios" to them. At first the patriarchs decided to place "dios" in the temples of the Great Mother, since surely he was one of Her sons. Dios thus began as a son of the Mother, but he changed as the patriarchal understanding of power over the matriarchies grew.

This jealous male god and son still exist today in great numbers (call them Jehovah, Christ, Krishna, Allah). Goddess worship continued, despite centuries of suppression and the four hundred years of horror known as the Inquisition. The patriarchs have not been able to burn, shoot or torture it out of existence. Goddess worship continues despite the atrocity of worldwide mass murders of women as witches.

Estimates by women historians and scholars today place the number of women exterminated during the witch "trials" at eleven million, and claim that even this estimate is conservative. There are records of certain towns where as many as four hundred women were burned to death in ONE day. During this shameful period, no male uprising occurred to stop the murder of women. No husbands, sons or lovers banded together to stop the hysterical slaughter of millions of women. Even in the years following, no one has called for an accounting. No witches have been avenged through trials of accountability such as those for the Jews at Nuremberg. There has been no apparent opposition to the wave of hatred which caused the flesh of the mothers to be burned.

At one point during the Inquisition, the patriarchs were burning or hanging children who were over a year old. At the end of this four-hundred-year period, however, they grew "milder" about the children and spared those at puberty or younger. But to teach these children to remember the "sins" of their elders, they led them around the stake at which their parents burned, while the patriarch whipped them. All this horror in the name of the Father God, in the name of Jesus, in the name of Jehovah. I am still filled with rage about this issue, because deep down, I want justice for women.

Epilogue

Judaism, Christianity and Islam, Buddha and Krishna are brothers. Judaism has an inherent backlash to feminist spirituality built into it. Christianity simply helped itself, through Judaism, to write its own sexist war story. At any rate, both made concerted efforts and succeeded in writing out the Great Goddess, Queen of the Universe, Rhea, Flow of Life. They took special pains to write out everything having to do with the lesbian Goddesses, thereby denying the women a choice of lifestyles.

It is fairly easy to see that Judeo-Christianity is anti-woman and exclusive in its intent. It is not as obvious in the case of the Eastern religions, which stole religion from Tara even earlier. Finding that there is a profit to be made from the spiritual poverty of the West, they are now in an excellent position to sell their brand of spirituality to the Westerners (some call it the New Age).

In the Orient, we find Tara, sometimes shown as the Tree of Life. She comes in green, because that is Nature's favorite color. Ever-young Tara comes in yellow for manifesting. She comes in white for the blessing. She is red for anger. She is black for the death aspect. Her temples still stand in India; Her worship preceded that of Krishna, the warrior on the chariot. Sometimes She is shown pregnant, and that image was taken over by Buddha, with the fat belly.

Death-oriented religions often encourage the killing of other people by promoting the idea that whomever you kill will be forced to serve you in the afterlife. Islam is a prime example. Christians too, used to bless their cannons before using them to kill innocent people. Waging war against each other is central to death-oriented, patriarchal religions. They revel in wars because war is a time when suffering becomes real on a grand scale. Everybody feels bad. At such a time, they are more easily able to attract members and appear important, offering false "protection."

In times of peace and abundance, a death-oriented religion does not have much appeal; you cannot attract new members to your religion by promising an end to all suffering and a heaven after death. Peacetime promotes concerns more oriented toward abundance, prosperity and pleasure—anathema to patriarchs who cannot deliver the goods in the here-and-now.

I am angered by some New Age religions which gain wealth by selling their liberalized versions of religion to spiritually-starved Americans. The token female leader of a particularly "disciple"-oriented group claims that when two women make love, all the energy goes to the devil—we never had such a nasty concept. Witches don't believe in the devil. That entire concept came out of the early patriarchal notion of duality: good/evil; black/white (racism); God/Devil. This and other patriarchal mythologies were created for the sole purpose of controlling the inner space of the people. The Wicca knows better and continues to deal in healthy multiples.

If religious stories are "good for the soul", then the believer will police herself into submission. In other words, the cheapest, most insidious and effective form of oppression is internal. This can only be achieved when someone goes all the way inside your soul and throws out your self-respect (self-love). This is the foundation of all kinds of oppression.

How we lost the Mother's Religion and why this continues to happen are not really the point. What counts is that it all has to do with a cycle—a Universal event—and that is related to the consciousness of a people. Whatever we think, we get. That is the very reason religions are all-important and all-political, and why they will always be that way. Religion can never be left alone while the people argue about whether or not we need it, whether or not it influences us, whether or not we can make it go away by not thinking about it. That's foolish ignorance, actively displayed only through futile debate and verbiage.

Just because the religions fed to us so far in the patriarchal scheme have been poison is no reason for women to totally reject their spirituality. The point is to be wise, to take our powers and think a way through—to find another way to feed our undernourished spirits. We must find a nourishing, healthy resource which will be the foundation for our spirituality, the basis for our rebellion against every kind of oppression, and our weapon for awakening and sustaining the Goddess within. And that's the future.

the one you insist to create for yourself. Here is
paradise. Here is destiny. When you seek her she is beneath
This is God. When you seek her she is food in
your feet. When you seek her she is love in
your mouth. When you seek her. You share
your heart, pleasure in your body.
her heartbeat.
The cosmic ride through space, with no
tickets, nor space suits, affirms your freedom,
which is natural. Internalize her love for you
and you'll be loving others. Love others and she
will reward you with rich peace within.
God speaks every day. God holds us in love
every day. Earthchildren, so fragile, we are God.
Channeled by Z Budapest

Medea speaks:
This is God, children, listen up well. The
beautiful blue planet, our mother, our sister.
She moves with 200 miles per second, yet
imperceptible; she offers the quiet of the lakes
and the rushing of her rivers, the vast expanse
of her oceans, the echoes of her mountains.
This is God, children . . . listen up well.
Lift your eyes to the heavens, and you behold
her sisters the stars, and her cousins with her
infinite beauty.
and nebulas, and fill your senses with her
This is God, children . . . and she has made no
other heaven but the heavens where you
already reside, and she has made no hell except

Conclusion

The Holy Book is but a fragment of our growing knowledge of Women's Spirituality. Yet it has changed women's lives and our herstory. No longer are Goddess worshipers mocked as silly in the Feminist Movement; no longer are we seen as threatening clouds on the political horizon, but as the very essence of Women's Politics.

Now there are more covens than can be counted, organically springing up like wild roses. Women who practice solo have increased, more conferences are planned, more newsletters of the Goddess are printed. And so it should be.

We don't pretend that we have covered all the areas of Woman's Religion, but we labored in love and we reap love. This book is published as the New Right is organizing against Woman's Rights, and when a new oppressive Christian era looms over us. Never before was an articulate Women's Religion more needed to sustain us. Never before was our endorsement in our own behalf more political.

When we started working on the *Holy Book* idea, Janet Roslund found a quote from Florence Nightingale: "Do you think it is possible for there to be a religion whose essence is common sense?" she asked.

I hope that with this volume, I can answer a proud "Yes" to the sister of the past.

May the Goddess bring prosperity to all who follow her Paths, and may we all be free to worship Her!

A Year and A Day Calendar

BETH (December 24—January 20)
January 6: FEAST OF SIRONA, Goddess of Rivers. Blessing of the waters.
January 11-15: CARMENTALIA, festival to Carmenta, Roman Goddess of childbirth. This festival was attended only by women, who called upon the Goddess to give an easy position for birth.
LUIS (January 21—February 17)
February 2: CANDLEMAS, celebration of the waxing light, initiation of new witches.
February 14-21: FESTIVAL OF LOVE, celebration of the Goddess Aphrodite.
NION (February 18—March 17)
March 20: SPRING EQUINOX, return of Persephone from the underworld to reunite with Demeter, her mother; rejuvenation of the life force in nature.
FEARN (March 18—April 14)
March 21-25: QUINQUATRIA, Festival of Minerva, Goddess of Wisdom and inventor of the arts and sciences.
March 30: FEAST OF ESOTARA, Goddess of Fertility.
SAILLE (April 15—May 12)
April 28-May 3: FESTIVAL OF FLORA, Goddess of Spring Flowers and Vegetation. This celebration is rather licentious.
May 1: BELTANE, the maiden Goddess coming of age; sometimes celebrated May Eve (April 30).
UATH (May 13—June 9)
June 1: FESTIVAL OF EPIPI, Goddess of the Dark. This celebration is always on the Full Moon in late May to early June and is an investigation of the mysteries.
June 7: VESTALIA, Feast of Vesta, Goddess of the hearth and home.
DRUIR (June 10—July 7)
June 13: FEAST OF EPONA, Goddess of Horses.
June 21: SUMMER SOLSTICE, sacred to the fire queen of love and celebration of the Goddess' power over men.
July 2: FEAST OF EXPECTANT MOTHERS.
July 7: NONAE CAPROTINAE, a feast under the wild fig tree and oldest of women's celebrations in Rome.

TINNE (July 8—August 4)
July 17: BIRTHDAY OF ISIS.
August 2: LAMMAS, celebration of Habondia, the Goddess of plenty, of fortune, and of the daughters of the Earth Mother.

COLL (August 5—September 1)
August 13: FESTIVAL TO DIANA, Goddess of the Moon. Women made pilgrimages to Nemi with torches and wreaths to grant children and easy delivery.
August 21: CONSUALIA, Celebration of the taking in of the Harvest. There were chariot races and horse races, entertainment, dancing and singing.

MUIN (September 2—29)
September 8: FEAST OF THE BIRTH OF THE MOTHER.
September 23: AUTUMN EQUINOX, witches' Thanksgiving, celebration of the harvest.
September 27: DAY OF WILLOWS, a Ceremony of Fire and Water.

GORT (September 30—October 27)
October 24: FEAST OF THE SPIRITS OF THE AIR.
October 26: FESTIVAL OF HATHOR, Egyptian Goddess of Productivity. This celebration occurs on the Full Moon.

NGETAL (October 28—November 24)
October 31: HALLOWMAS, Witches' New Year, celebration of the sacred gag aspect of the Goddess, the destroyer of life, essential for future life.
November 30: FEAST OF THE GODDESSES OF THE CROSSROADS.

RUIS (November 25—December 22)
December 13: FEAST OF BELISAMA, Goddess of Light.
December 15: CONSUALIA, Celebration of the sowing of the Harvest.
December 19: OPALIA, Festival of Ops, ancient Sabine Goddess of Creative Force and Agricultural Fertility.
December 21: WINTER SOLSTICE, birth of the sun Goddess, Lucina.

THE DAY (December 23)
December 23: DAY OF LIBERATION, DAY OF THE DIVINE CHILDREN, or DAY OF THE FOOL.

Suggested further reading

Margot Adler, *Drawing Down the Moon*. Beacon Press, 1987.

Richard H. Allen, *Star Names: Their Lore and Meaning*. Dover, 1963.

Jean Anderson and Yeffe Kimball, *The Art of American Indian Cooking*. Simon & Schuster, 1986.

Jose Arguelles, *The Transformative Vision*. Shambhala, 1975.

Alice A. Bailey, *A Treatise on White Magic*. Lucis Publishing Co., 1974.

The Beltane Papers, PO Box 8, Clear Lake WA 98235.

Pamela Berger, *The Goddess Obscured: Transformation of the Grain Protectress from Goddess to Saint*. Beacon, 1985.

H.P. Blavatsky, *Abridgement of the Secret Doctrine*. Theosophical Publishing House, 1973.

H.P. Blavatsky, *Isis Unveiled*. Theosophical Publishing House, 1973.

John Blofeld, *Bodhisattva of Compassion: The Mystical Tradition of Kwan Yin*. Shambhala, 1977.

Derk Bodde, *Festivals in Classical China*. Princeton University Press, 1975.

Anita Borghese, *The International Cook Jar Cookbook*. Scribner's, 1975.

Marion Zimmer Bradley, *The Mists of Avalon*. Ballantine Books, 1984.

E.A. Wallis Budge, *The Egyptian Book of the Dead*. Dover, 1967.

Calendar of Irish Folk Customs 1984. Appletree Press (Belfast), 1983.

Richard Carlyon, *A Guide to the Gods*. William Heinemann/Quixote (London), 1981.

Dolores Casella, *A World of Breads*. David White (Port Washington NY) 1977.

Carol P. Christ, *Diving Deep and Surfacing*. Beacon Press, 1986.

Ella E. Clark, *Indian Legends of the Pacific Northwest*. University of California Press, 1953.

June McCormick Collins, *Valley of the Spirits: The Upper Skagit Indians of Western Washington*. University of Washington Press, 1980.

Percy Dearmer, Ralph Vaughan Williams and Martin Shaw, *The Oxford Book of Carols*. Oxford University Press, 1975.

Christine Downing, *The Goddess: Mythological Images of the Feminine*. Crossroad, 1984.

Lawrence Durdin-Robertson, *Juno Covella: Perpetual Calendar of the Fellowship of Isis*. Cesara Publications, 1982.

Barbara Ehrenreich and Deirdre English, *Witches, Midwives and Nurses: A History of Women Healers*. Feminist Press, 1973.

Alvaro Estrada, *Maria Sabina: Her Life and Chants*. Ross-Erickson (Santa Barbara CA), 1981.

Louis C. Faron, *Hawks of the Sun*. University of Pittsburgh Press, 1964.

Louis C. Faron, *The Mapuche Indians of Chile*. Waveland Press, 1972.

Paul Friedrich, *The Meaning of Aphrodite*. University of Chicago Press, 1978.

From the Lands of the Scythians: Ancient Treasures From the Museums of the USSR, 3000 BC to 100 BC, exhibit catalog. Metropolitan Museum of Art (NYC); Los Angeles County Museum of Art, 1975.

Marija Gimbutas, *Goddesses and Gods of Old Europe*. University of California Press, 1982.

Goddesses and Their Offspring: 19th and 20th Century Eastern European Embroideries, exhibit catalog. Roberson Center for the Arts and Sciences, 30 Front St, Binghamton NY 13905, 1986.

Naomi R. Goldenberg, *Changing of the Gods: Feminism and the End of Traditional Religions*. Beacon Press, 1979.

Robert Graves, *The Greek Myths*. Moyer Bell Ltd, 1988.

Robert Graves, *The White Goddess*. Farrar, Straus and Giroux, 1966.

Florence Greenberg, *Florence Greenbergs's Jewish Cookbook*. Chartwell Books (Secaucus NJ) 1980.

M. Grieve, *A Modern Herbal* (two volumes). Dover, 1971.

Susan Griffin, *Woman and Nature: The Roaring Inside Her*. Harper & Row, 1979.

Pierre Grimal, editor, *Larousse World Mythology*. Paul Hamlyn (London) 1965.

Denise Guren and Nealy Gillette, *The Ovulation Method—Cycles of Fertility*. Ovulation Teachers Association (Bellingham WA), 1984.

Nor Hall, *The Moon and the Virgin: Reflections on the Archetypal Feminine*. Harper & Row, 1981.

M. Esther Harding, *Women's Mysteries, Ancient and Modern*. Harper & Row, 1976.

Jane Ellen Harrison, *Prolegomena to the Study of Greek Religions*. Ayer Company Publishers, 1955.

Kenneth Harrison, *The Framework of Anglo-Saxon History to AD 900*. Cambridge University Press, 1976.

William Harlan, *The Horizon Cookbook and Illustrated History of Eating and Drinking Through the Ages*. Doubleday, 1968.

Rhoda Hendricks, *Mythologies of the World: A Concise Encyclopedia*. McGraw-Hill, 1979.

Elizabeth Hickey, *The Land of Tara*. Dundalgan Press (Dundalk, Ireland), 1982.

Murry Hope, *The Way of Cartouche*. St. Martin's Press, 1985.

Ake Hultkrantz, "The Religion of the Goddess in North America" in *The Book of the Goddess, Past and Present*, Carl Olsen, editor. Crossroad, 1985.

Hallie Iglehart, *Womanspirit: A Guide to Woman's Wisdom*. Harper & Row, 1983.

Gertrude and James Jobes, *Outer Space: Myths, Name Meanings, Calendars From the Emergence of History to the Present Day*. Scarecrow Press, 1964.

Barrie Kavasch, *Native Harvests: Recipes and Botanicals of the Native Americans*. Random House, 1979.

Paul Kovi, *Paul Kovi's Transylvanian Feast: A Chronicle of the Most Remarkable Middle-European Cuisine*. Crown, 1985.

Saul Krieg, *The Alpha and Omega of Greek Cooking*. Macmillan, 1973.

E.C. Krupp, *Echoes of the Ancient Skies: The Astronomy of Lost Civilizations*. New American Library, 1983.

Manfred Lurker, *The Gods and Symbols of Ancient Egypt*. Thames and Hudson, 1980.

Jon Mikalson, *The Sacred and Civil Calendar of the Athenian Year*. Princeton University Press, 1975.

Patricia Monahan, *The Book of Goddesses and Heroines*. E.P. Dutton, 1981.

John Murphy, *Traditional Irish Recipes*. Appletree Press (Belfast), 1980.

Margaret Nowak and Stephen Durrant, *The Tale of the Nisan Shamaness: A Manchu Folk Epic*. University of Washington Press, 1977.

Octava: Newsletter for the Eight Feasts. PO Box 8, Clear Lake WA 98235.

Mimie Ouei, *The Art of Chinese Cooking*. Random House, 1960.

Better Homes and Gardens Heritage Cookbook. Meredith Corporation, 1975.

Martin Palmer, editor, *T'ung Shu: The Ancient Chinese Almanac*. Shambhala, 1986.

Nancy Passmore et al, *The Lunar Calendar: Dedicated to the Goddess in Her Many Guises*. Luna Press.

Marge Piercy, *The Moon Is Always Female*. Random House, 1980.

Marge Piercy, *Woman On the Edge of Time*. Fawcett, 1985.

Billie Potts, *Witches Heal: Lesbian Herbal Self-Sufficiency*. Hecuba's Daughters (Bearsville NY), 1981.

Adrienne Rich, *Of Woman Born: Motherhood as Experience and Institution*. Norton, 1986.

Jane Roberts, *The Nature of Personal Reality*. Bantam, 1984.

Herbert Spencer Robinson and Knox Wilson, *Myths and Legends of All Nations*. Litlefield, Adams, 1978.

Dane Rudhyar, *The Lunation Cycle*. Aurora, 1986.

Peggy Reeves Sanday, *Female Power and Male Dominance: On the Origins of Sexual Inequalities*. Cambridge University Press, 1981.

Jack Santa Maria, *Indian Sweet Cookery*. Shambhala, 1980.

Dorothy Gladys Spicer, *The Book of Festivals*. Gale, 1979.

Charlene Spretnak, *Lost Goddesses of Early Greece*. Beacon, 1984.

Charlene Spretnak, *The Politics of Women's Spirituality*. Doubleday, 1981.

Starhawk, *The Spiral Dance*. Harper & Row, 1979.

Diane Stein, *The Kwan Yin Book of Changes*. Llewellyn Publications, 1986.

Katie Stewart and Pamela Michael, *Wild Blackberry Cobbler and Other Old-Fashined Recipes*. Salem House, 1984.

Merlin Stone, *Ancient Mirrors of Womanhood: Our Goddess and Heroine Heritage*. Beacon Press, 1984.

The Time-Life Holiday Cookbook. Time-Life Books, 1976.

Tun Li-ch'en, *Ancient Customs and Festivals in Peking*. Henri Vetch (Peiping) 1936.

Barbara Walker, *The Woman's Encyclopedia of Myths and Secrets*. Harper & Row, 1983.

R. Gordon Wasson, *Maria Sabina and Her Mazatec Velada*. Harcourt Brace Jovanovich, 1974.

Youngsook Kim Harvey, *Six Korean Women: The Socialization of Shamans*. West Publications (St. Paul MN), 1979.

Youngsook Kim Harvey, "Possession Sickness and Woman Shamans in Korea" in *Unspoke Worlds*, Falk and Gross, eds. Harper & Row, 1980.

J.E. Zimmerman, *Dictionary of Classical Mythology*. Bantam, 1980.

Researched by Ariel Dougherty

About the Author

Zsuzsanna Emese Budapest was born in Budapest, Hungary to Masika Szilagyi, an artist and witch whose artwork and ancient spiritual beliefs had a tremendous influence on her. Z escaped her country after the Hungarian uprising of 1956 and studied in Innsbruck, Vienna and Chicago. She was married and had two sons, now grown and her friends. In 1970 she became a feminist and realized that her witchcraft background was a natural expression of alternative feminist spirituality; she has devoted her life to it ever since. She was the first to coin the term Feminist Spirituality, and advocated the idea that politics and spirituality are two sides of the same coin. This idea transformed the Women's Movement into a globally interconnected phenomenon.

Z originally published *The Holy Book of Women's Mysteries* under the title *The Feminist Book of Lights and Shadows*; this book served as the first women's spirituality work available anywhere in the United States or Europe; combined with the author's travels, public speaking, rituals and a rising conviction that women's liberation is not possible without spiritual liberation, it seeded the current Women's Spirituality Movement in the U.S.

Z was the High Priestess of the Susan B. Anthony Coven Number 1, the first coven active in Los Angeles, where she taught and trained for ten years. She celebrated the major holydays of the Earth and the Full Moons. In 1975, she was arrested for reading Tarot cards for an undercover policewoman, and tried as a witch. She was found "guilty" of predicting the future. This radicalized the spirituality movement, which up until then was non-political. Her fight against the anti-prophecy law lasted nine years. The law forbidding Tarot reading or other means of divination was finally found unconstitutional.

Z has published hundreds of articles on her subject. She has edited *Sister*, and contributed to *Thesmophoria, Women's Spirit, Beltane Papers, Lesbian Tide, Quest, Woman of Power, Goddess Rising, Circle, Mama Bears News and Notes* and *Plexus*. She has also reviewed spirituality-oriented books for the *San Francisco Chronicle*.

Recently Harper & Row published Z's *Anna Perenna: The Grandmother of Time*, a book of lost women's holydays, easy rituals and a history of the growing Women's Spirituality Movement.

Her work has influenced a score of writers and artists, and she is the most often quoted witch in history. Among the books that have discussed her work are *Moon Moon* by Anne Kent Rush (Random House); *Womanspirit Rising* by Carol Christ (Harper & Row); Gayle Kimball's *Women's Culture* (Scarecrow Press); *The Politics of Women's Spirituality* by Charlene Spretnak (Doubleday); Naomi Goldenberg's *Changing of the Gods* (Beacon Press); and *Drawing Down the Moon* by Margot Adler (Beacon).

Thousands of people have been acquainted with her work through San Francisco Bay Area radio and television, where she has read the Tarot, been interviewed on the origins of holydays and debated born-again Christians. She recently started her own cable TV program to broadcast more information on Goddess culture.

Z currently lives in the San Francisco Bay Area. She is the director of the Women's Spirituality Forum, a non-profit organization organizing events, lectures and retreats throughout the year, including an annual Spiral Dance on Halloween. She is available for women's festivals, conferences, lecture series and retreats. She also continues her work in the media educating people about the Goddess. Letters asking her for help are put upon her full ritual altar on Full Moons.

To write to Zsuzsanna Budapest, send your letters to PO Box 11363, Oakland CA 94611.

About the Artist

Masika Szilagyi was born in rural Hungary to Ilona, a suffragist who founded trade schools for girls and became the first congresswoman in Hungary's history. As a youth, Masika was a poet and medium. She wrote poems of invocations in trance states, and sometimes spoke ancient Egyptian. Through her poetry she won a scholarship to Paris where she began her studies as a ceramic artist and sculptress. She continued at Budapest University, and erected two statues in the city before she was 25 years old.

She went through much hardship during the war; afterwards she was the only artist to teach art to homecoming maimed soldiers: how to paint with their teeth if they lacked arms, how to throw the potter's wheel with only one leg, etc. She then worked in a factory and finally in 1956 began her career anew, winning many annual shows in Budapest.

Masika was a folk artist, maintaining Pagan symbolism and Goddess portrayal in all her works as well as honoring peasant rebels and other historical figures. She remained a beloved artist of the people, still reading the palms of those she loved and bringing back rich stories each morning as she communed with the dead in her dreams. She died April 19, 1979, to the deep sorrow and loss for us all.

Blessed be!